exploring

CHARACTER DESIGN

exploring

CHARACTER DESIGN

Kevin Hedgpeth
and
Stephen Missal

THOMSON

DELMAR LEARNING

Australia Canada Mexico Singapore Spain United Kingdom United States

Exploring Character Design

Kevin Hedgpeth and Stephen Missal

Vice President, Technology and Trades SBU:
Alar Elken

Editorial Director:
Sandy Clark

Senior Acquisitions Editor:
James Gish

Development Editor:
Jaimie Wetzel

Marketing Director:
David Garza

Channel Manager:
William Lawrenson

Marketing Coordinator:
Mark Pierro

Production Director:
Mary Ellen Black

Senior Production Manager:
Larry Main

Production Editor:
Thomas Stover

Editorial Assistant:
Niamh Matthews

Cover Design:
Steven Brower

Library of Congress Cataloging-in-Publication Data:

Hedgpeth, Kevin.
    Exploring character design / Kevin Hedgpeth and Stephen Missal.—1st ed.
        p. cm.
    Includes bibliographical references and index.
    ISBN 1-4018-6296-9 (alk. paper)
    1. Characters and characteristics in art.
    2. Graphic arts—Technique.
    I. Missal, Stephen, 1948–
    II. Title.
    NC825.C43H43 2005
    741.5—dc22

NOTICE TO THE READER

dedication

The authors would like to dedicate this book, Exploring Character Design, to our good friend, artist and colleague, Terrance Yee, who passed away in 2003. His friendship, excellent advice and all-around decency will be sorely missed.

table of contents

Preface   viii

Introduction   xviii

1 **What Is Character Design?**   2

An introduction to character design and its relationship to stories, scripts and other narratives.

2 **Research-O-Rama!**   26

How research in literature, mythology, history, science and other resources helps provide valuable information in the development of character and creature design.

3 **Characters: Archetypes, Life Forms and Worlds**   56

An examination of the various kinds of characters and creatures available to the character designer and how they relate to storylines and historical and physical environments.

4 **Character Concept and Construction**   90

How we come up with ideas for character and creature design and how we go about translating them into actual artwork through various methods and media.

5 **Synthesis: Two and Two Makes Five**   120

An in-depth analysis of synthesis and how it contributes to character design solutions.

Color Section

Examples of character and creature design in color.

6 **Stylin'**   140

An overview of style and its relationship to character design, with a look at such related issues as silhouettes, model sheets, and the stages of the refinement of a design.

7 Expression and Emotion or Vice Versa 176

A study of the relationship of expression to character design, with an in-depth list of expressive language cues and modes, analysis and examples of dramatic action, facial expression and a look at how culture affects expression.

8 Anatomical Correctness 202

An introduction to the nature of human and non-human anatomy, and how each significantly affects character and creature design.

9 Come On and Do the Locomotion with Me! 232

A look at types of locomotion, both human and non-human, and the ways in which these might influence the development of character and creature design.

10 The Resources that Time Forgot 262

An example of a research category and how it can be used as a resource for character and creature design, utilizing prehistoric reptiles, mammals and other vertebrate and invertebrate creatures as visual raw material.

11 Not of this Earth: Alien Design 306

A look at why alien designs can diverge from standard character and creature design, and how environments may influence the final results.

12 The Power of Design Technique: Final Thoughts, Demonstrations and Illustrations 336

Showing how the various themes of this text fit together as a complete methodology for the solving of character and creature design problems, along with a final look at inanimate and animal character design issues.

INTENDED AUDIENCE

Exploring Character Design is the first book to comprehensively deal with all major aspects of character and creature design. Although students and professionals may find many books that discuss designing characters in certain stylistic modes or building characters through computer programs, they will not find any books that talk about the nuts and bolts of character design theory. The aspects of designing that trouble all artists are the ones this book addresses directly: research, conceptualization, style, synthesis and construction modes, expression and emotion, anatomical issues and locomotion, and corollary subjects that flesh out these topics. Numerous illustrations and demonstrations have been included with the text to help guide student and professional alike in solving character and creature design problems.

Exploring Character Design is written for a wide variety of audiences. Many of the people who read this book will be two- and four-year college-level students (or advanced secondary) planning a career in one of the many visual arts fields. Others will be individuals working on their own towards professional careers. Character design is integral to a multitude of entertainment industries. Artists in such diverse disciplines as illustration, comic or graphic novel (sequential) art, game art design and animation must master this skill. Whether in an animation, illustration or game art program in college or as an individual working to prepare a portfolio for professional presentation, any artist can utilize this text towards a successful outcome. Because of the wide spectrum of people who will be able to utilize this text, it has been written without a particular bias towards any single career avenue. Anyone with a modest drawing technique, will and curiosity can use this text to help them become a successful designer of characters and creatures.

EMERGING TRENDS

Character design, like so many fields, has been greatly influenced by the emergence of computer technology. With the advent of complex and dynamic software programs, artists find themselves with new and sometimes overwhelming tools at their command. They are given a project to complete, only to discover that they still need the command of certain basic, foundational techniques and methodologies to succeed. Character design has been partially absorbed by this new technological paradigm, and many younger artists emerging from school settings or individual study rely too heavily on the software packages to rescue them when faced with design difficulties. New software capable of rendering designs in multifaceted ways is overtaking and improving the natural look desired by artists and art directors. 'Libraries' of images have been created for general use, and generic figures abound, needing only some 'tweaking' to produce a character design. Online character building, game development and competition have taken advantage of these new resources to give anyone the ability to construct simple, viable characters that operate in a game context.

Another consideration is the multi-verse of cultural influences now affecting character design in this country. Asian, particularly Japanese, culture has produced several mainstream styles that have had broad appeal among a younger audience in the United States and Europe. Other cultures and "popular" cultural trends will likely continue to blend with the mainstream of style in character design for years to come, as the merging of American and world culture in general produce new and unusual ideas. Technology will provide templates for artists to use, and this temptation will make it difficult for creativity to emerge. Many fields still have considerable traditional skills involved in character design, and the preparatory steps to constructing characters have the same validity whether done by hand or digitally. It will take strong will and steadfastness in the face of all of this change to produce the great character art of the future.

BACKGROUND OF THIS TEXT

Character design as a field is replete with lavishly illustrated "how-to" books that give some basic drawing techniques, tricks for construction of narrow fields of character development, and a few tips on expression. Some books detail the technical ins and outs of computer software programs. Others are simply showcases for their author's talents. Unfortunately, none delve in a thorough way through the full spectrum of skills and techniques needed to become a fully developed character design artist. The intention of this text is to give a learning artist the tools necessary to compete in this fascinating field. The artist is given a background in research, conceptualization, synthesis and refinement that go hand in hand with the basic drawing techniques for developing characters. Additional chapters involving expression, locomotion, character choice and so on produce a package that covers the full gamut of skills in this field.

Information in this text was arrived at in two ways. The first is years-long experience in professional and academics contexts—that is, practical application of projects and 'what works' information. Secondly, more technical information was derived from many sources, both text and electronic, reduced to general data, and formulated to grant easy access by the reader. Where possible, personal insights were added to enhance the original information. All illustrations are original, including versions of such things as locomotive gaits and anatomy. Student and professional sources of imagery have been added to give a broader stylistic sense to the book. The use of student work was a way of showing how high quality design solutions can happen within an academic setting.

TEXTBOOK ORGANIZATION

This book is organized into twelve chapters, with a color section containing examples of finished character design. The book is full of illustrations showing various types and stages of character design. We begin Chapter One with an exploration of what character design actually is. Chapter Two proceeds to the vital skill of research, involving many types of sources. In Chapter Three, the issue of how to choose a character and its typology are introduced and covered at length. Chapter Four gives the reader an analysis of conceptualization, with the emphasis on the utilization of an idea sketchbook. The chapter then moves into modes of construction, from modular to gestural. Next, Chapter Five describes and explains the process of synthesis, the use of differing (in our case visual) sources in combination, and how this important tool allows the artist to develop original character designs. After a color section showing actual finished examples of character and creature designs, Chapter Six plunges into refinement, materials, model sheets, and other practical considerations of character design. Chapter Seven covers the essential topic of expression as it relates to character design, with a lengthy listing of many word triggers. In Chapter Eight, anatomy and its influence on character development and creature development are discussed. In Chapter Nine, locomotion, the movement of living things from one place to another, is explored, with examples and general considerations for many commonly encountered situations found in human and animal movement. Chapter Ten explores, as an example of category research in greater depth, prehistoric creatures as a rich and valuable resource for character design, and Chapter Eleven takes this a step further, with an overview of possible other-worldly alien character issues. Here, the more specialized realm of design based upon possible alien anatomies, environments and cultures are explored. Finally, Chapter Twelve gives the reader valuable examples of characters and creatures built in visual steps, along with a number of student and professional final designs. Professional profiles are also included with examples of their artwork, and student designs of high quality are interspersed throughout the book.

Exploring Character Design is structured deliberately to follow a practical path for the reader. The nature of what constitutes character design is followed by research, then conceptualization and construction. Although these could have been reversed, it has been the experience of the authors that the subject of research has been almost totally neglected by most curriculums and individuals, and needs to be addressed before the reader progresses to actual ideas and means. Synthesis is then introduced as one of the prime means for design solutions. Style follows because it is at this point that final choices in 'look' need to be made. Expression, the most fluid ingredient, comes next, with examples of visual and verbal emotional cues examined. This allows a further refinement of the design solution. Anatomy and locomotion, more technical realms, are now given some space. These are essentially two resource chapters for those needing this type of exact information relating to their character or creature design. In Chapters Ten and Eleven, two specific areas of character resource and parameter are given. Neither is intended as a final word in themselves, but as resource examples that clarify the nature of resource and specific character development. They are not included earlier to avoid a prolonged delay in exploring critical issues like synthesis and expression. Finally, a summary of the book follows, with examples of work and demonstration designed to help the reader evolve their own technique.

FEATURES

- Objectives clearly state the learning goals of each chapter
- Illustrations are used generously to enhance the concepts learned
- Profiles of successful character designers give important industry advice
- The entire character creation process is covered, from concept to final product—including research, conceptualization, synthesis and refinement.
- The relationship between drawing skills, anatomical knowledge, locomotion and character design is introduced.
- Actual demonstrations in a step by step format are given along with numerous examples of character design.
- The preliminary planning and concept development stages that are so important to young designers are stressed.
- Color section depicts fully developed character and contexts in various media.

SPECIAL FEATURES

▶ Objectives

Learning Objectives start off each chapter. They describe the competencies the readers should achieve upon understanding the chapter material.

▶ Notes

Notes provide special hints, practical techniques, and information to the reader.

▶ Sidebars

Sidebars appear throughout the text, offering additional valuable information on specific topics.

▶ Professional Profiles

In the Professional Profiles, various artists with working experience in industries utilizing character design have their experiences chronicled and offer advice and tips for students and professionals alike. In addition, character designs of theirs are exhibited as examples of solutions within the professional world.

▶ Student Showcases

The Student Showcases give an opportunity for actual students of the authors of *Exploring Character Design* to exhibit their own character design solutions. They clearly demonstrate that a high level of competency can exist within so-called student level artwork, and are the outcome of education, will and talent.

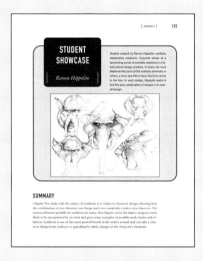

▶ Review Questions and Exercises

Review Questions and Exercises are located at the end of each chapter and allow the reader to assess their understanding of the chapter. Exercises are intended to reinforce chapter material through practical application.

E.RESOURCE

This guide on CD was developed to assist instructors in planning and implementing their instructional programs. It includes sample syllabi for using this book in either an 11 or 15 week semester. It also provides chapter review questions and answers, exercises, PowerPoint slides highlighting the main topics, and additional instructor resources.

ISBN: 1-4018-6297-7

ABOUT THE AUTHORS

Stephen Missal is an artist, author and educator, currently teaching in the Animation and Game Art departments of The Art Institute of Phoenix. Stephen, whose degrees are from Wichita State University, is well grounded in figure drawing, having taught that subject at the college level for over thirty years. He has also been a wildlife, commercial and gallery fine artist, selling his paintings and drawings nationally. His works have appeared in Wizard's of the Coast *Call of Cthulhu* gamebook, various magazines such as *Prehistoric Times* and *Vim and Vigor,* several educational publishers, and on various web fantasy and science fiction e-zines and sites. Missal's artwork can be seen in various public collections, including the New Britain Museum of American Art, and are found in many private collections, including Frank Sinatra, Gary Owens (*Laugh-In*), Itzhak Perlman (concert violinist), producer Samuel Arkoff, and Joshua Logan (film producer: *Camelot, Picnic*). His listings include: *Who's Who in the World; Who's Who in America; Who's Who in American Art; Who's Who in American Education;* and *2000 Outstanding Intellectuals of the 21st Century*. He is co-author of the college textbook *Exploring Drawing for Animation,* published by Thomson Delmar Learning. A member of the Southwest Paleontological Society, Stephen is also a published poet.

Kevin Hedgpeth teaches and administrates as Assistant Academic Director in the Media Arts & Animation and Game Art & Design departments at The Art Institute of Phoenix, where he also continues to sculpt, draw, paint and produce ideas for future visual projects. A graduate of Arizona State University, he has 15 years of experience in commercial stop-motion animation, 2D animation, illustration and character design. Clients include: the NBA, The Arizona Heart Institute, and Sunwoo Animation. Kevin worked for VAS Communications' Clay Studio on several clay-animated commercials, including a Charles Barkley fitness ad; contributed maquettes of prehistoric proboscideans to the Mesa Southwest Museum (recently featured in a Charles R. Knight exhibition) and designed the official logo for the 2001 National Day of Puppetry. Kevin is also a contributor of images to *Prehistoric Times Magazine*. Former President and active member of The Phoenix Guild of Puppetry; he is the Animation Consultant for The Puppeteers of America, Inc. He continues active participation in this arena, as well as exploring the world of paleontology. He is also the author of a profile of Japanese animation director Hayao Miyazaki in *Shade* magazine, and is collaborating with several colleagues in animation projects at The Art Institute of Phoenix. Kevin makes his home in Phoenix, Arizona, where he actively pursues a dual career as artist and educator/author. Kevin is co-author of *Exploring Drawing for Animation*, published by Thomson Delmar Learning.

Both authors continue their fascination with H.P. Lovecraft; Kevin still fancies gorilla images for his personal icon, and Stephen still thinks that squids and octopi are essential to happiness.

ACKNOWLEDGMENTS

The authors would like to acknowledge their dads, patient spouses and children, who, as with their previous volume, sat with, fed and otherwise maintained the authors during many writing and drawing sessions. The late Terrance Yee, Art Institute of Phoenix instructor and a fine nationally-recognized illustrator gave us valuable artwork as well as his patience and generosity to help in our project. We are also indebted to our wonderful students and colleagues who provided us with excellent artwork on short notice: Landon Armstrong, Joshua Barker, Dan Garza, Ramon Hippolito, Ryan Yee, Daniel Campa, Cesar Tafoya, Tamara Ramsay, Darcie Banfield, Danny Beck, Matt Mocarski, Dave Dawson, Cameron Forsley and Cesar Avalos. As with our first book, we are deeply indebted to the patient editors at Thomson Delmar Learning: Jaimie Wetzel, Tom Stover, James Gish, Nicole Stagg, and Niamh Matthews.

Thomson Delmar Learning and the authors would also like to thank the following reviewers for their valuable suggestions and technical expertise:

Mar Elepano
Animation & Digital Arts Department
School of Cinema-Television
University of Southern California
Los Angeles, California

Robb Epps
Animation & Illustration Department
International Academy of Design & Technology
Tampa, Florida

Matt Jackson
Art Department
Citrus College
Glendora, California

Ruth Lozner
Art Department
University of Maryland
College Park, Maryland

Lee Lanier
Media Arts & Animation Department
Art Institute of Las Vegas
Henderson, Nevada

Royal Winchester
Media Arts & Animation Department
DigiPen Institute of Technology
Redmond, Washington

Kevin Hedgpeth and Stephen Missal
2005

QUESTIONS AND FEEDBACK

Thomson Delmar Learning and the authors welcome your questions and feedback. If you have suggestions that you think others would benefit from, please let us know and we will try to include them in the next edition.

To send us your questions and/or feedback, you can contact the publisher at:

Thomson Delmar Learning
Executive Woods
5 Maxwell Drive
Clifton Park, NY 12065
Attn: Media Arts and Design Team
800-998-7498

Or the authors at:

Stephen Missal
c/o The Art Institute of Phoenix
2233 W. Dunlap Avenue
Phoenix, Arizona 85021

Kevin Hedgpeth
c/o The Art Institute of Phoenix
2233 W. Dunlap Avenue
Phoenix, Arizona 85021

INTRODUCTION: EXPLORING CHARACTER DESIGN

Artists beginning their journey in character design are, by and large, inventing by instinct and imitation. After getting some modest early success, they discover that coming up with original and consistently competitive creations isn't an easy task. It turns out that designing characters is not as straight-forward as the artist imagined. What is needed is some kind of path to follow. As an art career, character design is extremely popular among young artists because, frankly, it's fun. The main protagonists and antagonists of popular culture hold huge attraction in terms of fantasy, role models and just plain enjoyment. Cool creatures that roam about doing mayhem and otherwise chasing the local populace have enormous appeal for the artist as well. Designing these can be enormously gratifying. The trick is to avoid the pitfalls of mere imitation without producing art so obscure that it loses its audience. This book is a path that the learning artist can use to help solve the problems of successful character and creature design.

Character design is a broad term that actually includes production of prototypes and final versions of everything from small secondary creatures that inhabit an alien world to the heroine of an action film. What they have in common is the fact that they are generally biologically alive or at least, as in the case of a robot, a life *mimic*. Trees, bushes, rocks and other natural parts of backgrounds (with a few famous exceptions) are not generally considered characters. So we can see that the character can either be aware and part of a plot in a sentient way, or be simple and instinctive like a wild animal. They can have aspects that are totally foreign to our sense of what a creature is, and yet still function as a character. The issues are what to choose, where to look for useful related information, and how to construct the character design. These are the three basic pieces of the skill. Further, we must determine what would be an appropriate style for the character. It must fit into a story or general project's overall design sense, enhance its story or surroundings, and often carry the plot forward by weight of its appeal. That is a lot for a character to do. Other questions to ask: does it have expression?, how does it move?, does it have a costume or props?, and how does it fit into an historical or cultural context? To achieve this, the artist must understand good drawing skills, have a working knowledge of human and animal anatomy, know how to find costumes, be able to juggle several ideas at once and produce a new idea, and...well, it's a long list. To help achieve this we have divided this path into several bite-sized chapters, each of which deals with some important aspect of developing a character. Taken as a whole they do, in fact, form a road that the artist can follow to finally solve the challenge of character design.

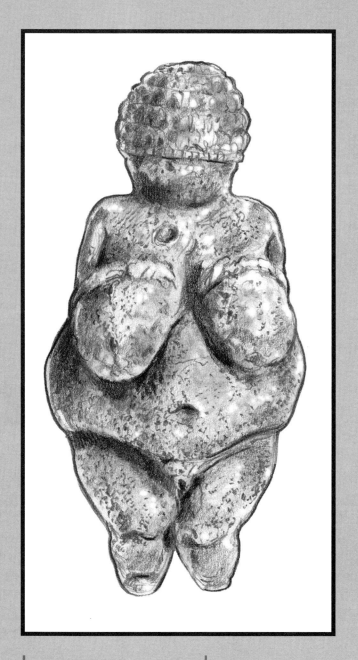

what is character design?

1

introduction

Most young artists wander into creating their own characters like someone at a restaurant eating dessert first. Because they love art and they want to have an immediate creation, they skip the main portion of the meal and don't even know that there is an appetizer. What character design involves is a full package, like a full meal, with preliminary steps including research, concept development, sketching, and so on. Only after these preliminary processes have been accomplished can the artist conclude with a full-blown character. But, you ask, what do you mean by "designing" a character? Isn't design a process that you go through to create a logo for a company, develop a layout for a magazine ad, or create blueprints for an engineering project? The answer is "yes," but the term *design* covers a lot of territory. We'll get to that concept shortly.

We hope to be "on the same page" as you, gentle reader, and so we shall start this journey into character design by defining what is meant by the term *character:* the initial word in "character design." The first definition found in Random House *Merriam-Webster's Collegiate® Dictionary, 10th Ed.* defines "character" as "the aggregate of features and traits that form the individual nature of a person or thing."

Definition 9 describes the term as "a person represented in a drama, story, etc." Definition 10 says "(of a theatrical role) having or requiring eccentric, comedic, ethnic or other distinctive traits."

The Dean of Animation Directors, Chuck Jones, spoke about characterization in his first autobiography, *Chuck Amuck:*

> "Character always comes first, before physical representation. Just as it is with all living things, including human beings. We are not what we look like. We are not even what we sound like. We are how we move; in other words, our personalities. And our personalities are shaped by what we think, by where we come from, by what we have experienced. And that personality is unique to each of us."

These three apt descriptions (and Mr. Jones' insight) apply to what this tome is designed to delineate about the fundamentals of character design. It is our hope that students and professionals alike will find valuable information on the process of character design. Research, design theory, practical art production skills, and their applications to character and creature creation are discussed in this book.

Character design is all of these things and more. Designing really refers to the whole process (in art) of constructing a visual end product. That process often involves many steps (some of which are already mentioned), with the end result being something with which an audience can interact visually. This product can be as mundane as a flyer left on a doorstep advertising the services of a handyman, or it can be as complex as the development of the visuals for a full-length animated movie. In this book, we refer to design for characters as the process having the goal of creating a visual character and all the look and context that go along with that character. A character is an individual entity—man, woman, beast, alien, or the like—that can be derived from the story, but sometimes stands alone from an overall storyline. Characters can be living beings, inanimate objects (like carpets or salt shakers), robotic, or undead (like Dracula) and are usually the central focus of story development. Characters are what the audience follows in an emotional way: by loving them, hating them, or just being fascinated by them, but in any case, by identifying with them.

In short, a character is what makes a story worth reading or watching, and character design is the means by which artists put together planning, sketching, concept, and refinement to produce a character. Even when the character is not specifically tied to a storyline, we are invited to respond emotionally to its appearance. Characters, for our purposes, also include creatures, which can also elicit emotional responses, but they don't normally live in a self-conscious manner and so more rarely involve themselves in the concepts inherent in a plot. Both character and creature design use the same basic foundational approach in conception and construction. Ultimately, if they lack visual and emotional appeal, they have not succeeded. To create successful characters, then, we start the artist's journey from beginning to completion of a character or creature design. This journey starts in the past, with the early origins of characterization.

Masks and Puppets and Spirits. . .oh my!

What is the origin of the character? Ever since man became an image-maker, he has been characterizing the world around him and worlds unseen by him. Early characterization can be seen in such images amongst the cave paintings of Lascaux and the voluptuous prehistoric sculpture deemed the "Venus of Willendorf." These images are derived from the need of the artist to interpret the basic characteristics that define a living creature (Lascaux) and the simplification and exaggeration of physical elements that define an archetype (Venus). These images become symbolic.

The world was most certainly a dangerous and perplexing place for early humans. Natural phenomena, wild beasts, and the nature of fire had an effect on the psyche and imagination of ancient people. The basic human need to understand and exert some control over one's environment must have been a key factor in the development of image-making and storytelling. Personification, or the projection of human-like attributes on nonhuman creatures, objects, and phenomena, became the methodology through which man described the world around him.

Shamanism, animism, and the rudiments of religion were affected by personification. Trees, rocks, and rivers gain a spirit presence. Awesome powers of nature are ascribed to deities: thunder personified becomes the god Thor of Norse mythology, for instance. It was difficult for the "primitive" mind to grasp the nature of the world's phenomena, much less get in touch with their relative spirits. The idea of the spirit "trap" was an early attempt to speak to the powers of the unseen world. This trap was some representational vessel of the spirit in question and was created to allow communion. Personification of the spirit trap allowed early humans to relate to the spirits.

Early "visual arts" and other means of expression laid the foundation for religion and its related aspect of storytelling: not only invoking the supernatural continuum but also describing what goes on there. Mythology relies heavily on legends and fables to teach behavior and morality. Deities and other preternatural entities were undoubtedly the first characters. Their likenesses become manifest in painting and sculpture (idols and totems) and in ceremonial forms of worship wherein masks and, later, puppets are used to invoke otherworldly denizens.

Early man's imagery, both two and three dimensional, were founded on basic observations of the physical world coupled with basic art-making tools. The origin of the "style" was founded as much on that tool use as it was on imagination. Pigments applied to a cave wall with fingers or sticks give a certain characteristic line quality. Pigment sprayed from the mouth to the rocky surface creates tonal variations in the coloration.

The quality and quantity of stone (and other resource materials) for use in tool-making (and as raw sculpting material) affected early man's dimensional art-making attempts and the possibilities for stylistic advances.

Figure | 1-1 |

Hypothetical cave painting: mammoth.

Prehistoric man, like children or other naïve artists, observed the structure of an object and reduced it visually to its simplest core shapes and elements that characterize its form. The object is reduced to a symbolic, often stylized, representation. How might a prehistoric artist with no formal image-making skill set visualize a woolly mammoth? How might a child do the same? The answer is that these individuals would define the observable characteristics that "mean" mammoth. Trunk, long and curving tusks, big body, big head, four columnar legs, large ears, little tail, and fur coat: these are key elements that define the mammoth's physical appearance.

The awesome nature of such a beast can also affect the observer, causing him or her to exaggerate elements to create a more imposing symbol. This reconstructed example of a bull's head painting from the caves of Lascaux in France suggest strong, symbolic forms that say "bull." In making such modifications to the visual aspect of a creature, the basic groundwork for character building has been put into place.

Like our imaginary example of the mammoth, a human being can and has been caricatured to the point of becoming a symbolic character at the hands of the primeval artist. A case in point is the famous figurative carving known as the Venus (or Woman) of Willendorf, named after

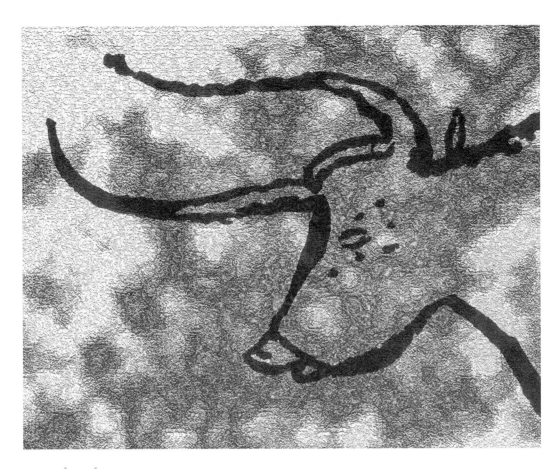

Figure | 1-2 |

Lascaux bull.

the Austrian town nearby its place of discovery in the early twentieth century. This statuette, scarcely over four inches tall, was carved from fine, porous limestone and is dated somewhere between 24,000 and 22,000 BCE (Before the Common Era). The Venus shows some residue of red ochre pigmentation.

This little sculpture is visually defined by an exaggeration of female sexual characteristics: giant pendulous breasts, pronounced hips, and enlarged genitalia. The hands, feet, head, and facial features are significantly reduced in scale and detail, rendering them visually unimportant and even nonexistent.

This "character" becomes symbolic of woman and what may be a corporeal example of an abstract concept: fertility. Woman as a life-bringer may be the theme represented through this caricature. Portraying an idea or concept related to human thought or emotion is a key element in designing a character.

Man was not content to rely on his totems to aid him in his desire to speak to spirits, but continued this early characterization by temporarily disguising himself as the spirit trap and acting out his relationships with the supernatural forces. To heighten the drama and mystery of shamanic rituals (i.e., keeping the parishioners interested), religious performers began to develop secretly guarded "special effects." One such development was the addition of articulated mask features, capable of movement (the lower jaw, for instance), as seen in the mask work of Native American tribes living on the northwest coast of the United States.

Soon, the need to invoke the sympathetic magic through more advanced storytelling caused the development of totemic figures capable of motion via human manipulation. Some movable figures were attached to early masks—a marked transition to puppetry. Once these figures became freed from the constraints of being an elemental part of masks, the puppet was born. These characters originally served as instruments of religious tale-telling and only much later served as purveyors of popular entertainment and satire.

Now spirits and deities had a tangible, recognizable form as characters.

Mask-and-puppet rituals began to give way to more complex religious practices in which the magic of language (originally in a pictographic form) became increasingly important in the development of symbolic forms and abstract ideas. The "sequential" storytelling art of the ancient Egyptians and Mayans define character archetypes: scribe, slave girl, warrior, and gods of the cultures. In a pictographic sense, these images depict the basic characteristics of these figures without describing specifics. This is the nature of the archetype: stereotypical features defining the representation of a type of figure—male, female, deity, king, and so on.

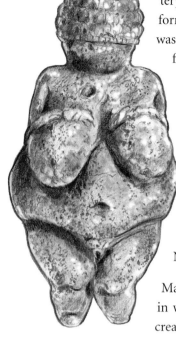

Figure | 1-3 |

The lovely and talented "Venus" of Willendorf.

Enter Mr. Punch, Stage Left. . .

The development of characters is often affected by cultural factors and may be influenced by different theatrical forms. A prime example is the evolution of puppetdom's favorite rapscallion, Mr. Punch. The origins of this traditionally English, irreverent character go back perhaps as far as the Roman Atellan farces, with such archetypal characters as Maccus, the country bumpkin, or Bucco, the comic servant. It is generally believed that theatrical character satire of the early Italian Renaissance's Commedia dell'arte derived its characterization from these earlier forms. The prototypical Punch was Pulcinella, the big-nosed, womanizing miscreant and was played by a masked actor. A physical characteristic that was developed for Pulcinella and followed his later incarnations was the

Figure | 1-4 |

Northwest coast tribesman in articulated mask (after Baird).

humped back and protruding paunch. Physical deformities were ripe topics for comedy and ridicule at the time, and became synonymous with buffoonery. Some believe that Pulcinella's distorted features are a caricature of an individual suffering from acromegaly.

As his character developed, Pulcinella became Polichinelle in France and Punchinello in England, where he was incarnated as a marionette. The powerful proboscis and the impudent attitude stayed with Punch, as did his ubiquitous hunchback and paunch. The former deformity began to take on an increasingly symbolic structure, until its final manifestation became a sort of curved fin and was now essentially a design element incorporated into his costuming. Punch was, and remains, the incorrigible Everyman, thumbing his nose at authority.

While characters have a symbolic nature, symbolism precedes characterization.

What, you may ask, is the meaning of symbolism? For our purposes, symbolism refers to visual iconography that describes or gives clues to the nature of a more complex idea or image, usually within a predetermined context. For instance, if you showed a red octagon to an (adult) American citizen, he or she would likely draw a visual connection to the stop sign, lauded in the legend and lore of driving as an obstructer of roadway progress. However, if you were to show the same symbol to a lost tribesman living in some remote jungle territory, it would be unlikely for him to have the same recognition.

Some symbolic recognition does not require a cultural context. As human beings, we can make observations that are common to virtually all people. For example, we will go out on a limb and say that all human beings have seen another human or at least their own reflection. Therefore, if we ask a person to draw a human face, it will (depending on the skill level of the artist) look something like view A in the following figure. The attempt to replicate the appearance of life is apparent.

However, our intimate knowledge of the way people look allows us to identify a visual arrangement of simple forms or marks as meaning "face," as seen in view B of the same illustration. Behold the power of symbolism!

Figure | **1-5** |

Mr. Punch.

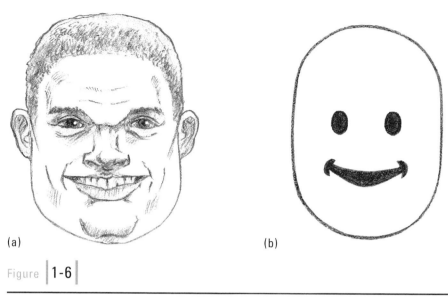

(a)   (b)

Figure | 1-6 |

Faces: realistic (view A) vs. symbolic (view B).

Characters and Storyline: You Won't Watch if No One Is Home. . .

Let's ask a question: Do we have to have a storyline in order to have a character? The answer is "No, not necessarily." However, without a story of any kind, it is difficult to understand and develop a character. Why would this be so? The explanation is simple. What we mean by a character is a particular set of traits and physical descriptions, and these are valid in the most meaningful way when operating in a "real," specific setting (and one that has its own description and history). This is because the two modify each other. A story and its physical setting change and limit the character's actions, and the character influences its surroundings and the running history of the same. They change and complement one another. One is inseparably part of the other. Why the character looks and acts the way it does is derived from where it lives and how it grew up. After brief contemplation, this is self-evident. This does not mean that an interesting *looking* character can't be designed without a story to go with it. But that same figure remains something of an enigma, a possibility only, until given a world within which to operate. Of course, in choosing characters for simple ad illustrations, we need not probe the depths of story or emotion to effectively design a character or creature. Within the mainstream entertainment industries, however, this approach does not work very well.

It is easier to give some examples of this interdependence than to talk in the abstract about it. Suppose we have drawn a character with close cropped hair, perhaps military looking, with a black eye-patch over the left eye. The character is male, perhaps 40, wearing a complex leather outfit replete with weaponry.

It begs the question, why the eye-patch? Is this a warrior of some sort? Does he exist in the past, future, or present? Does he live on this planet or somewhere far away, perhaps not on a planet at all? Despite being intriguing, the character is caught in limbo, a story that could unfold with just a little more information. Now, giving the fellow a name begins the process. Why? Because a name focuses the viewer's attention on the character *as an individual*. Whether female or male, or something bizarrely alien, the name provides a handle, so to speak, that allows us to connect with the character.

A moniker does two other things: first, it connects the story through similarities to other names and places within the story, and second, it may give some sense, through the sound of the name, what the character might look like. This, although not obvious at first, is something writers know all too well. You can have a great character and a useless name. So this is where we start.

There are two ways to concoct a character. The first is to make one up out of "whole cloth," without any connection to a specific narrative or storyline. The other is to *derive* a character from a story or plot so that the character is bound to and meaningfully shaped by the story (or in some cases, actually concoct a story based upon a character invention). All artists have doodled in their sketch pads, fiddling with this shape and that, coming up with ideas for characters.

This is not just normal, it is necessary. Without explorative drawings it would not be possible to create characters at all, because there would be no visual backlog of ideas to work with. That being said, it is the story (or ad campaign or cartoon situation) within various entertainment and illustration industries that drives the formation of the character's qualities. Because we go to the movies or buy a particular video game in response to advertised stories and imagined worlds, we expect to see characters that help tell the story and act out the plots to our satisfaction. Here is the reciprocal aspect of character design. The character also influences the plot or story as well. It is much like casting performers for a live action movie. Would an older, seasoned actress be more appealing as the gritty heroine in an action movie, or would the character (and story) do better with a sultry, kittenish starlet? Each might have its pluses and minuses, and although we might have our own opinions as to which would be better, it ultimately is the economic outcome that probably will influence the decision the most. Within the pure aspect of character design, however, we should note how the differing actresses changed the feel and momentum of the storyline, by virtue of their own pace, emotive capabilities, and look.

Figure | 1-7 |

Ol' Eye-Patch.

Figure | 1-8 |

Character doodles.

In any character construction, this result is inevitable. You cannot design a character and not influence the story. We can see how by simply varying the age of the character, the possible physical limits are enlarged or reduced. One of the actresses would be an athletic, robust character full of physical activity and pushing the boundaries of her environment. The other would be more cerebral, perhaps acting more like you and I, producing empathy for her character because of her limitations. Fully developed character design will have the identical result for both the viewer and story; the story is what fills the audience's minds and what drives to a great extent the story itself.

Action stories might become more reflective, thoughtful vehicles with a character that must move and act in a more deliberate way. Tragedies could have comic overtones simply by the reworking of a main character or a subcharacter, giving the character humorous aspects that would reflect into the story. Many more examples could be imagined.

Several aspects of a story or narrative help to define the *look* of a character. Each narrows the parameters for what logically can be used to create a visual representation of a specific character. These would be such things as culture (related to specific peoples), world and local history (of this particular world), personal history (of the character), environmental qualities (such as forest, urban), and time frame (whether the story unfolds in the past, present, or future and the ramifications of each). Further limits and possibilities come from whether the story is action oriented, comical, tragic, lusty, surrealistic, or one of a host of other genre types. These qualities affect everything from species identification of the character to gender, costume, age, technology, weaponry, transportation, and even the character's role (villain, heroine, and so forth). Some of these design variants are illustrated in the following figure.

We introduced some of the qualities of a character that the artist (and writer) must address. To cover this in more detail, let us list some of the major qualities that should be part of a character design. No character operates in a complete vacuum. Even if the artist is just "doodling," the visual ideas that make up any new character design are for the most part derived from other sources. This topic is covered in greater detail in Chapter Five: Synthesis. But what we want to know at present is what to worry about when drawing up designs.

Figure **1-9**

Actress vs. actress.

PLEASE TAKE NOTE!

The following is a good preliminary list of character qualities:

- Type of being or creature (for example, a humanoid-derived character with some modifications) to start the process
- Scale or size of the character (relative to understandable objects or scenic contexts)
- Costume (if any)
- Props (if any), ranging from a weapon to a space suit to a pipe
- Emotive capabilities (can it show emotions by facial or body gestures?)

- Surface texture, if applicable
- Colors
- Anatomic peculiarities that need clarification or "readability"
- Locomotion capability and mode
- Gender issues
- Style issues (relative to others of its kind or the story context in general), possibly including hairstyle, makeup, and so forth
- Level of realism (realistic, stylized, or cartoon-like)
- Ability to manipulate its environment and means to do so (such as hands, talons, or tentacles)
- "Morphing" capabilities or evolutionary changes (shape and detail change)
- Role in the story (e.g., hero, anti-hero, villain)

In Chapter Five: Synthesis, we revisit many of these categories and explore them within the context of assembly, disassembly, and reassembly. Some examples of these as applied to a character design are seen in the following figure.

These and other more derived qualities will, when put together, give a preliminary character design. We must remember that even the way we draw the subject can influence its "look." This might mean the line or paint quality, whether it ultimately will stay hand-produced or will become a computer-generated image, and even in what program it will be completed.

As stated earlier, characters and creatures can be designed without any storyline whatsoever. Purely conceived as visual stand-alones, done just to satisfy the artist's personal desire, these characters might inspire a story or be inserted into one (or just an action sequence), or they might end up as "eye-candy" in the middle of a coffee table book. These types of character and

Figure | 1-10 |

Guys, girls, ghouls, and guns: synthesis and variation.

Figure | 1-11

Mix-and-match of men and mutants.

creature designs are completely valid, with their great shortcoming being their lack of context, other than what might be provided by an invented background. Still, a great many excellent designs have been constructed by first-rate artists that have no relation to any script, story, novel, or related narrative form.

Enter Design, Stage Right

Although we have enumerated a number of specific qualities concerning the character construction, we still have to give a more specific answer to what *design* means in relation to characters. Design, when taken in the visual arts, usually means *the manipulation of basic visual elements (line, form, color, value, texture) in the service of a particular image.* The image may be abstract, as in a series of shapes and colors on a brochure cover, perhaps containing some photo inserts, or it may be a literal imitation of something that we would construe as real, like a person or place.

There are a vast number of stylistic modes within which design can operate. Geometric, colorful shapes can predominate both the general design and any particular parts (including images), or there can be exotic textural and color passages that swirl and blend together (as often accomplished in computer graphics and image manipulation programs). Simple, starkly real images can also be the key feature, or humorous cartoon images might catch the viewer's attention. So, to review, we can say that there are two aspects to the design issue. One would be how the abstract elements that make up any visual phenomenon are used (as in choosing hard-edge green, geometric forms with no lines versus a soft-edged set of complementary colored shapes connected by varied lines). The second modality would be more intimately tied to images derived from our real world. In this arena, the artist can run the gamut from photorealistic renderings (or actual photographs) to extremely terse, almost abstract cartoon versions of objects and characters. There can be a mix, or several mixes, of stylistic content that modify each other and the whole. The following images are some examples of (but by no means exhaustive of) stylistic modes.

Obviously personal taste is one governing factor. Another limitation would be a stylistic/design mode into which one must fit the artwork. In the real art industry, we rarely get to choose our own stylistic path exclusively. Instead, we more often have to meet the expectations of a producer, art director, or intended audience. For example, if you intend to produce genuine horror, it would be absurd to render your characters in a silly, humorous comic strip style.

If the need of the art director was for a light-hearted visual romp through childhood, it would not be recommended that the characters and backgrounds look like the denizens of a Victorian gothic novel.

These ideas may be funny because of the incongruity of the images, but it gives a direct sense of what is *appropriate* to the character design.

We now return, in a more complete way, to how the story (and its audience) impacts the visual choices we make in character design. There are story-telling modes as well as direct visual design modes, and these two intertwine to produce a *look.* The same story can be rendered in several differing styles, and now it is up to the artist and art director to choose what path to take.

Figure | 1-12 |

A smidgeon of styles.

In more narrow parameters, there are common design styles relating to characters that should be taken into account here. In these, it can be seen clearly what design style does to a character. For example, one often occurring style is a kind of generally reductive cartoon design (as seen in animation, advertising, and comic strips), in which the features and physique are reduced to simpler shapes and linear descriptions.

In this design system, there are many substyles. Some styles use heavy, geometric lines.

Others have more subtlety in the shape and line.

We could change directions entirely and render the figure in a more "realistic," albeit stylized manner, such as an action comic look.

Later in this book, we look at this topic in more depth, covering various stylistic issues and types. But this taste of specific styles should give the artist a glimpse into actual design modes and how they can vary when applied to the same character. Design here really gets defined as a group of visual signals that have a common appearance (in a character design) and insert into a plot in such a way as to both reinforce it and enhance it. That is quite a mouthful, but it is important here to realize how many aspects of a project will be influenced by our design choices. The advantage of a team approach to total story and character design is now clearer. There are so many parts to this process that it is easier for several talented artists, writers, and designers to work together than for an individual to try to create the whole package.

Figure | 1-13 |

BOOO!!! Too silly to be scary.

Before the artist reading this says "Whoa, I *want* to do the whole thing myself," let us reassure everyone that many successful solo and small group projects have been accomplished. For example, Bill Plympton is an animator who traditionally creates almost all of his design and animation work himself. It can be done and done well, but it is a daunting enterprise. Depending on the needs of the project (and the budget), the size of the staff undertaking it can vary greatly, from one to many hundreds. Graphic novels are another realm where individuals have shined as both artist and storyteller. As an artist, perhaps the wisest course is to first get fundamentally good at creating various kinds of characters and not to worry about major projects until this skill is mastered.

Figure | 1-14 |

Too sullen to be silly.

Figure | 1-15 |

Goofus and gladiatrix: reductive line style.

Originality versus Cliché

One final issue (and one we will return to often) is the problem of originality versus clichéd imagery. To have originality in our character design gives freshness and induces interest; uniqueness is probably impossible, because of the derived and synthetic character of most creativity. That is, although new types of design can (and should) be constructed, the bits and pieces that go together to make that new design are typically pulled from preexisting sources. Even so, great design (art, music, and so on) can be produced from known, smaller units.

Think of the classical composer Wolfgang Amadeus Mozart. He took a style, along with general phraseology and instrumentation, and even thematic sections, and turned them into magic. He is recognized today as a monumental genius, and yet he didn't invent notes, instrument design, or any other parts that went into his music. Instead, he found novel ways to combine them to give us moving, remarkable music. His father, although a capable musician, produced compositions that were, to be generous, ordinary. The music that came from the father was more predictable and did not vary much from other examples, thus condemning it to obscurity.

The upshot of this discussion is that we would like to surprise the audience, at least a little, in order to sustain interest in our production, and to give a new or deeper look at a subject that might have been done many times before. Much work done today is stylistically repetitive, with the end result being that not a lot of original work stands out. When we encounter inventive character design, we are usually moved to look at it many times because of its appeal as something new and unexpected. Old story lines can be reinvigorated by just the inclusion of creative character design.

Let's face it: As a culture, we are inundated with "mass media" that has become increasingly massive. The internet, television, motion pictures, comic books, and graphic novels hammer us with ideas. Even though these resources can hold inspiration for character designers, they often sneak into our thoughts when we are not expecting it and present a challenge to the character design process. Here we are trying to be original, but our minds are being bombarded with a myriad of preexisting character concepts. The truth of the matter is that we can't be "design hermits" holed up in a cave creating characters and so we will experience the phenomenon of analogous design. A multitude of characters in so many styles have been developed through the years to the extent that it would be difficult not to be influenced by their existence. The trick is to put a twist on your idea. How is it different

Figure | 1-16 |

A very graphic Kris Kringle.

Figure | 1-17 |

Demetrius: subtle yet stylized.

from a competitor's in the marketplace? For example, if you receive the professional assignment to design a group of crime-fighting reptilian humanoids that wield martial arts weapons, there is a strong likelihood that an audience could draw a parallel to the ever-popular Teenage Mutant Ninja Turtles. As a designer, it is your responsibility to create interesting characters capable of telling a good story while not infringing upon the copyrights of others.

This being said, it is possible to be overly concerned about the possibility of different characters expressing similar visual traits. If the law of the land were so heavy-handed that it throttled the life out of any analogous design, no one could ever create another bipedal bunny character, much less two female superheroes in magenta tights. However, there are still some producers who throw a fit over lesser character design issues. Let's take Milo, for example. Milo, a friend of the authors, worked as an art director at a small production house, developing animated series projects for syndication and Saturday morning television. He had just completed a character design for a current project, when the producer walked in, looked at Milo's renderings, and began fussing.

"We can't use that character. It looks like Baby Huey," the producer said. (For those of you who are not familiar with Harvey Comics' Baby Huey, he is an oversized infant duck decked out in a diaper and bonnet, made popular in animated shorts by Famous Studios.)

Milo had to explain to the producer that his creation was actually an ostrich in purple lederhosen and was only similar to the aforementioned duckling in that both were large avians with girded loins.

Temporarily placated by logic, the producer left Milo to his designing and was not heard from again in that particular capacity. The "Baby Huey Alert" became the stuff of legend and a long-standing joke amongst the art department denizens.

Figure **1-18**

Super action guy and Jack Kirby homage.

Too Big for Our Britches

Artists are made not born. This applies to character designers, in-betweeners, portrait painters, and so on. Many artists have the unfortunate idea that they possess greater skills than they actually have. Unlike Mark Twain's comment that Richard Wagner's music was "better than it sounded"; artists are no better than the quality of their imagery. We're only as good as our last drawing, painting, or animation.

This is not to say that raw artistic talent does not figure into the mix—it does. However, it is the raw material from which greatness in creating, drawing, or designing occurs. We're building on

STUDENT SHOWCASE

Joshua Barker

Student artwork by Joshua Barker: heroic warrior. Barker gives us an example of a character niche, the powerful, heroic warrior. We see him examining the general form, costume, and props appropriate to such a character. Barker chooses elements that are consistent in shape and cultural cues that an audience will identify without much difficulty.

a knack. The authors themselves were not always functioning at their top form as young people. One often looks back with a modicum of humility (and possible embarrassment) at having cranked out some stinkers along the way.

The authors, as instructors, see in our students ourselves: often brash, proto-artists coming into the college arena from high school having been a big fish in a little pond and trying to coast on raw talent alone. This is not to say that some individuals, through extraordinary talent and hard work, have a nigh-on professional edge. This is the exception, not the rule.

You see, there are a series of factors that must come into play to develop the proto-artist into the professional artist. These factors apply to character design:

- A good education
- Developing observational drawing skills
- Practice!
- Developing core design skills
- Mentoring (i.e., working with a talented instructor or peer)
- Observing art

Understanding these concepts and applying them as part of your professional development will aid you in becoming a successful artist with the skills necessary to create good character designs.

SUMMARY

This chapter deals with the definition and basic parameters of character design. As used in the visual arts, character design is the combination of the elements of design united with the story aspects of a character to produce a finished product. Many different parts go into the creation of a character, and the relation of design to character construction is paramount in importance to the artist. Design for the artist is separated into both abstract and realistic qualities, where such things as shape, color, and texture unite with the dramatic needs of a story to give us a character's appearance. An artist needs to examine specific qualities of the character as derived from a story, or at least to have a sense of a general genre look in which to explore various options visually. By remembering to "cover all your bases" in terms of what goes into a character creation, you as an artist have a greater chance at success by meeting more needs and possibilities of your character. The goal ultimately is to be original but functional: we want something interesting but still useable for various types of visual projects.

exercises

1. Look up various different character designs for the same story, and compare and contrast them in terms of style and success.

2. Using a known literary resource, create a range of sketches for character designs that meet the needs of the story.

3. Design a character and then change its appearance from realistic to cartoon. Note what it took to transform the image.

4. Modify an existing character (respecting copyright laws) by changing certain parts of its appearance. Try physical changes, costume changes, or surface color or textural changes.

5. Using your own story fragment, create a central character design, paying close attention to uniting the story to the look of the character. List the various attributes of the character and how the character fits into the world you have created.

in review

1. What is meant by design in reference to character design?

2. Name some of the types of visual categories that modify a character design.

3. How does a story influence the look of a character?

4. What are some of the properties of abstract design elements that can be used in character design?

5. Why would originality be a worthy goal of the character design artist?

research-o-rama!

o b j e c t i v e s

Learn about various types of sources for visual subject matter.

Discover the potential in literature and mythology.

Explore historical and cultural material.

Learn how to use scientific resources.

Discover other means for visual source material.

i n t r o d u c t i o n

This chapter gives guidance in the hunt for visual resources applicable to character design. All artists learn as they encounter both personal and professional projects the need for obtaining visual resources to help construct imagery. Addressed here are specific categories of information and ways and means of getting at that storehouse of images and ideas. Types of categories for visual imagery are surveyed in brief, with possible outcomes from the use of each and images suitable to the categories as a resource. The importance of reading and the use of written resources are emphasized, with examples of illustration derived from such sources as fiction and mythology being represented. Other types of image resources are introduced as well, including scientific literature and contemporary entertainment styles.

RESEARCH-O-RAMA!

A Short, Yet Brief, Look at Sources

What are the categories available to the artist for research into character development? As you can see above, they might be broken down into general historical information, including war, exploration, and the like; cultural resources (for our purposes, social tales and description, such as the "anglers," or grave robbers, of the middle ages, and other "colorful" types from historical records), literature in general (from novels, short stories, and novelettes to poems and epic poems), mythology, the stories rooted in the development of archetypal imagery of all cultures; scientific resources, from paleontologic papers to museum offerings; and contemporary and historical visual resources, that is, such cultural visual icons as comic book characters and similar subjects.

Mental Field Trip or the Wonderful World of World Literature

Rummaging around for new visual ideas can be frustrating or an amazing adventure. Most of us in the creative industries are prone to look for the quick fix, an idea that probably has already been done to death, because of time pressure or just sheer ignorance. Unfortunately, the other common reason for such a solution is laziness. Our recommendation is to strike out into unknown territory, because without a doubt, once you have seen what is actually available for resources, it becomes difficult to return to the worn-out ideas permeating current creative thinking.

One arena that is always available as a resource for fresh ideas is that of world literature. We can see many of you running off, shrieking "I will not read a *book*!" While it would behoove you to do so, you don't have to read an entire book to get images, nor do you have to plow through a thousand pages of Tolstoy's *War and Peace* to find something satisfying. You do have to research a bit, finding out what sorts of books or even collections of short stories might have what you need. To this end, your local, friendly librarian can be an enormous aid to the search. They can point you to a multitude of pieces of literature that you probably didn't even know existed. Many great stories were written in languages other than English and have been ably translated for your benefit. Many of these books and stories have been illustrated by excellent artists. This alone might be worth the price of admission. Such artists as N. C. Wyeth, Gustave Doré, and Howard Pyle have created lasting illustrations for many famous novels, epic poems, and the like.

Novels and shorter length written narratives have the ability to convey detailed, psychologically driven portraits of their characters, complete with descriptions of their surroundings, history, and contemporary social milieu. It is easily seen why artists would investigate these sources for visual ideas; the writers are of a very high standard, and give ample and original information useful to the artist. Within these stories are hate, love, jealousy, crime, war, heroism, supernaturalism, and many other passions and qualities attractive to the illustrator or designer.

Among the wonderful characters in these books are hobbits, wizards, fire-breathing night things, a reincarnated Mark Twain, demigods, pirates like Long John Silver, Sherlock Holmes,

Dracula, Fagin the thief, Natty Bumpo, the Count of Monte Cristo, Martian swordsmen, Captain Nemo of the submersible Nautilus, otherworldly dream creatures like the vertical-mouthed Gug, dread Cthulhu and the elder things of H. P. Lovecraft, and the dual-personality of Dr. Jekyll and Mr. Hyde. Wandering in extraordinary landscapes of endless forests, archaic black-stoned cities, Victorian England, Middle Earth (borrowed from the Norse by Tolkien), and on deserted Caribbean islands, these remarkable characters conjure up a wealth of imagery and ideas for the artist. Read Algernon Blackwood's short story "The Willows" and you will think twice about a boat ride down any secluded river. H. P. Lovecraft called this the greatest fantasy horror story of all time.

Literature comes in different flavors. Some major categories include historical romances, science fiction, fantasy, horror, drama (including everything from Aeschylus to Dickens), tragedy, comedy, and the supernatural. Each category has many subcategories, and these in turn have their own branching paths. Medieval allegories, poetry and epic poetry, and plays further enrich the depth of literature. Some religious books like *Pilgrim's Progress* have become classics in their own right. Many of the Greek plays set the stage for parts of twentieth century psychology. The twentieth century introduced theater of the absurd, with minimalism and surrealism lurking in the story plots (or lack thereof). The field of poetry is enough to provide an astonishing array of characters and situations. Milton's "Paradise Lost" and Walt Whitman's "Leaves of Grass" come to mind readily. Epic poems that straddle the gray zone between myth and literature abound, as in the story of Beowulf, with its famous monster, Grendel.

These do not even begin to touch the tip of the iceberg of literature available to artist or reader. There are so many remarkable stories and images contained in those stories that it would take a heavy book or two just to make more complete, long lists like the next page. Explore the bookstore shelves, wander through the library, talk to the resource librarian, go on the internet and type in key search words for book subjects. By these simple means, you as an artist can open up almost unlimited worlds. Some literature is now online and can be searched or even skimmed for source material. We don't recommend losing the ability to read, but sometimes a quick search is all that is possible in the time available. There are really two ways to go about using these books. The first is to plunge in "without a program" and just see what turns up. Although this is a longer process, in the end it provides more material because of its unknown nature, rather like digging for fossils or archeological artifacts. The second method is to narrow your search by subject before reading (e.g., adventure from the Middle Ages), thus eliminating much wandering on the sideroads of information.

Hit or Myth

Another realm for exploration is the world of mythology and epic story. *This category is explored in greater depth to demonstrate just how broad any category can be.* Even in a brief introduction such as what you encounter here, the amount of visual source material is stunning. In addition, much of the story lines and plotting for novels, short stories, and related written material relates to the structure of myth.

REDOUBTABLE READING REFERENCES

A *very, very, very* short list of novels and longer literature to be investigated might include the following works:

20,000 Leagues Under the Sea by Jules Verne

Gulliver's Travels, by Jonathan Swift

Kenilworth, by Sir Walter Scott

The Sea Wolf by Jack London

Ben-Hur by Lew Wallace

The Prisoner of Zenda by Anthony Hope

The Strange Case of Dr. Jekyll and Mr. Hyde by Robert Louis Stevenson

Ivanhoe by Sir Walter Scott

David Copperfield by Charles Dickens

The War of the Worlds by H. G. Wells

Quo Vadis by Henryk Sienkiewicz

Robinson Crusoe by Daniel Defoe

The Hunchback of Notre Dame by Victor Hugo

The Last of the Mohicans by James Fenimore Cooper

The Legend of Sleepy Hollow by Washington Irving

The Count of Monte Cristo by Alexandre Dumas

The Woman in White by Wilkie Collins

Dracula by Bram Stoker

Kidnapped by Robert Louis Stevenson

The Hound of the Baskervilles by Arthur Conan Doyle

Iliad by Homer

Odyssey by Homer

The Three Musketeers by Alexandre Dumas

The Moonstone by Wilkie Collins

Dreamquest of Unknown Kadath by H. P. Lovecraft

The Case of Charles Dexter Ward by H. P. Lovecraft

Oliver Twist by Charles Dickens

A Christmas Carol by Charles Dickens

Treasure Island by Robert Louis Stevenson

The Arabian Nights by Princess Sheherazade

Stranger in a Strange Land by Robert Heinlein

The Lord of the Rings trilogy by J. R. R. Tolkien

The Worm Ouroboros, by E. R. Eddison

The Night Land by William Hope Hodgson

The House on the Borderland by William Hope Hodgson

The White Dragon by Ann McCaffrey

Riverworld by Philip José Farmer

Fahrenheit 451 by Ray Bradbury

Lysistrata by Aristophanes

At The Earth's Core by Edgar Rice Burroughs

A Princess of Mars by Edgar Rice Burroughs

Figure | 2-1 |

Shantaks and Martians and Gugs . . . oh my!

A myth is a story set in the past, outside of any particular time frame, that has supernatural overtones or parts to the unfolding of the story. They often deal with religious (one man's religion is another man's mythology) and culturally universal themes, such as seasonal rebirth, the afterworld, and so on. All cultures have myths, from the Native American stories to the tales of the South Sea Islands. What is particularly attractive about mythology as a derivative source is that it contains larger-than-life characters, great drama, and the suspension of natural laws and a strong sense of the fantastic. All of these qualities are useful for the construction of an interesting character. It would seem that the underlying psyche of humans universally needs and creates these types of stories, whether in the vastness of the Pacific Ocean or in the lush mountains of South America. No matter where humans find themselves, the expression of the drive of the species finds its way into written, oral, and visual storytelling of a monumental nature. Epic stories often involve

CARL JUNG

Carl Jung, the famous Swiss psychoanalyst and researcher in the world of the mind, concluded that the human mind has an underlying structure that is universal in nature. In his theory, we literally *share* an unconscious mind that has preexisting forms that then make their way through the individual minds and reveal themselves through symbol in dreams and waking behavior. He called these *archetypes*. Their functioning and particular traits ultimately shape the nature of actions and thus stories that emanate from actions: archetypes beget myths, and myths are the raw material for an infinite number of stories. Myths have a profound sense of predating "real-time" world activities and are powerful because they relate to some (perhaps Jung's) underlying universal themes and drives. A myth is a story set in the past, outside of any particular time frame, that has supernatural overtones or parts to the unfolding of the story. Myths often deal with universal themes, such as seasonal rebirth or the afterworld. They are a collection of archetypal sets that produce a significant impact and path for humans. Dreams partake of this structure as well. Archetypes are what Jung called a "preconscious psychic disposition that enables a (man) to react in a human manner." What is a general "disposition" or thematic sense can show up in many variations when it emerges in human consciousness. Basic archetypes can therefore be disguised through symbol. We do not consciously produce these images ourselves as an individual being, but rather *react* to them when they appear in our dreams or spontaneous imagery. Jung felt early on that how we had developed as human beings had given us a link through our bodies to archetypal information. Later, he strongly felt that the archetypes actually were inherent in nature, shaping both it and the human mind. These elemental forces were the source for the concept of "gods" and "goddesses" and "elemental

continued

spirits" in ancient legend and thought. This was the "Universal Unconscious."

The basic archetypes are the Shadow, the Anima or Animus, the Syzygy, the Child, and the Self. A basic exposition of them is as follows:

The *Shadow* is the possibility of encountering the unconscious part of ourselves, the "dark" side. This more universal part of our psyche contains some difficult urges and is often referred to as a wild place (wilderness). Negative aspects of this area can be projected onto others when it is uncomfortable for us to assimilate it in ourselves. From this comes prejudice, judgmentality, and so on; we personify the unconscious drive and place it on others. One aspect of mythos is to reintegrate this part of ourselves to the conscious mind (and also in Jungian psychoanalysis).

The *Anima or Animus* is the soul. Anima is male, Animus female. The theme here is our "other" half, male or female quality, that is, again, not integrated. One may have a mentor that appears in dreams that is our projected Anima or Animus, and it may provide wisdom or solace for the dreaming mind. Myths often have these two opposites being reconciled or divided.

In the order of archetypes, the *Syzygy* follows the Shadow and the Anima/Animus; it is the unity of the outer and inner psychic world.

The *Child* is the archetype of renewal, the urge for the retrieval of paradise, and new beginnings. Circles are one of the images associated with this archetype.

The *Self* is the final and ultimate archetype. This is the divine, or god image. Human and divine merge. This is the world of spirit.

Myths spin these archetypes into stories of quest, renewal, treachery, loss, rebirth, and ultimate enlightenment. A myth is often, in great extent, the working out in one mode or another the separation of and reintegration of these parts of the human psyche.

heroes in quest mode, saving their peoples or involved in complicated and dangerous combat with antagonistic forces.

As a historical, scientific subset to this category, we include sociologic studies of human behavior that meld with myth making, but in the real human arena. A prime example of this type of source is Sir James George Frazer's *The Golden Bough, A Study in Magic and Religion.* This comes either in a 12-volume set or a single-volume condensation. Topics include such things as sympathetic magic, taboo, magicians as kings, Isis (the Egyptian god), the ancient deities of vegetation as animals, and so on. It is an altogether fascinating, and we might add, stunning look at humans and their magical/psychological history. Although it is not mythology per se, it does weave in and out of that subject and reflects it in human behavior repeatedly. A few images related to this type of subject matter are shown on the left.

Returning to mythology, most readers have at least a passing familiarity with Greek, Roman, and Norse myth, with such gods and characters as Jupiter, Mercury, Odin, and Thor. Disney Studios used some of these (Greek) gods and characters in their epic animation *Fantasia*, during the sequence involving centaurs, cherubs, pegasi (flying horses), Zeus, and Bacchus. Other

Figure **2-2**

Mystic architecture and mystic.

fantastic creatures that evolve from myth and epic story are dragons, trolls, giants, and golems (living clay men). Myth inhabits all lands and cultures. The sheer unfamiliarity of Western culture with some of the Asian and Native American myths lends itself to the development of a raft of new ideas in character design.

Religion and myth intermingle in many cultures, with a prime example being the Egyptian pantheon of gods and attendant deities. Although there is strong evidence that ancient Egypt was oddly monotheistic underneath the facade of the multigod drama, it is the latter that catches our attention. Greek, Roman, Norse, Native American, African, Polynesian, and many other cultures' myths also often have this mythical/religious dual purpose. Both the internet and library are valuable resources for exploring this realm. In no particular order, we take the liberty of listing some (but by no means all) mythical resources, including names and some locales given in the stories.

To start with the more familiar, we take a brief look at Greek mythology. Because there are so many mythos creations in so many cultures, this brief overview is intended to show what a myth can look like and how many interesting and useable characters it might have. After this look, we introduce the reader to a number of other myth sources without such (modest) detail.

It's Almost All Greek to Me

These Greek stories, like those of many other cultures, include world creation myths, starting with the almost universal idea of a primordial, description-less Chaos, from which generated the first generation of gods, namely, Gaia (mother earth, a very universal symbol), Tartarus (the underworld, realm of death), Eros (love), Night, and Erebus (darkness). These generated other theme-based godlings, which typified all the varied behaviors from murder and crime to doom and deceit. Gaia and Uranus (the sky) had many children, which had among their denizens the Cyclops (a one-eyed monster), and the Titans, a second generation group that included various earth gods such as Rhea and Themis, Oceanus (god of the sea), Hyperion (god of the sun), and Cronus, the strongest and smartest of the lot. After much mayhem, Cronus and Rhea begat gods of the more familiar Greek pantheon of Zeus, Hera, Hades, and their fellow deities. This third generation of gods made their

Figure 2-3

Zeus, looking vengeful.

home on Mount Olympus, where they finally wrested control from Cronus, emasculating him, and sending the Titans to the underworld. Atlas ended up having to hold up the world on his shoulders, and Typhon, a last son of Rhea, with 100 heads and flame covering his body (this alone would make most artists salivate at the prospect of designing), ended up having a more mundane job of producing the lava for Mount Etna. With the help of the hero Heracles (Hercules), Zeus consolidated his rule, getting rid of another bunch of unlovelies, the Giants, and finally ruling a more or less stable roost.

This very modest level of detail gives the reader some idea of the richness inherent in this particular field of information. In fact, as you examine these stories, you will run across a flood myth, to be repeated in Mesopotamian and Hebrew stories, and rebirth myths. The archetypal nature of these images seems to be part of the fabric of all human experience. The stories of the Greeks evolve into how fire was discovered and used, how evil wandered into the world (Pandora's box, actually a jar), and a host of other bits and pieces of human experience. The famous stories of the *Odyssey* (by the blind poet Homer) and the *Iliad* (also by Homer) tell of the travails of the hero Odysseus and the Trojan-Greek war. They abound in imagery, such as the Cyclops Polyphemus, the monsters Scylla and Charybdis, and the lovely voiced but deadly Sirens in the *Odyssey*.

The Romans borrowed much of the Greek mythos, expanding it to suit their own needs, substituting names like Jupiter for Zeus, Mercury for Hermes (the messenger of the gods), and so on. They additionally used Egyptian, Persian, and Middle Eastern ideas in their myths, probably borrowed as they expanded into these areas by conquest. The poet Ovid drew upon much of this storytelling to produce several works, principally the *Metamorphosis*, which expands the

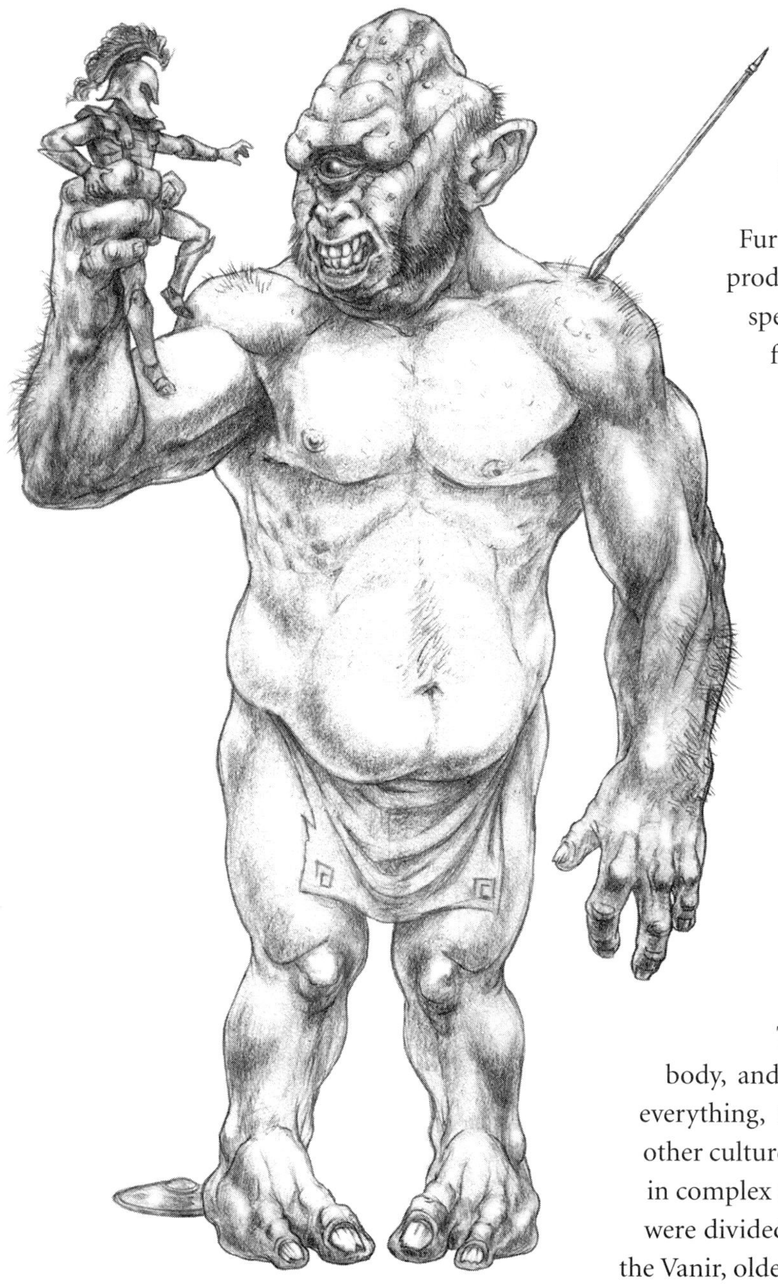

Greek and Roman tales into even more complex and fascinating intrigues and conflicts.

Way Up North

Further north in Scandinavia, the Norse produced a brand of storytelling and myth specific to their society. The chief sources for their stories are the *Poetic Edda*, *Prose Edda*, and *Saga of Volsungs*. There was not much that was happy or pleasant in their myths, which may be attributed to the difficult and strenuous lives they lived in such a harsh and demanding land. Like the Greeks, the Norse had the world starting in a kind of "nothingness" called Ginningagap. Spontaneously evolving from this is Ymir, the ancestor of the frost giants. From him comes a long list of giants, ultimately including Odin, who, rather like Zeus of the Greeks, eventually wrested control from the older gods to himself and his cohorts.

The world was made from Ymir's body, and the world tree Yggdrasil grew over everything, resembling other similar images in other cultures. From this point the stories develop in complex (and rather violent) ways. Norse gods were divided into two main groups. The first was the Vanir, older fertility gods, and the second group was the Aesir, more contemporary (for the Norse) gods with warlike attributes. Odin, the one-eyed ruler, had a wife, Frigg, akin to the Greek Zeus and Hera. Loki, the trickster, was Odin's foster brother. He was, among other things, a shape shifter. His children were quite interesting, including Hel, a daughter, who was half alive and half dead, and Jormungand, who was a giant snake that eventually wrapped around the world (like the worm Ouroboros of other legends from other cultures). Another child, Fenrir, was a huge wolf.

Figure **2-4**

Perturbed Polyphemus and friend.

Thor was the god of order and had a mighty hammer called Mjolnir. Tyr, the son of Odin, was a war god, with only one hand (the left). Freur was apparently the god of fertility, perhaps a deity developed from old Gaia or earth mother models of prehistory. Heimdall was associated with the seas and served as watchman of the gods. Njord ruled the seas, resembling Poseidon of the Greeks. Balder, whose death began the final world battle, was the wisest and kindest of the gods. The goddess of love and lust was Freya (counterpart to Greek Aphrodite). Thor's wife, Sif, ultimately ended up with hair of gold (literally), and Idun was the goddess of the Apples of Youth. The Norse characters also included giants, dwarves, elves, trolls, and dragons.

Popular fiction has certainly had its way with Scandinavian mythology as a story and character resource. J. R. R. Tolkien borrowed mightily from the Norse legends to produce his masterwork, *The Lord of the Rings* trilogy.

Even a brief glimpse of a mythos can lead to many possible visual resources. Going into even minor detail would turn this chapter into a book unto itself. Remember, take in the heroes, heroines, gods, and goddesses with their total contexts, as this will both explain and enrich the nature of each "character."

Figure | 2-5 |

The lofty Mt. Olympus.

A Sphinx, Methinks

Egypt, like other cultures, had various versions of their main mythic stories. Depending upon the era and place, the gods could interchange identities and even roles. Some representative deities include Ra, the sun god, who aged through a day from young to old; Osiris, brother and husband of Isis (children of the old sky and earth gods: Nut and Geb); Seth, the brother of Osiris and Isis, murderer of Osiris, and depicted as part pig (or anteater) and part wild donkey; and Horus, son of Osiris and Isis, later god of the sky, who is often associated with a hawk representation. Other deities include Thoth, the moon god, shown as a baboon, ibis, or man, associated with magic and the mythic Book of Thoth; Bastet, the cat goddess; Bes, a roly-poly dwarf with a lion's mane and tail; Selket, scorpion goddess; Sekhmet, the lioness goddess; Hathor, goddess of fertility; and Anubis, who had the head of a jackal.

Among the images associated with Egyptian myths are pyramids, the Sphinx, mummies, animal cults, and the Book of the Dead.

A common multicultural design theme in myth, predominant in ancient Egypt, is the attribution of animal characteristics to humans and vice versa.

Hindus and Don'ts

India, with the great Hindu religion, gave us a whole pantheon of deities and subdeities. Hinduism replaced the earlier Vedic religion, whose great writings (including the *Upanishads* and the *Rigveda*) influenced millions of people up to our present era. In Hinduism, the Great Epics (including the *Mahabarata* and *Ramanyana*), plus the collection of stories called the *Puranas* give us the basic cosmology and mythology of this religion. Brahma was the creator god, often shown with five heads facing in differing directions. Vishnu performed the duty of guarding humans and the truth of the religion. He could appear in several forms, each with a different name. Among these are Kurma, the tortoise; Varaha, the boar; Parashurama, the Brahman; Krishna, a beautiful blue being covered in jewels; and Matsya, the fish. Each performed different duties and fit into the stories in fascinating (and often ribald) ways. Some older Vedic gods remained in relation to the newer deities, including the warlike Indra, god of the atmosphere. Shiva, the Hindu god, is known as the destroyer, and had a necklace of skulls and possessed a third eye in his forehead. Goddesses include Devi, whose avatar represents several different goddesses. Another well-known figure is Durga, a warrior goddess. Kali, a terrifying hag, dark and hideous, had long fangs, and sprang from Durga's head when the latter was angry. Kali fought demons and could become drunk with blood. Manasa was the goddess of snakes; Mata the mother goddess, a sort of earth goddess, was not unlike the European Gaia. As with other mythos stories, these characters interacted in complex ways, and are extremely visually colorful and interesting.

Figure **2-6**

Not-so-jolly *jotun,* or Norse giant.

Figure | **2-7** |

Thoth, Horus, and Anubis, left to right.

Go East, Young Man!

Traveling to China, we encounter an Eastern culture whose mythology retained ideas that meld with the common mystical themes of other cultures, including the idea of the "world egg" that becomes the sky and earth.

In Chinese lore, Pan Gu was the first human. Like other progenitors in so many myths, he died after his chores were done, and his body parts became the various pieces of the world. A different creation myth has a goddess, Nu Gua, fashioning the world. Her creation stories make for intriguing reading.

Japan gives us further sources for imagery. Most early Japanese mythology was recorded in the ancient document *Kojiki*. In it, the earth was devoid at first of anything, until five gods presented themselves, and thence begat seven generations of gods following. Ultimately the first man and woman appeared, and, as usual, fumbled about in their first adventures on earth. The first-born child was a leech-child and was cast adrift. After some practice, they produced other children, which became the islands of Japan, and such gods as Kagutsuchi, the fire god. The Japanese had an underworld, like other cultures, and named theirs Yomi. The sun was represented by the goddess Amaterasu, who, like most other gods, ended up having a rather soap-operatic existence.

Other creatures inhabit these stories, including dragons, Oni (devils) with horns and cloven feet, ghosts, magical foxes, and cats. Another interesting mystical entity from Japanese lore is the kappa, a short humanoid creature that appears to be half monkey, half turtle. This amphibious critter has a hollowed out "bowl" in the top of its head that contains water. This water is the source of the kappa's mystical abilities. As long as the bowl is full, the kappa keeps its supernatural powers. Kappas may be helpful or harmful to human beings.

Would You Believe Feathered Serpents?

Latin America has a rich tradition of mythology from the Aztec, Olmec, and other historical cultures. North America's many Native American myths further enrich this mine of visual stores. From the Olmec rain god, part human and part Jaguar, to Quetzalcoatl, the feathered serpent god of the Toltecs (and other folks), the synthesis of animal and human in divine form pervades these myths. In the Mayan book *Popol Vuh*, a flood appears to destroy the first bad attempt at making humans. Floods appear in many cultural stories, indicating a kind of archetypal strength to this story mechanism.

Figure **2-8**

Elephant-like Ganesha.

Mayan gods include Cizin, the god of death (and *their* underworld), Ix Chel, the moon goddess, and Ah Kin, the sun god (who in the underworld was a jaguar). Aztecs had a head god, Tezcatlipoca, "Lord of the Smoking Mirror," Huitzlopochtli, the sun god and war god, Xipe Totec, god of springtime (i.e. rebirth), and Ehecatl, the wind god, who had aerodynamic temples. The Incas of Peru had a creator god, Viracocha, who also used a flood to destroy his first creation attempt. Their sun god was Inti and the moon goddess (the moon is "female" in many cultures) was Mama Kilya. Ilyap'a, the god of rain, used the Milky Way star band to obtain water. Among the more well known and interesting of the Southwestern Native American stories are those of the Zuni kachinas (ancestral spirits) and Kokopelli, the flute player, a common image for many cultures of that area.

Many other mythical beings and beasts abound in these stories. Some are animal-derived, like the trickster, Coyote, of the Southwest Native Americans. Bear, wolf, bird, and other "deities" walk the earth and converse with people in many tales.

Figure | 2-9 |

Bishamon, Guardian of the North and unidentified kappa.

Mything Links

In other cultures, animal-derived or purely fantastic beasts are plentiful, from the Medusa of the Greeks with her snake hair to the clay creature of Jewish tradition, the Golem. Griffons, harpies, chimeras, and unicorns: these and other wonderful characters and creatures beckon to the artist for interpretation or just as resource.

We can see the depth of the mythologic field for artists. By investigating this field in even minor depth, we can see the riches it holds visually. It has many varied typologies and visual options useable as a starting point for character development. The modest survey

Figure | 2-10 |

Krazy kokopelli.

Figure | 2-11 |

Clever coyote.

herein by no means covers, as with the literature section, the full scope of this category. By using the myths outlined here and by following up with other stories from other cultures, from Africa to the South Pacific, the artist, with a modest investment in research, should find plenty of new material available for character derivation.

History and Culture, or Vice Versa

History provides an amazing source for visual information. The nature of historical records is to store for future generations all types of information relating to actual events and people from the past. Within these records are everything from small anecdotes about day to day living for the peasant in medieval France to the tragic and dramatic romance of Cleopatra and Marc Antony. To sort through historical sources, we recommend getting a general text from the library, one either covering the whole gamut of human activity or one from a particular historical era (or place). One excellent source is *The Story of Civilization* by Will Durant, a series of extremely well written and accurate historical surveys of different times and people. With some judicious skimming and index reading, sources related to your search or just generally interesting information should be available in short order. Frequently other sources are pointed out in the text or bibliography.

Encyclopedias and summary texts like them also contain much that can be used. Topics can be sorted by category (e.g., plagues, the Renaissance, and exploration of the New World) and by place or culture. What makes the search more effective is to get at least some preliminary sense of what direction you might wish to go and then by index to sort out various possibilities by era and place. As an adjunct, look through art history books of the same time frame. They frequently have sources of visual reaction to events of their time, or at least they give a temper of the type of image available within that time frame. Stylistic slants on imagery that an artist might not conjure on his or her own may be found in these paintings, sculptures, and other artistic artifacts. Here we have a double-barreled attack on possible sources of images for character development.

Costumes, weaponry, armor, and related image categories comprise another realm to be explored in the historical locale. Oddly enough, the juvenile section of the library proves to be superior often to the general library resources because of the heavy pictorial content of young readers' books. Larger prop imagery such as Viking ships or Colonial carriages fit in here; architectural resources are almost limitless within historical research.

Innumerable books detail everything from Scottish castle ruins to Gothic church architecture. Some books even give cut-away views and construction scenarios that could be useful to an artist.

MYTH ADVENTURES

Author and researcher Joseph Campbell outlined the basic formula for a general myth, sometimes called a *monomyth*. This is the famous "hero's journey" that many readers may already be familiar with. *Star Wars*, *The Lord of the Rings*, and *Monty Python and the Search for the Holy Grail* are all examples of variants of this theme. It fulfills much of the archetypal drives to integrate various parts of the psyche through symbolic or actual means. Much of world literature also partakes of this thematic base. In it, the "hero," which can actually be any of us, male or female, is moved from a normal, perhaps comfortable status quo to embark on a journey that is life-altering. The phases of this journey are as follows:

1. The Call to Adventure. A herald or sign disturbs the equilibrium of the hero's (or heroine for all that follows) life. He must respond, often because there is a triggering event or set of circumstances that allows no other option. Therefore, he at least begins the mindset if not actually the journey of adventure. This is the "departure," or "separation." Later in the journey he will experience the "return" phase of the journey.

continued

2. Sometimes there is a refusal to the call; the hero is not ready or needs further provocation to heed the call to adventure.

3. Helpers/Amulet. After finally accepting the call, the hero may encounter a figure or circumstance that bestows upon him a device (magic or similar instrument) that is an aid to his adventure. This is often known as the "boon."

4. Crossing of the Threshold. In this, the hero departs from the comfortable, known surroundings for the unknown. Sometimes the threshold is literal: a barrier. Often it is merely a change of context.

5. In the Belly of the Whale. Often the threshold crossing leads to a "dark world" or difficult world—the belly of the whale—which the hero must negotiate in order to emerge and begin the "initiation," a realm of tests.

6. The Road of Trials. This begins the real set of tests for the hero, a series of bouts, trials, or adventures that test him in various ways.

7. The hero may meet with the Goddess. This can take the form of an ultimate prize or a literal feminine (or perhaps masculine for a heroine) partner. The other side of the goddess is as temptress, someone who can lure the hero away from the quest.

8. Symbolic Death. The hero may experience a symbolic death, in which he loses his original self preparatory to his new persona emerging. This can take a literal and sometimes terrifying form in a story.

9. Atonement/Recognition by Father. The father figure represents a higher power, such as God, or Logos, or a similar theme.

In this stage, the hero must reconcile with this "figure."

10. Apotheosis. Through reconciliation and trial, the hero experiences an apotheosis, or elevation to a new, higher status.

11. The Ultimate Boon. Now the hero is in possession of a great boon, which can be enlightenment, a physical prowess, a great gift, or substance that is needed or can be dispensed to others.

12. The Return. Once the hero has reached this stage, he may experience a reluctance (or be held back by some force) to return to the "real" world.

13. Refusal of Return

14. Rescue and Magic Flight: others may have to intervene to rescue the hero from his predicament; once this has been accomplished, he makes a perilous journey back with his boon.

15. A symbolic rebirth may occur here, rather than earlier in the story, with the hero crossing another threshold that has an opposite pairing with the first threshold he crossed at the beginning of the journey.

16. Master of Two Worlds. The threshold crossed, the hero is now master of two worlds, that is, an integrated psyche, which may be demonstrated by a literal ability to move between the two worlds in the myth at will.

17. Freedom to Live. After completion of the journey, the hero is free and able to dispense his boon to others.

Although this format is rarely followed completely in all its detail, much of the structure can be found in part throughout various myths and stories.

Figure |2-12|

Ye Olde Scottish castle: environments affect characterization.

Real Characters

Within the historical category, we find numerous examples of colorful characters. Whether real or quasilegendary, they are a gold mine of possible source material. A few names thrown out here gives some idea of the staggering number of possibilities: Blackbeard the pirate, Mary Queen of Scots, Julius Caesar, Jack the Ripper, Charles the Bald, Genghis Khan, Ramses I (and all the other Rameses) of Egypt, Nero and Caligula, Aristotle, Alexander the Great, Leif Erickson, Chief Joseph, Anne Frank, Faust, Queen Victoria, Nefertiti, Plato, Huang Po, Confucius, Dogen, Rasputin, Caligula, Audie Murphy, Plato, Benjamin Franklin, Simon Bolivar, and Malcom X. The list is endless.

As with the literature, the supply of information will easily outstrip the demand of the artist. Eras give much to provoke thought on character development, for example, the years of the Black Plague, a disease that ravaged Europe and Asia from the 1300s onward.

Images can also be culled (and imagined) from the landscape of severe cold weather during the Little Ice Age (when a mild return to the Ice Age conditions of several thousand years ago occurred) of about 1400 to 1800, in which the English channel sometimes froze over, allowing wolves to travel from the continent to England.

Figure |2-13|

Ever-lovin' Ben Franklin.

The pre-Renaissance artists Pieter Breughel, Hieronymous Bosch, and others painted scenes derived directly from the feel and actual events of the time; some are allegorical in nature as in Bosch's *The Haywain*, and others are realistically descriptive. Explore the art history books at your local library for examples of such imagery.

Figure **2-14**

Plague remnants. Props set the stage for character development.

Miscellaneous Comments

One can see that the context often drives the character, as we have mentioned before. Obviously we can't even attempt to be a history primer here. Rather, we want to point out a direction for the artist to take. History often provides us with circumstances and images beyond what we thought possible. Even contemporary history is replete with overwhelming scenes of joy, pathos, and drama. The advent of the photograph has greatly enlarged the resource of recorded imagery from the recent past. Pictorial archives are abundant, and can be retrieved through the library or research desk at the library, or over the internet. Copyright laws in relation to more contemporary images should be respected; if in doubt, contact a library staff member to help you determine whether you need to get permission from an estate or other legal entity to use an image.

Figure **2-15**

Ice Age, Jr. Surroundings support acting and story.

Figure | 2-16 |

Baba Yaga on the loose!

Tales of Wonder

As we have previously discussed, stories and characterization developed thousands of years ago as a method for groups to create communal bonds while trying to explain the uncanny forces of nature. The oral tales were not only instructional but also used for amusement, support of cultural morality, and enlightenment of the listener. These "wonder tales," so called because of the marvelous element introduced as part of the story line, were tied to the beliefs and customs of the people who told them. These stories were the original fairy tales.

This type of tale does not usually approach the magnitude of mythology, but rather might simply involve a tale of magic, human passion, or adventure set within the context of the particular feel of a certain place and time. There are several distinct types of folk tales. Some are traditions and legends, more along the lines of mythology. They may also include semihistorical figures, and even cover creation or the origins of a tribe or people.

True fairy tales (especially later works) are more formularized, and involve fantasy creatures or the like "beyond the normal" activity and characters. Snow White is an example of this type of story.

Witches, ghosts, animated inanimate objects, distressed princesses, giants, and talking animals figure into these legends, amidst a wealth of other character types. All cultures have tales relating to animals, as we were once much more intimately involved with them and nature. These creatures, heroes, and villains have formed the archetypal basis for many characters that we continue to redesign and visually explore to the present day. Western cultures know many of these characters by heart: Sleeping Beauty, Rumpelstiltskin, and Tom Thumb, to name a few.

The rural south in America produced ample numbers of folk tales about swamp critters and ghosts and gullible humans. Within the Native American tradition, folk stories are the norm. Morality tales, scary stories, and simple humor are scattered throughout these delightful tales. Europe, Asia, Africa, Australia, island nationalities, and South America: explore these areas and you will find thousands of smaller stories or folk tales embedded in the traditions of the various peoples of each land.

Figure **2-17**

Threatening prow of a Viking longship.

As we delve more deeply into the folk tales of specific societies, we come up with interesting thematic character variants. In Russian folklore, for instance, resides the witch, Baba Yaga. Instead of flying around on a battered broomstick, this hoary hag traverses the ether in a giant mortar (pestle included). If that isn't weird enough, Baba Yaga lived in a wooden hut that tramped about on giant chicken legs! Such tales are food for thought when it comes to designing interesting characters.

An Inordinately Brief History of the Literary Fairy Tale

As organized religion and "civilized" thought began to relegate wonder tales to the venue of the uneducated peasantry, these oral traditions became virtually lost to all but the lowest classes of many cultures. The transition of the oral folk tale to the written folk tale was an arduous process. Most of the people who shared strong oral cultural traditions could not read, and the fables had not been modified to suit the tastes of ruling classes.

The predominant intellectual and literary language through the late Middle Ages was Latin, so written resources were not widespread because of the illiteracy of the populace. Literary fairy tales and their characters needed a receptive audience and a framework that was understandable. Religious instruction incorporated such tales to give their lessons a cultural context. Such manuscripts as the *Gesta Romanorum* (circa 1300) were used to provide moralistic instruction for young Christian boys via anecdotal stories.

The publication of *The Pleasant Nights* (1550–1553) by Giovan Francesco Straparola created a group of stories that were originally designed to entertain him and other exiled Milanese aristocrats, but the text became popular for mixed-class audiences of the time. Gradually, the literary fairy tale and its characters were brought to light in a vernacular that could be understood by a wide range of people.

As the years progressed, the literacy rate grew across Europe as cultural activity increased and commercialism prospered, and from 1690 to 1714, the literary fairy tale came into vogue. France was a key source in spreading literary fairy tales, which became gradually accepted in literary salons. Fairy tale recitations and games were of special interest to aristocratic women. The most prodigious French fairy tale writers of the period were Mme. Marie-Catherine D'Aulnoy and Charles Perrault, known for the tale "Puss in Boots." A veritable "golden age" of the fairy tales spread over Europe over the following hundred years, with old and new fairy tales being preserved by such collectors as the Brothers Grimm.

The means to finding these stories is through the library or internet, searching via the term "folk stories" or "cultural tales."

Scientifically Speaking

In the field of scientific literature, we find ourselves with an even more substantial amount of information available to the artist. What does the term *scientific literature* mean? It refers to the vast accumulation of studies, monographs, papers, books, and notes covering humankind's exploration of the universe. Much of what is extant has been produced within the last 50 years, driven by the astonishing surge of technology. All theological and metaphysical arguments aside, just as a visual resource, this storehouse of facts and imagery is an excellent place for the artist to rummage about. Science has the virtue of being able to be categorized somewhat more easily than some of the sources discussed earlier in this chapter. Let's look at some basic ways it can be broken down and used by an artist interested in character design.

Popular magazines that have as their audience interested laymen are in many ways the best source for scientific imagery and information. These have excellent artwork and photographs accompanying stories that are written in accessible language. Many such magazines have come and gone, but certain ones have stayed the course. Some magazines are more for the informed reader, but still have the virtue of excellent graphics and reasonably understandable language. Well known among these are such publications as *Scientific American, Lancet,* and *Discover.*

They command fairly wide readership, and have well written and usually quite interesting articles written by researchers in a dizzying array of fields.

Each area of scientific study has journals oriented to those in the field, and although they can be daunting reading, oftentimes gems of information and interesting pictorials lie in these publications. Paleontology, archeology, physical and social anthropology, astronomy, physics, meteorology: These don't even touch the beginning of the varied fields covered by such journals. The student or artist researching this arena would probably be best served by initially searching the internet for organizations and sites that lead to both hardcopy reading and online articles. Narrowing by category (e.g., saber-toothed cats or trees of the rain forest) begins the search in earnest. Museums and large academic websites are sometimes poorly organized, and it is recommended that the artist contact individual researchers or groups or clubs associated with the larger organizations to find imagery and information suitable to their topic. Inspired amateurs often have websites that are goldmines of visuals and readable text, along with electronic newsletters and subject-related "chat rooms." Individual monographs published within each discipline are another road to be taken, and with patience the artist can find skeletal reconstructions of prehistoric beasts, for instance, and other difficult-to-locate imagery from the researchers themselves. Researchers often will be pleased to give out the names and websites of colleagues who have related information: We have repeatedly found this to be true.

Books detailing the evolution of various inventions, discoveries, and overviews of different disciplines fill shelves at libraries and bookstores. They have the advantage of not having to be printed from a computer or of being as fragile as magazines. Artists frequently have their own mini-library of science; our own libraries contain surveys of animal species and anatomy, astronomical images, dinosaur and mammal fossil history, and so forth. Coffee-table books that are basically "eye-candy" can be had for a little more money. Look for such tomes in the library, where they can be borrowed for free.

Getting Cultured

Popular culture and related media give the artist a further area of visual exploration. Pop icons and entertainment stars often inhabit visually stunning contexts, both living-wise and costume-wise. Their lifestyles give interesting ideas for character development and background invention. Various popular magazines available at the newsstand or bookstore can, with the proper editing, provide a villainess or sidekick character by close scrutiny of their photo-stories. General magazine resources that mirror more mundane cultural mores still can provide such information regarding costume, architecture, hairstyles, and the like.

Posters, promotional material, videos, and movies are slickly constructed by professional teams of artists and directors: These provide both a "norm" of the cultural times and additional visual resources for the artist. The downside to this element is the creative inhibiting factor of trying to emulate the look of the contemporary in order to be viable in the marketplace. Here artists must be able to use elements and yet forge their own path visually. Not doing so will doom them to following rather than leading. Of course, not all artists can be in the stratosphere of creative thinking, but it is nonetheless a worthy goal.

Lose the Trenchcoat!

Popular imagery in the media is often and unfortunately a primary target of reference for many artists. While this area can afford wonderful fuel for the fire of the imagination, it presents some pitfalls that are problematic for character designers. One ill-used medium that often presents difficulty is the comic book. Don't get us wrong; we love well written and illustrated comic books, but care must be exercised in using them as a reference.

A huge problem with comics as reference is "style creep." As certain artists in comicdom gain popularity based on a new or intriguing visual style, many other artists seem to begin to "develop" a similar style in order to capitalize on another's notoriety.

This problem leads to a bunch of bad knock-offs. While we as artists grab stylistic "chunks" from other artists as we develop our style, direct replication of someone else's style should be avoided. The Japanese manga style of comics is a good example of a style that can be interesting, but it has developed an almost cult status among American artists to the point of being overdone.

Another "style creep" issue that affects both comic books and films is the adoption of a certain genre "look" that is implemented and then summarily beaten to death over the course of many comics and films. The "brooding-pseudoGothic-vampire/antihero-in-a-black-leather-trench-coat-with-swords-and/or-automatic-pistols-and-sunglasses" character that has reared its head in multiplicity over recent years is an example of such an overused subgenre type. As a researcher, it is as important to consider what *not* to take from a resource subject as it is to choose what to use.

Other cultures provide paths to be followed prudently as character design reference. One obvious example is the aforementioned anime craze sweeping our country. This visual import from Japan has a distinctive stylistic approach that many young artists find attractive (and practical to copy). The large number of titles available on video or DVD that are animated in this or related styles can be a good source for visuals, especially in the area of backgrounds. The Japanese have extremely accomplished background artists and the products that they turn out make good sources for ideas and stylistic solutions. China has, of late, provided cinema that is both refreshing and exciting visually. Grand epics, adventures, and genre films give the artist a look at a world quite unlike the West. India, South America, Europe, Australia, Canada, and Central America: All these and more have their own unique cultural properties. *National Geographic Magazine*, among others, is an excellent resource for plumbing other cultures and the looks they can provide. Travel magazines are other resources in this area. Tourism is a large industry and because of its importance to many countries, their governments often produce slick, interesting brochures of packaged tours and trips to the particular area. Within these lie many possible visual sources. By contacting the consulates or other representatives of various countries, an artist can provide themselves with an abundance of full color material about another culture.

Sport is another arena for research. Topical magazines such as *Sporting News* and *Sports Illustrated* give ample supplies of action photographs of sports figures. From ancient times to the present, athletic activity has provided much in the way of imagery. Frescos and wall murals from ancient civilizations like Rome and Mycenae show acrobats and wrestlers performing and competing. Contemporary culture has raised sports figures to the level of icons, with the result that there are whole industries devoted to the use of sports imagery. This particular area provides an abundance of colorful characters ripe for use as reference material. One can think of Wilt Chamberlin, Ted Williams, Pelé, or the many Olympic athletes that thrill us every few years. Their exploits have been recorded on film, in books, and on videotape and DVD; all of which are accessible by library or the internet.

The fine arts contribute their share of visual information too. Composers and performers such as Paganini, Brahms, and Berlioz were all colorful characters worthy of exploration, and all had paintings and portraits (and not a few scandalous cartoons) done from their likenesses. The painter Caravaggio died on a beach after being stabbed in retribution for a crime he had committed. Leonardo da Vinci constructed war machines as well as the Mona Lisa, and was himself a fascinating-looking man. The artist Frida Kahlo, now the subject of a well known movie, exemplifies the gender-blind aspect of this category. Her tragic life and startling visage certainly inspired more than a few creative thoughts.

This explorative adventure could be added to indefinitely, but the general idea has been made. With a little thought, any artist can productively research imagery and information useful to projects at hand. The appendixes give a small peek at an enormous world. It is estimated that there are about 300 million websites available on the internet. That is a staggering number. Although only a fraction relate to our visual research theme, it is still a rich lode to be mined. With the addition of libraries, bookstores, and other publication outlets, there is no limit to what is available to the creative mind.

SUMMARY

This chapter has emphasized the importance of research in the actual practice of character development and design. As with all good creative endeavors, it is the preliminary work that makes the end result so satisfying. If an artist or artist in training takes the time to uncover and use the wealth of information available for character design, then that artist will discover that being original and eye-catching are still possible, even in today's marketplace.

Categories introduced in this chapter include literature, mythology, folklore, scientific literature, and popular culture, with the expectation that the artist or student will use the recommended resources, namely, libraries, bookstores, and the internet to do further research. When

STUDENT SHOWCASE

James Thayn

Student artwork by Jamus Thayn: Thor and youthful character. Thayn has used a mythical Norse god for one of his characters, choosing to portray him with strong Viking overtones. The other character is more generic. Both reveal a commonality of style in line and structure that show their common artistic source.

using the internet and looking at potential sites listed, it is a good idea to review the cache under each site. This often eliminates useless wandering in tangential sites. Each category listed is quite broad and complicated; our intent is to help narrow the preliminary search by pointing out larger groupings of information and providing the ways and means of looking through them. Some areas such as mythology are given a more in-depth description, partly to show how any category can be great in depth and partly to portray the richness of a specific category of knowledge.

exercises

1. Pick two types of characters. Using the categories listed in this chapter, develop several sources for each type, noting the bibliography of each and how the material could be used to further refine the characters.

2. Find several illustrators' art for some literary sources. Using these as a guide, redo the characters in your own style.

3. Create a scientific illustration with characters based on a scientific source listed in this chapter.

4. Create an extended list of contemporary comic and graphic novel genre magazines.

in review

1. What are the major written categories of visual resource for the artist?

2. How can mythology and folk tales be used as visual resources for character development?

3. What are some of the ways these resources can be explored? Give several options.

4. How does using one of the sources listed in this chapter enhance the artist's own imaginative resources?

notes

characters: archetypes, life forms, and worlds

objectives

Gain an introduction to some main categories of characters and creatures.

Learn about humanoid oriented characters: heroes, heroines, villains, supporting characters, and their related ilk.

Learn about characters and life forms that are not humanoid: aliens, robotic entities, animals and animal-related characters, plant characters, and others.

Investigate the natural world and its limiting effect: ecology, body systems, reproduction, ancestors, migration, and isolation.

Discuss fitting the character to the story line: do's and don'ts; the importance of description and plot; theme.

Explore characters and context: history, culture, locale, and environment.

Learn about how costumes and props affect character typology.

introduction

This chapter concerns itself with the various categories of characters and creature and some of their modifying criteria. This, in plain language, refers to the kind of character (hero, human, female), their style of presentation (cartoon, realistic, industry style), their particular elements (armor, hairdo), and their limiting context (historical context, environment). We also deal with nonsentient (nonthinking/reasoning) creatures in much the same way, although their categories concerning behavior are much more at an instinctual level. Again, it is impossible to cover every conceivable type and circumstance of character choice; however, by dealing with most of the more well known niches and modifiers, we show the reader some basic design paths that have been laid out and how, in some measure, to follow them. With this said, the following goes through some of the basic ways artists and designers construct character and creature design within these constraints, prefaced by a brief historical note.

CHARACTERS: ARCHETYPES, LIFE FORMS, AND WORLDS

Archetype Setting

Eons before humans like Gutenberg were setting words in type, they were using images to transfer ideas at a symbolic level (Mayan and Egyptian pictograms), and then much later at a "realistic" level (Realist painters). Where some of this picture-based idea exchange would later develop into linguistic forms, another path would lead to a refinement of pictorial elements that could describe the nature of its subject as an individual. This is basic characterization. The addition of modifiers (exaggeration, for instance) further define the nature of the character.

Culture and tradition weigh heavily in the history of characterization and the development of archetypal character forms. Before this train of thought chugs any further down the tracks, let us stop to define the term *archetype*. *Webster's Third New International Dictionary* defines the term *archetype* as follows, in definitions 1 and 3a, respectively:

> "The original model, form, or pattern from which something is made or from which something develops."

> "A primitive generalized plan of structure deduced from the characters of the numbers of a natural group of animals or plants and assumed to be the type from which they have been modified."

As previously discussed with characterization in the form of the Venus of Willendorf and Mr. Punch, an archetype represents a sort of ultimate form of a living being or character: man, woman, hero, villain, etc. Idealization, based on cultural influences, modifies the archetype. What is the ideal form for a beautiful woman? What elements physically define a villain? Idealization (which may be positive or negative) usually involves an exaggeration of the original form.

Stereotyping, in which physical, emotional, and cultural elements are developed in a pronounced form to establish specific audience recognition, is a staple of characterization. Unfortunately, stereotyping is often thought of as a negative term because of its often inappropriate application to racial or ethnic groups. Through stereotyping, the character design is able to draw upon visual elements that act as socially ingrained clues to stimulate audience recognition:

> Low forehead, buck teeth, blonde hair = stupidity
>
> Bald, stooped posture = old
>
> Fat, hairy, pig-eyed = oafish; bestial

These examples are a miniscule thought on the exhaustive generic methods by which stereotyping is used as a characterization tool. Remember to approach this method with care, so as to avoid being inappropriately insulting.

Pick A Path!

What do we mean by choosing a character? It sounds simple enough, like saying "eenie, mee-nie, minie, mo" or rolling a pair of knucklebones. Well, "simple" is a relative term and the choosing process, which may be challenging, means two things, actually:

1. Picking an initial concept to develop into a character design
2. Thinking about character development by choosing specific character types or archetypes to use as a base form to build on

Following these choices are two primary paths that lead to artistic character development and modify our choosing process. These are motivations through self-interest and project-driven creation. The self-interest path refers to developing a character based on individual preference and ideas. This path is typically chosen based on some interesting idea that we have brain-stormed or may have simply started from a thumbnail drawing in a sketchbook. The fact that we as creators have come up with a "cool" idea for a character is our primary motivation for getting it out of our heads and onto paper. Whether or not this character serves a purpose as a part of a story line may be secondary in some cases.

The project-driven path requires that characters be generated as part of a particular story idea, game concept, or toy development idea. While project-driven characters may relate to personal artistic concepts, they are typically related to such projects as films or comic books, which are meant to be marketed for monetary gain. Often, character and story development in a profes-sional studio environment are controlled or supervised by nonartists. This reminds us authors of a story. . .

The Slings and Arrows of Outrageous Fortune Seekers

Once upon a time, a friend of one of the authors, Penelope, worked as an art director in a very small studio, with a very small artistic staff (herself and one other artist). This studio developed animation projects for film and television. The owner/producer of the studio was predominantly a businessman, who fancied himself as an idea-man of some renown. One day, he burst into the room where the artists were hiding and announced that he had come up with a great idea for a new animated television series. "It's called 'Amoebas'!"

Then, as he left the room, he asked them to get to work developing characters and a story line for the series immediately.

Reeling from incredulousness, Penelope and the other artist finally regained their senses after a few minutes and wondered how in the heck they were going to hang the entire premise for an animated television series on one word. Penelope decided that their first step would be to have the artists do some brainstorming individually on how the term *amoeba* could translate into character designs and then regroup later to discuss their concept sketches. It ended up that both of the artists came up with some really neat character and story ideas, and that the design problem facing them had actually been an opportunity for a "free reign" implementation of their character design skills. By the end of that day, they had at least two strong treatments to go along with several color and black-and-white character designs. The boss was pleased and the "Amoebas" development forged ahead for some time. Unfortunately, the characters were soon found to be too close visually to the designs used in Warner Brothers' animated film *Osmosis Jones* (which was undergoing clandestine development as Penelope and her group were developing their characters), and was scrapped after that film's release. Oh, well. *C'est la vie!*

The moral of this story is "If you're afraid of your producer, find a better place to hide." Not really. The real moral of this saucy little anecdote is that professional character designers rarely work on their own ideas and are most often creating character concepts based on story ideas that may or may not come from an artistic personage. These are project-driven character designs. The challenge of the character creator is to take these rudimentary concepts and turn them into some plausible character ideas.

Character Ingredients

To create a character, an artist needs to have some idea of where he, she, or it will fit. Is the character for a story, film, game, or other type of visual communication? What is the emotive nature of the story? It might be drama, tragedy, comedy, satire, parody, slapstick, action hero/heroine vehicle, military/combat, historical, science fiction, fantasy, horror, or just plain weird. Once this has been determined, then an artist, as we have and will again allude to, must avoid clichés and stereotypes, unless directly ordered to produce just that. Cultural sensitivity is another issue relevant now; we should try to avoid representing various population groups in ways that are offensive and blatantly untrue. With the story in hand, the role of the character needs refinement. (Main categories are discussed later.) To clarify what the character is, we can ask certain questions, some of which are listed previously:

- What is the environment of the character?
- Where does it live now?
- Does it have a name, family, clan, tribe or other affiliation?
- Is it based on myth, legend, someone's writing, or other sources?

Other questions ensue:

- How was it born (hatched, created etc.)?
- What are its physical characteristics?
- Does it have strengths or flaws in its personality?
- Is it educated, literate, illiterate, intelligent, crafty, stupid, dull, or some other related trait?
- Does it have a job? Skills?

- What is its financial status (if there is such a thing in the story)?

- Does it have tool savvy?

- How about favorite foods, hobbies, or other tastes?

- What sort of body language does it use?

- Does it have a costume or other coverings or accessories (including props or mechanical contrivances small enough to fit an individual being)?

- Is it "cartoony," realistic, or fitted into some other stylistic genre? (This latter question is addressed more fully in Chapter Six).

- Is the character disguised?

- Does it have a certain range of emotional states?

- Do servants, harems, business associates, or other characters flesh out its feel or characteristics?

- In its history, are there triumphs, failures, traumas, or other significant events?

- Is it generous, selfish, superstitious, oafish, clumsy, petulant, or some other of a host of other possible personality qualities?

- If an action-type character, would it be characterized as more offensively or defensively oriented? What are its physical capabilities?

More questions may ensue related to a specific project:

- Will the character be animated? What is the size of the character in relation to its surroundings?

- Will the camera (if filmed or similar) be close or far?

- What is the size of the character in relation to the other characters?

- How many angles will it be viewed from?

- How much movement will it have?

- Will we see the face, with emotions, and will it speak or utter any kind of sound?

After stumbling through these and other defining types of questions, the artist and director (or author) can settle down to more specific art creation and development of the character—story relationship.

Putting the Pedal to the Metal

Characters drive story. This is probably the most important piece of theoretical information about character design that we are providing in this illustrious tome. Characters and story are forever bound to each other. Hypothetically, we might think of a story as an automobile, let's say a station wagon, with the story's protagonist as the driver. The protagonist is the main character (or in some cases, multiple principal characters) around which the story line focuses. A hero is a typical protagonist. We might think of the story's antagonist as riding along in the front seat. A villain is a typical antagonist, or principal adversary, to the protagonist in a drama or narrative. Please understand that these roles can be, and often are, reversed. An example of this kind of role inversion is seen in John Gardner's novel *Grendel*, a retelling of the epic Anglo-Saxon story from the point of view of a more sympathetic monster.

We could perhaps place the entire supporting cast for our story in the back seat of the station wagon. These characters include sidekicks, minor adversaries, henchmen, friend, pets, and "background" characters. In motion picture terms, many of these characters would qualify as extras or "thug 1" and "thug 2" in the credits. In role-playing game terminology, these characters or creatures would be NPCs or "nonplayer characters."

Then we might imagine a gleaming Airstream trailer in tow, carrying a load of other elements that are key factors in storytelling: backgrounds/environments, accessories, props, costumes, and the script.

With this visualization exercise in mind, the relationship between character elements and story in a narrative environment becomes clear.

Cheers, Tears, and Jeers

Larger-than-life heroes fill our television and movie screens: tragic tales of lost souls wrench a few tears from the eyes (and we pretend that it was just a bit of dirt that got in under the eyelid) or a villain wreaks mayhem on an innocent village and we are outraged. Perhaps we are watching a drama unfold on a faraway planet, where strange, unearthly creatures lurk menacingly in a methane river, threatening the well-being of the space explorers. In every case, we, the audience, are being drawn into a story through the use of character and creature types. When we say character or creature types, we are really talking about the role they play within the story.

Story lines for games, movies, comic books, graphic novels, and related venues are driven by similar emotional mechanisms. We mention elsewhere the underlying setup, conflict, and resolution; within this structure, certain types of characters show up repeatedly to fulfill the need of the story and to give the audience personally identifiable individuals. This is necessary because the anonymity of large groups or pure symbols is difficult for the average viewer to penetrate and relate to. So the storyteller and designer produce characters that allow the viewer to personify various kinds of human (and unhuman) traits.

Emotion is the primary tool that entices a viewer. He or she wants certain outcomes because of the emotional attachment to the characters in the story. This provides the source for the storyteller to give each character motivation, the meaning for what the character does and *who* the character is. The main characters in any story line are the protagonist (good guy) and the antagonist (bad guy). We often call them by other names, such as hero, villain, sheriff, or outlaw (and they can be female as well as male), but by any name they drive the story forward

Figure | 3-1 |

Several types of heroes.

through the resolution of their conflict. Even if missing, the roles still play out in some fashion nonetheless.

A type of a character is in reality its role within a story (or implied story). There are *generic* role types, and these are used to manipulate the audience's emotions (and pocketbooks) as "plugged" into a particular script. A hero or heroine provides the protagonist for a viewer. We identify with this character in a fairly personal way. This character type, however, rises above the normal everyday limitations that ground most of us. A hero performs amazing deeds that transcend normal human performance and typically is able to deal with imposing odds. Within this category, we find characters that move from ordinary to heroic, some who begin as more than ordinary, and those who seem almost godlike in their abilities. Examples of each are numerous: Gary Cooper as the sheriff in *High Noon* might fit the first description, Arnold Schwarzenegger as the military man who triumphs over the alien in *Predator* could fit the second type, and any Marvel Comic hero would fulfill the last category. In all cases, the audience roots for the hero/protagonist to prevail; we identify with, in fact live vicariously through, these characters. Whether on screen or in an action game, the feeling is identical for the person watching or playing.

Good guys (or girls) aren't necessarily heroes. They may perform in a much more ordinary way than a hero could, yet still fulfill the role of protagonist, because their motives are more pure or less threatening than others within the story. Comedies and other types of story lines contain this type of character in droves.

Villains provide a target for our pent-up anger and personal devils, or they provide general relief from stress, if, and this is a big if, they are vanquished. If the villain wins, then the tables have been turned, and the audience experiences either defeat, or, as in the case of the horror/gore

Figure | 3-2 |

Examples of other protagonists that aren't heroes.

genre, indulges in the sensation of fear and mystery. This perverse bit of human behavior is a common experience for all of us. Its analog is the screaming roller coaster ride: We pretend to be in danger, and our bodies, oblivious to the rationality of the situation, react as though we really are! Villains are the antagonists, the personalized force that allows the hero to function. Even if this is in the form of a mindless, hideous creature, the result is primarily the same.

As with heroes, villains come in various forms. There are ordinary or "good" people gone bad or there are people who have never had a lot of ethics or compassion, like the career criminal.

Figure |3-3|

Hiss! Boo! Some examples of villains.

Figure | 3-4 |

Other character types.

Then there are the psychotic or sociopathic personalities that plunge through society destructively, without any regard to consequence, completely imploded in their motive and awareness. As with the protagonist, there can be rather ordinary bad guys, those whose personal traits are more irritating or petty than those of the more monumental, Stalin-like villain. This might be the head cheerleader who merely torments the bookworm-ish girl in the high school class, or it could be an overbearing manager at work.

Other than the protagonists and antagonists that are often the central plot movers, we have many other roles available to the artist and designer: comic relief; sidekick or friend; lusty babe or desirable hunk; oafish boor or jerk; scheming plotter (not a main villain) as in a social climber; fool; hedonist (pleasure pursuer); village idiot; weakling; mundane laborer, clerk, or homebody; elderly type; recluse. Each of these fulfills certain plot needs and help drive the story forward (if there is a story).

As an example of these other types of characters, we look at the sidekick category. A sidekick is someone, male or female, who gives dramatic or comic relief to the main protagonist or antagonist, who may give advice or simply be the ear for venting, and who normally fulfills the role of friend without encroaching on the main character's audience draw. Examples of this type of character include Gabby Hayes (of the old movie westerns), the talking mule of Shrek, and Santo Panza, Don Quixote's loyal companion.

Within a script or story line, as in any design, we need to flesh out the entire design (story) with elements that are not as flashy or dominant as the main elements. This gives it completeness and breadth, authenticity, and variety. There are obviously many more types than we have enumerated, but these cover much of the available plotting found in various forms of entertainment. It is interesting to note that these types can be found in alien characters as well as human(oid) ones, assuming that the motivation for them is similar. Ultimately, all of these characters must have appeal; they must draw the audience in and make them interested in following the story.

Average Joe Animal

Not all characters are humanoid, and there are some that seem human-like but are certainly different upon closer examination of physical or other traits. Animal based, some living, moving elements of a story are not particularly high on the IQ charts (e.g., a toad), and partake from a little to almost nothing in the way humans appear. This large world is the world of beings and beasts that populate many fantasy, science fiction, or horror stories. For thinking animal characters, we must remember that stories like *Watership Down*, with its sentient rabbits, or the *Secret of NIMH*, again with intelligent rats, don't easily fit within certain boundaries. Nor does *Winnie the Pooh*, and a whole host of other sometimes delightful, sometimes grim tales. Fairy tales, myths, and legends abound with animals, hybrid creatures, and the like that exhibit a wide range of intelligences and emotional states. So in general, there are familiar animals set within both expected story contexts and altered story contexts. They may exhibit behaviors that are associated with their known status in the animal kingdom, or may talk and wear costumes, perhaps even have some slight body modifications.

Figure | 3-5 |

More examples of other subsidiary types of characters.

Figure | 3-6 |

Animals as characters.

Similar to Humans, Only Different

Within this very broad expanse, we can separate and define such beings in the following ways. First would be sentient (thinking) and somewhat human-like beings. These could include everything from vampires to human/machine hybrids. Their appearance seems somewhat like

Figure | 3-7 |

Human-like, but not human characters. Too close for comfort though. . .

ours, but their motives, abilities, and general behavior take other and often surprising turns. Included within this category are many such familiar characters as Dracula (who once was human), Frankenstein (same issue, with multiple sources), the Golem (living stone creatures), lycanthropic characters (Wolfman, bird-man, in fact, any human turned animal), and the Creature from the Black Lagoon.

This category is sometimes the most disturbing, rather like the sociopath or psychotic killer, because their resemblance to an ordinary person is enough that when they behave in other, often outrageous ways, our sense of reality is shaken to its roots. This is their great value as characters, rather like a mask that when pulled off reveals the true, and often scary being beneath. Not all of them are bad or frightening. Some merely muddle along like us and can have great comic or even tragic potential.

Once we move beyond human resemblance, the field becomes cluttered with a myriad of creatures and characters.

Aye, Robot

Inorganic characters (creatures as well) such as robots and androids fit another niche. These have been made either by another intelligent life form or by other robots or similar non-organic organisms. In this sense they arrive full blown, without much in the way of development, unlike living creatures. There may be preliminary versions, or more advanced types, but the changes occur in the main because of intervention by another agency. Often their bodies (if we can properly call them that) are constructed from metallic, plastic, or other exotic materials. These characters may mimic human behavior, animal behavior, or be without any discernible emotions whatsoever. They tend to be great fun to create, due to the types of materials, surfaces, and combinations possible in such entities. In Chapter Five, we discuss ways and means of constructing characters and creatures, and it is obvious that a mechanized brontosaur would present an interesting challenge to the artist.

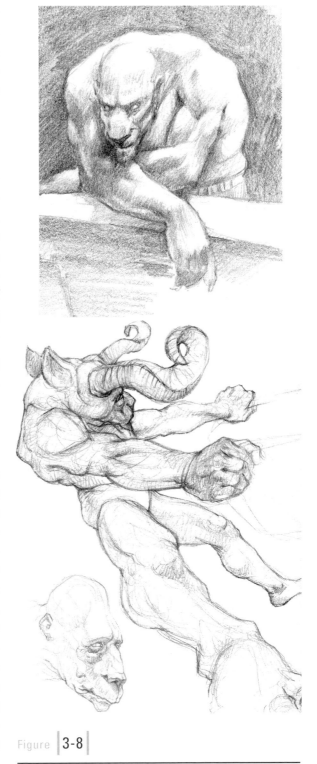

Figure 3-8

Some other weird, but humanoid characters.

| NOTE |

The term *robot* comes from the Czech word for compulsory labor; *robotnik* refers to a serf, the lowly peasants who worked in slavelike fashion for large land owners. Used by the Czech writer Karel Capek in his play "R.U.R." from the early twentieth century and referring to automatons that resemble humans, the word has entered our language as an everyday noun, with a great boost from the wonderful science fiction author Isaac Asimov (*I, Robot*). We can see where the heritage of "slave" and "labor" combined with the machine age to produce a new character type.

Androids are robots that have been made to resemble humans (or perhaps other entities) so closely that we would be barely (or completely) unable to distinguish them from the real thing. An android would have, as a character, the unusual characteristic that its *differentness* was implied, rather than directly visible, unless one perhaps opened up its arm and discovered the servo-mechanisms that operated the limb (as in the movies *Terminator* I, II and III, with actor Arnold Schwarzenegger, who plays an android with military and very violent capabilities).

In Chapter Five, we discuss ways and means of constructing characters and creatures. Those that partake of mechanical and computer-aided elements comprise a type of creation that, as a synthetic design, needs to account for both the living beings it might resemble and the machine parts used to mimic the same. Hybrid characters or creatures combining both living and machine elements have the further problem of synthesizing the two into a design that is both functional and aesthetic. A mechanized brontosaur would present an interesting challenge to the artist. The following illustration shows a design that is an example of a hybrid living and mechanical being.

Figure | 3-9 |

Mechanical brontosaur and other robotic characters/creatures.

Other versions range from human-like (as in the Japanese giant biped robots that often contain a "driver" and wreak havoc on the environment and each other) to merely functional; in truth, a computer is in essence a robotic "brain," but it is certainly not very visually compelling. Other types can have distinctly emotive responses from the viewer:

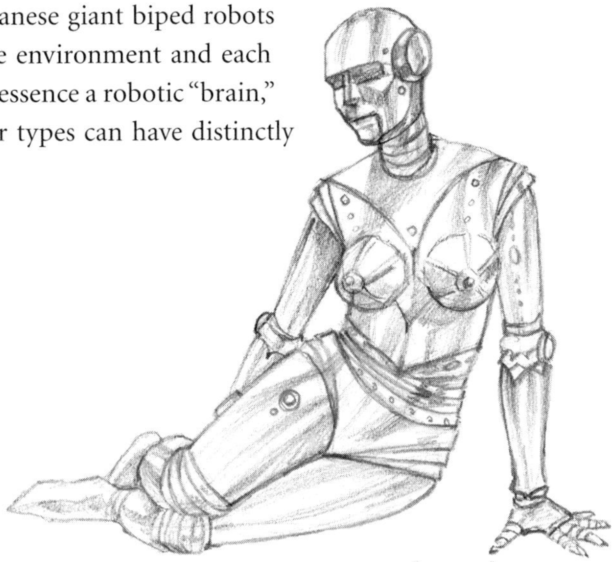

Figure | **3-10**

Hot stuff for the robot crowd.

Or, they can be just plain interesting to the eye:

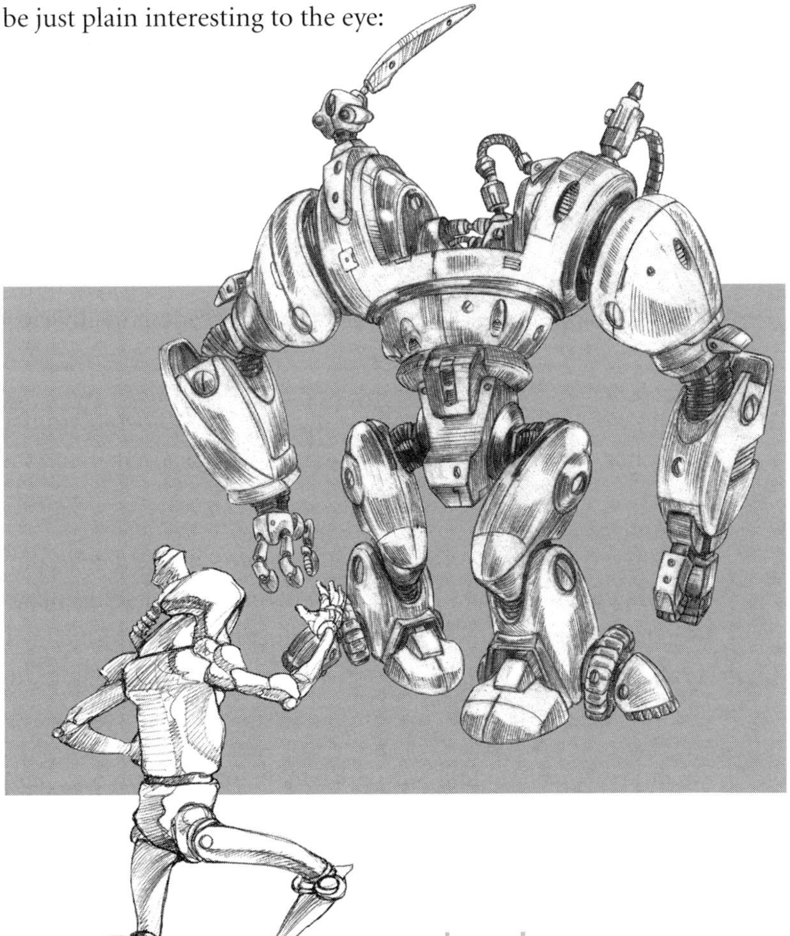

Figure | **3-11**

More robots, androids and mechanical bipeds.

Animals, Plants, Hybrids, and Lowbrows

Let us return to the general animal kingdom. Practically speaking, this can be divided into two parts. The first involves animals we already are familiar with: cats, birds, snakes, insects, etc. As we have seen, these can be modified by scale, costume, intelligence, or other attributes.

A second category covers synthesized (hybrid) creatures (purely animal) and alien creatures that we would generally categorize as more like animals than the vegetable kingdom. In fan-

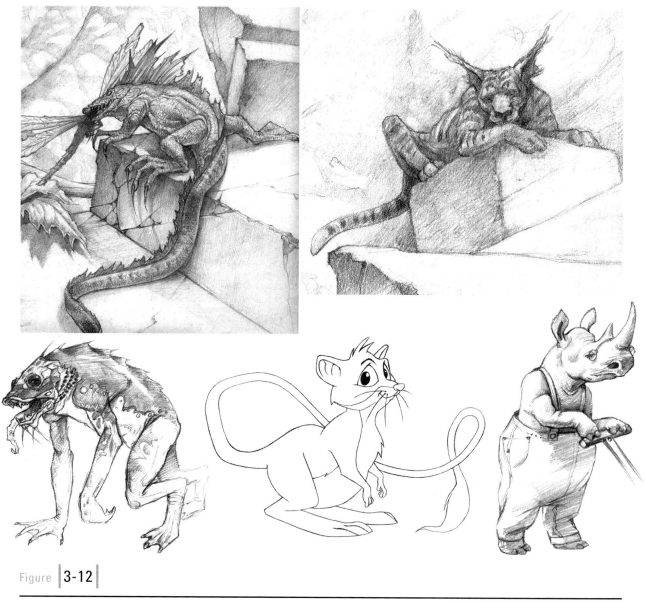

Figure **3-12**

Yet another menagerie of animal characters.

tasy, we often produce hybrids that combine qualities of two or more familiar creatures (sometimes involving human traits as well).

In these characters or creatures, we can clearly recognize image cues from familiar sources, although they may be presented in unusual ways. So there appear to be two relatively straightforward ways to use extant animals: modify existing ones or combine attributes of two or more of these creatures to make a new, synthesized animal (or character). The modifications can follow the paths outlined in Chapter Five, and can sometimes "hide" the original animal source until it is well nigh unrecognizable. All this occurs within a particular style or mode, which is addressed more fully in Chapter Six.

The plant kingdom provides another realm that can be mined for visual information in character and creature design. Using the elements found in this area of living things follows in main the methodology outlined above for animals. There are straightforward modifications of obvious plant sources, and the synthesis of two or more plant sources to produce a new result. Another option here is to combine plant and animal into an entirely new type of hybrid, one that combines qualities of both.

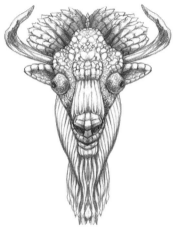

Figure | **3-13**

Hybrid designs derived from familiar sources.

What mainly must be remembered when using plants as sources is that they often have differing metabolisms, minimal locomotion (if any), and unique reproduction methods that only vaguely resemble that of animals. Their methods of eating and excreting, for example, seem quite different from their distant living animal cousins. Photosynthesis is not something that has an easy animal analog. The lack of a nervous system and senses that interact with the environment (at least as far as we know) make us feel that the plant kingdom is very limited behaviorally. Indeed, "intelligent vegetables" conjures up a kind of oxymoronic feeling; the terms seem to be mutually exclusive. Yet that introduction of intelligence could be the ticket to a great character design. The invader from another planet in the original 1950s version of the science fiction film, *The Thing*, was, in fact, an intelligent plant biped, albeit not terribly friendly.

Another science fiction story from the 1960s had another world inhabited by beings that had tamed and utilized motile (capable of locomotion from place to place) and semi-intelligent plant forms, whose appearance and abilities mimicked animals like cattle or similar beasts of labor.

Other life forms, like bacteria, viruses, and similar living things, can be useful in design, but often are limited because of their scale or means of functioning. Yet even these may provide some visual basis for design. The flagella, inner workings, spike-like protrusions and overall configuration still are useful for larger, macro-scale characters and creatures.

Natural Systems and Living Thingies

Characters and creatures are living beings. As such, they are limited by certain repeated environmental and species parameters. This is a fancy way of saying where they live and how they are built. We can examine these briefly under the following categories: ecology, body systems, including genetics and reproduction, and modifications by time and environment.

Since this isn't a biology textbook, we're really only going to touch on a few significant points that would affect character or creature design. Since our beings that we are creating have to live in some environment, we need to pay at least a little attention to what the nature of that environment is, because it will be a prime factor in many of the physical and behavioral elements of our character or creature.

Ecology is a term that covers a lot of territory. It really refers to a whole complex of interacting phenomena that produce the structure of living things in a particular locale (a pond or a planet, depending on your scale of investigation). Just saying the above sentence can make the mind blur a bit. All we are really stating here is that the interaction of weather, geography, and animals, plants, and other living beings existing at a particular time gives rise to a system. Some animals and plants will thrive, while others will not fit in. New varieties evolve and a few die out.

Figure **3-14**

Plant critters/characters, representing the best in vegetable intelligence.

Figure | 3-15 |

Hopefully intelligent plant characters and friends.

The whole system can be looked at in different ways. Where the animals and plants exist together in a local living "community" (we don't mean towns), their common shared interaction with each other occurs within a physical locale called a *habitat*. A "biome"is the actual living part of this habitat; it is the presence and mutual interaction of the living things. The habitat more refers to the physical location, perhaps a pond or valley, or other quasi-localized area. Habitats can be huge, like the Serengeti plains in Africa, or it can be very small, like your backyard.

Because living things need to nourish themselves, a "food web" exists. It is the total sum of all the living things and how they feed and interact within the behavior of feeding. A "food chain" is the hierarchy from the "lowest" (bacteria, fungi, plants) to animals that feed on them (insects, herbivores) to those who feed on the feeders (predators like birds and lions). The higher you go in the food chain, the fewer the animals existing there. This number is constrained by the real availability of food for each part of the food chain. Fewer plants mean fewer herbivores;

fewer herbivores mean fewer predators. Each depends on the other for existence. If the rains stop and drought occurs, plant life diminishes and changes, as we see in areas of our world which are suffering from desertification. For example, the Sub-Sahara of Africa has undergone an immense change within historical times, causing the deaths of many animals and people, along with wholesale change in every mode of living. You would need to ask some of these questions about your creature or character:

1. Is it a consumer or a producer?

2. Are its behaviors passive or aggressive, predatory or herbivorous (or other?)

3. Is its population structure appropriate for its habitat? Biome?

4. Where does it fit in the food web/chain?

5. What does it use as an energy source (is it an intelligent plant?)

Other issues to be resolved are the aforementioned body systems and modifications by time and environment. As artist and designers, we obviously take note of first how the physical being we are creating fits into its environment. An air-breathing biped would have a rough time under water (or in liquid methane, for that matter).

Figure **3-16**

Micro-critter sources and some designs derived from same.

Its body is suited to where it lives. That's why, without seeming too obvious or "duh!" that astronauts wear space suits and undersea divers have aqualungs. They have to adapt to the environment through artificial means. Natural adaptation takes much longer. As an environment changes, the local population's gene pools hopefully have enough variance to give rise to offspring that will harbor the "right stuff" to live in the new surroundings. More on this in a moment. Right now, we need to think about *what* our particular critter is made of and how it is put together. Now we can see the obvious links to the habitat and biome (both small and large for each). *A living thing physically mirrors its environment.* As designers, this brings up the "two C's rule: continuity and compatibility." Continuity refers to repetition and linked families of forms, colors, tones, textures, and intensities. Compatibility is about whether new elements (or shuffled-around old ones) work together visually (and in this case, "realistically" in terms of real world survival). This now shows up in a dramatic way when we try to fit a character or creature into an environment.

Survival. That word is the key ingredient to solving much of what we encounter physically in any living thing. What it is made of, and how the parts look and fit together, is anything but random, although sometimes errors or mutations produce superfluous physical traits.

Animals have the following systems: circulatory (blood and lymph), respiratory (breathing or oxygen consumption), digestive (eating), excretory (numbers one and two), skeletal (internal or external support), and nervous (brains, spinal cords, or similar apparatus). In addition, they must reproduce, and they have evolved myriad and fascinating ways in which to accomplish this. Our own obsession with this system is an obvious example of its importance to the biological being. We might ask the following questions: Are the species divided into sexes? Male and female? Other odd varieties or variations? How do they reproduce? By intimate means or by some sort of flyby, as do some fish or starfish species? Or by some completely odd or unfamiliar technique?

Animals and plants have genetic material. As it passes from one generation to the next, changes (mutations) naturally occur. If the change produces a physical trait that is advantageous, then that living thing becomes a better survivor. That word crops up again. Some species can interbreed, while others are completely isolated genetically from one another. This raises further prospects of design hybrids (see Chapter Five). As artists, of course, we are less limited by the actual genetics. Frankly, we can do as we please, as long as it has the appearance of logic, or immense design appeal.

Figure | **3-17** |

Girl with bubbling mouth underwater, clearly surprised.

Figure | **3-18** |

Context compatibility; sometimes good, sometimes not.

Plants and animals have other biological modification issues. Other than gene mutation, adaptation, gene flow (the change and transmission over time), and similar internal changes, the options for change include the following:

1. Isolation (living on an island without means of leaving, for example)

2. Migration (leaving the habitat for another)

Figure **3-19**

Mutations: critters that went wrong.

Figure **3-20**

Hybrid fun (unless you are a carrot).

Last, we would want to have some sense of the past (fossil) record of the living being. This would only be important if the story demanded an accounting of how the creature got to be how it is. In Chapter Nine, we examine this issue in greater detail.

The Play's the Thing

Chapter One gives some detail about tailoring the character or creature to a story line. Again the importance of continuity and compatibility shows up. This time it is both visual and conceptual. A character or creature needs a *description* of some kind, at least inferentially. Some stories deliberately avoid too much detail in a description (e.g., H. P. Lovecraft's work) in order to let the reader's imagination help out. Nonetheless, as artists we need something to go on in order to make visual creations.

Within the story itself (if there even is one), a *plot* exists. What is a plot? We could say that a plot is the development of the interactions and confrontations of character to character (perhaps creature) or environment until some conclusion is reached. The conclusion would hopefully resolve the conflict (see the note on three-act structure in Chapter One) or finish the development of some activity, growth, or other story element. A character is, again, both the focus and a device to develop and complete a plot.

Contained in a plot we have an underlying meaning or sensibility to what is happening, called the *theme*. A theme is a focused message or emotional content that remains throughout the story. Characters again are both the object of a theme and one of its driving mechanisms. Choose the wrong character, and the theme is lost, masked, or distorted. This is a bit of reiteration, but it cannot be emphasized enough. As an example, comedic characters fit poorly within action movies, unless they are very carefully crafted and linked to other, bolder character types. Not only do living things mirror their environment, but characters mirror their plots and themes. Both must be considered.

Cultures Not Found in a Petrie Dish

We have already touched on the environment, and how it influences the character or creature. If the living thing is sentient (thinking and self-aware), then it probably has a *culture* and a *history*. What are these? Culture refers to the accumulated social behaviorisms and their physical counterparts for a particular people (or sentient creature). How they talk, communicate in total, dress, behave in differing situations, react to their mortality, neighbors, and environment in general, and many other bits of data all link together to form a culture. The Hottentots of North Africa have a culture quite different from the shepherds of Basque, Spain. Although there are some shared characteristics, much of what has evolved socially fits the local environment and the history of the people. And it is this history that defines much of what we encounter. Small and large events change the manner in which everything from language to costume evolves. An invading people add their cultural details to a local people, sometimes obliterating the original culture altogether. Migrations and isolation now become clearer modifiers for this character element. Accumulated history is, in a sense, equivalent to the culture of a people, when biology and environment are entered in.

Figure **3-21**

Apropos props.

Other factors include plagues and natural disasters. These are like wild cards that can suddenly shift the needs and look of a culture.

Social details are so numerous as to be impossible to enumerate in a book like this. Our chapter on research (Chapter Two) refers to ways and means of locating information relevant to our projects. The story hopefully contains enough information for the artist and designer to construct characters and environments. Their own research will add immeasurably to the richness of the actual creations.

Of Shovels and Evening Gowns

What are props and costumes? For sentient beings, these are the physical items they use and with which they cover their bodies. A prop can be almost anything, but usually refers to something within the same general physical size of the character. Props can be as large as a vehicle or throne, and as small as a ring or microchip. Each is some physical object that is usually (but not always) character made or modified. Within a story, props act as elements that drive a plot forward (as devices or things used by the characters for various purposes—anything from ritual to the mundane) and as visual "eye candy." The range of props is limited only to the imagination.

Clothing or costumes are generally not considered props, although the line between the two is a bit blurry at times. Some costumes, like a spacesuit, really act more as a prop. For the most part, however, clothing is a functional and decorative physical element that covers part or all of a character's body. It can have many functions. There is purely utilitarian clothing, like simple slacks or tunics, which keep body heat in, or protect against the sun, or have other functional purposes.

Figure | 3-22 |

Utilitarian clothing as costume.

Some clothing has seductive overtones, like harem pants, and some has definite social inferences, such as an evening dress or tuxedo.

Uniforms, denoting specific organizations and duties, are another type of clothing or costume. They clearly show a role that the character or being plays within the society, like a policeman or military person.

Props and costumes represent an endless font of possible solutions. Here again, the principles of continuity and compatibility weigh in. If the body and social needs do not fit the prop or costume, then a new solution is needed. These elements mutually influence and are influenced by the characters they serve. All characters can be enhanced or made ridiculous by appropriate or bizarre choices in props and costumes.

Figure | 3-23 |

Harem pants on girl.

Figure | 3-24 |

Uniformed characters of differing types.

Figure | 3-25 |

Appropriate or odd props and costumes.

STUDENT SHOWCASE

Dan Garza

Student artwork by Dan Garza: Fuzzy Bob, pirate. Garza gives the "pirate with an eye patch" a new twist by using a bold and simple style to enhance the character's gruff posturing. The hint of skull structure at the nose makes the figure a bit more sinister. Several developmental sketches show us part of the path Garza took in developing the character..

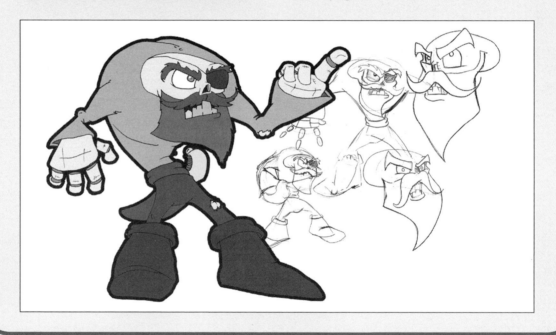

SUMMARY

This chapter deals with the introduction of main character categories and forms, as well as how story, props, environments, and natural systems apply to character design. How to choose characters and the importance of the character—story relationship in the matter of character design are discussed. In addition, this chapter describes key archetypes and character forms, emphasizing the important role that each of these elements plays in practical character development and design. The character design process depends on our knowledge of such paramount concepts as culture, stereotypes, and natural systems to support our creative process in this area. Related to these important design factors, this chapter discusses style of character presentation, modification of individual character elements, and limiting design contexts, as applied to human and inhuman characters.

exercises

1. Pick two types of characters: humanoid and nonhuman. One is a villain and the other is a hero. Using the suggestions listed in this chapter, develop and analyze a list of physical and mental attributes that can be ascribed to the said characters.

2. Develop two character designs based on some form of living or extinct flora: one sentient and the other nonsentient. Do the same exercise with living or extinct animals.

3. Create a character whose occupation and uniform or clothing play an important role in design and characterization.

4. Develop a character based on a concept provided by a friend or colleague.

in review

1. What is the definition of an "archetype," as applied to character design?

2. What descriptive tenets can be applied to a heroic character? A villainous character?

3. What is the "the two C's rule?"

4. What role do props play in character development?

PROFILE

cesar avalos

"One cannot emphasize enough the importance of following your passion. I grew up in the quiet town of El Paso, Texas and was lucky to be one of those kids who found the perfect outlet through drawing pictures. To combat boredom at school, I sketched and doodled things on the dustcovers of my schoolbooks and made silly flip animations on the edges of the book pages. As most kids who like to read comics and draw, I came up with my own stories and characters with the full intention of one day drawing the entire comic book myself. About 1976, I won the Hillcrest Junior High Vikings yearbook cover contest with an ink drawing of a stocky Viking character, which was taken right out of a *Conan: The Barbarian* comic book, the perfect research for that assignment. The prize: One free copy of the yearbook, and a little extra attention I would not have otherwise received. The same Viking was ultimately painted as a huge mural on an exterior wall of the gymnasium. In high school, I came up with my own renditions of Beowulf and his nemesis Grendel to teach myself watercolors. It was an exchange agreement with my literature teacher; the posters would exempt me from the tough exams on the Lord of the Rings Trilogy.

"In my first year studying art at the University of Texas El Paso I sold a color illustration of a penguin character, which was inspired by Chilly Willy, to the owner of an automobile and truck refrigeration company. I drove a hard bargain on that one: Fifty bucks. I thought it came out pretty good. He used it for his company hats and shirts, stationary and there was even a fluorescent bulb sign erected out front of the shop. After the penguin, I begged a college pal of mine to get me into the company he was drawing fashion illustrations for. He did because he was going back to New York anyway. He gave me a quick lesson on the style they wanted, and I was in. This is where all those life-drawing classes helped me immensely because they wanted stylish yet realistic drawings of people.

"My home town was not moving fast enough for me so in 1985 I moved to Phoenix, Arizona and I went on to a productive career in silk-screen T-shirt print design throughout the remainder of the decade. Eventually I burned out on the ruthless, soap opera-like politics of the industry and the small-time, bargain-basement, swap-meet market bonanza mania. To continue expanding my horizons, I went into traditional animation in 1991, landing a job working as assistant animator for a freelancer who was doing 30-second commercials. He took me under his wing and was very generous with his knowledge. I learned from him the entire production process of creating high quality animated films. This inspired me to come up with the Rhinoboy story and that cast of characters to produce my own animations for my reel with motivated characters.

"With the experience I gained there, I moved on to animated feature films. In 1995, Fox Animation Studios came to Phoenix and I landed a job as a Key Clean-up Animator on the animated films *Anastatia*, *Bartok the Magnificent*, and *Titan A.E.* On *Titan A.E.* I was able to learn character design from the director and the big boys themselves because I helped out in the character layout department while we were in pre-production.

"After that company left town in 2000, I went back to college (Arizona State University) to finish my painting degree (more life drawing) and re-tool in order to compete in the market of the new millennium. I had to upgrade my knowledge of the software being used to create 2D and 3D animation and adjust to the optimization needs of the increasing speeds and bandwidths of the ever-expanding web. I was able to obtain employment at an ASU math research foundation, doing traditional animation of characters needed for entertaining and interactive math lessons on websites, CDs, and DVDs. I have been happily teaching art and animation classes at the Art Institute of Phoenix since 1997, which I find very rewarding and plan to pursue the completion of my own animated short films.

"The important thing to remember about character design is that it is always based on human anatomy, so one needs to become very serious about life drawing and learn about proportion and the perspective of simplified geometric solid shapes. I believe a good character designer is one who is an alert observer of people's mannerisms, gestures, body language, idiosyncrasies, as well as a student of psychology and acting."

character concept and construction

Gain an introduction to the importance of conceptualization.

Investigate how ideas can be generated and manipulated.

Learn about problem-solving theory.

Understand the importance of basic drawing technique.

Find out the importance of the sketchbook and why we use it.

Be introduced to the basic building blocks of realistic characters: anatomic issues and how to start from gestures and modules to construct characters and creature design.

Be introduced to the basic building blocks of simple and cartoon characters: the use of simple form or modular drawing to construct characters and creature designs.

Find out more about media used to produce these concept drawings.

i n t r o d u c t i o n

Like all creative processes in art, once the research has begun to affect the possible visual out-comes, the artists must turn to their own technique to begin the actual early renderings of their character design ideas. *Conceptualization means literally the formation of ideas. As it relates to character design, conceptualization refers to the process wherein ideas and images in our minds are tossed about, reassembled, and finally put on paper.* It is here that the importance of funda-mentally sound drawing technique looms large. As we will find out, differing styles of character design demand somewhat different approaches to the construction of the characters, but each is still built on the foundations of good drawing technique. In addition, the "portable resource file" (i.e., our idea sketchbook) becomes an integral part of this process in that we produce ideas in it and access them at a later date for character development. Here, technique and old fashioned preliminary idea production in the form of a sketchbook combine to produce concept drawings.

Cartoon, stylized, and realistic characters have somewhat different beginnings technically, and this chapter looks at what each entails. We can choose different materials to produce initial concept art. Part One of this chapter involves the process of coming up with ideas, that is, conceptualization. Part Two concerns the mechanical means by which we begin to trans-late these ideas into visual products: gestural and modular drawing and the worlds to which they belong.

Conceptualization: The Art of Ideation

The bane of all artists is "artist's block," that is, the terrible void in imagination that sometimes appears when we are under deadline to produce a creative piece of art. Despite our frantic efforts, the block persists, and we end up in despair, creating some dreadful compromise between cliché and functional. There are several paths through this thorny thicket. The first line of defense is sound technique. This includes the understanding and use of gestures, anatomy, and modular drawing. The second is to have a storehouse of sketchbook ideas already available and to learn to use stimulus like word association and exploration of random visual sources. Third, understand and be able to research in the rich variety of sources outlined in Chapter Two. Next, we can use different types of exercises, word association, and visual games to initiate visual ideas. And finally, be familiar with the technique of synthesis, which is discussed in Chapter Five. This chapter concentrates primarily on using sound technique and sketchbooks to advance the cause of creativity.

Before examining the steps outlined above, let's take a look at how ideas are generated and what we can do with them after that. Without going into neurophysiologic theory, let us assume that the brain, along with its attendant awareness, is awash in memories and memory relationships. An artist is able to draw upon these to produce either copies of old ideas or to reshuffle the information to create new ones. (We do advocate practicing "right-brain" activity, such as physical exercise, manual chores in general, fishing, or whatever it takes to release the potential of this nonlinear, creative part of the brain.) That being said, you have to have something to retrieve in order for this process to work. If there is no input, then drawing on nonexistent memories is fruitless. As one famous (or infamous) mind theorist said, "You don't know what you don't know."

We have to have some prior input in order to create. This consists largely of event memories coupled with static imagery derived from books, movies, and other sources. Art imagery, specifically character images, comes from both events and static images stored in our minds. "Archetypal" figures, like the intimidating vice principal from middle school, for example, loom large in our emotional storehouse and can be used successfully as a template for a character design. Without intending to, we mix these images with those of other people, artwork, and mass media pictures to produce "character designs." If you doubt this, just record your dreams for a couple of weeks, and see what pops up. Because no one really knows how the brain fully accomplishes this, we would rather focus on techniques for *enhancing* this process. By the way, dream imagery is another, completely viable realm to explore for ideas related to art and character design in particular. If we try too hard, it seems that the creative juices refuse to flow. That's where the following sections come in handy.

One of our children was watching as we wrote a chapter for this book. He noticed an open page of reference material that showed cross sections of animal skulls. What chiefly attracted his attention was that each different cross section resembled a face and that each was distinctly different. In fact, they were almost complete in themselves, without enhancement or development.

What he had encountered was the use of random visual input (and not so random sometimes) to stimulate the association game the mind plays. Upon seeing some visual piece of information, the mind automatically begins an elaborate process of identifying the piece, often running through multiple look-alikes until it is satisfied with the identification. When we are aware of this process, it can be used to produce images based upon the resemblance of one or more items we are looking at; they give us a jumping off point to begin sketching ideas.

Word play is another means of introducing visual stimulation for the artist. How do words accomplish this? Words trigger the associated memories: They are the doorway to visuals. Combing through the dictionary, encyclopedia, or thesaurus can be enough to start the process. Cloaked by boring book covers, these volumes secretly hold a multitude of images. Another means of getting images "started" is to look at visual symbols like the infinity sign, a simple circle, or a Native American animal totem. These function as image triggers as well; they may in fact be associated with archetypal imagery common to us all. Mutual word games between consenting adult artists also qualify as image boosters. Puns, that often derogated joke style, actually are a great source for pictures. Words picked randomly out of a hat, a la the Surrealist artists of the early twentieth century, gave them poetry, literature and image ideas for art.

All artists play-act stories in their own imaginations as a part of the process of ideation. Fantasy and fantasizing are a normal part of the human psyche, and we can use this inherent ability to our own ends as artists. By "storytelling" in our heads, we formulate at least some of the look that could be used with a particular setting, character, or creature. One of the worst possible scenarios for artists is to see a movie based on a book before reading the book. It is almost impossible to "undo" the images from the movie. We should start out the creative process without being saddled with everyone else's solutions first. Children actively fantasize for years, and this rich ability is still present in adults, albeit often buried under a lot of mental debris. Dreams are a prime example of how the mind can produce absolutely bizarre or fantastic images in otherwise rather "mundane" folks.

Taking an image and deliberately messing about with one of its elements can produce unexpected results, especially if the addition or change is not predictable. You are probably familiar with the game in which several people draw consecutively on a folded sheet of paper, unable to see what the others have drawn. Because there is no ability to see the previous effort, succeeding drawings have the richest possible field to play in; namely, no limits other than where to start.

The Game's Afoot: Problem Solving

Ideas relating to art production mean one thing for all artists: they are in a problem-solving situation. Artists have an initial decision to make *always*: what does the client/workplace want, or, if there is no client, what is the personal goal of the artist in this particular project? What is the project? Before you can solve something, you must have something to solve—simple idea, but basic to starting the process. Once this has been identified, the artist/designer (or team of same) proceeds to the solution portion of the creative process. Crucial to this is the ability to communicate with both the source of the project and each other on the team. Artists cannot run off madly creating for someone if they are uncertain what that person wants. Students are particularly susceptible to this "disease" when given assignments in class. Often losing their syllabi or assignment sheets, they forge ahead anyway and can produce wonderful but totally inappropriate images.

So, we have the assignment or idea urge; next we define the problem in terms that are meaningful to artist/designers. The problem is analyzed and reduced to bite-sized parts. By simplifying the problem so that its main issues are dealt with first, the artist avoids getting lost in the details before solving the essential visual issues. Often here we resort to the ideation and mental gymnastics to which this chapter is chiefly devoted. What are the visual issues that go with this assignment or image? Once these are identified, their relationships are examined, because solving one may significantly involve the solution of another (or many other) elements. Size may influence role, gender, or other aspects of a character, for example.

Choosing one idea over another is sometimes the most difficult part of this process. Ultimately, artists/designers must trust their artistic "noses" here; it is not a bad idea to bounce these ideas and images off of other people. Their reactions may surprise (and depress) you, but they are valuable nonetheless. Some famous movie producers would be well advised to listen to their creative staffs a bit more often.

After roughing out solutions, a few or perhaps only one is chosen, and then the refinement begins. Refinement is an entire subject in itself. Suffice to say that as parts are polished and rethought, a final product does emerge.

So, the process might look something like this:

1. Identify the artistic problem/assignment.

2. Define the problem in functional terms: What is actually involved?

3. Maintain ongoing communication with the client or workplace to keep on track with the problem.

4. Break the problem down into manageable parts.

5. Examine how these parts will recombine to produce a final solution.

6. Create initial thumbnails/rough solutions and parts of solutions to work with.

7. Edit the roughs by group/client participation or by self-editing.

8. Refine and combine the roughs into one or several optional solutions.

9. Choose a final solution and refine.

We said we would talk about foundational technique and the use of rough concept art as a means to help create character design. Why would good technique matter? Why can't we sort of erupt onto the page with a dynamic burst of creativity? The main reason for this is that *although our minds can produce images, it takes a whole set of skills to translate that information onto a flat surface and eventually into different media.* Those skills do not come prewired in all their fullness in our brains. We have to learn them by practice. We have penned an entire book relating to this topic, *Exploring Drawing for Animation.* Although directed to the animation industry, it has principles about drawing that apply to all fields of creative endeavor.

Under Construction: Building Gestures and Anatomy

To actually make drawings that eventually become final designs, artists use various ways of organizing the elements involved in constructing a design. Their main intent is to figure out how to start with simple, easily manipulated visual information that can then be modified in a number of stages to finally produce the desired result. The first of these techniques is the gesture drawing.

Gesture drawings, sometimes called quick sketches, scribble sketches or preliminary drawings, involve a kind of shorthand visual notation of what the artist intends to finish later in a more polished form. Generally speaking, they give form, proportion, scale, and action in a few simple lines. This could be for anything from a landscape to a cartoon character. For our purposes, they are used to build ideas for character design without having to commit to a finished drawing every time we put pencil to paper. In fact, trying to always produce final versions from the beginning is self-defeating, because we are unable to "play" with the image, modifying it in various ways before deciding on the final outcome. In a gesture drawing, the line of action and general lines for the pose are combined with some anatomic markers or simplified forms along with a few contour lines to construct a preliminary, loose sort of engineer diagram/action analysis drawing. It's easier to understand by seeing, so the following are a few examples of types of gesture drawings.

Our sketchbooks will be filled with drawings in many stages of finish, from gesture to finely polished renderings. But it is the gesture that allows us to visualize quickly and either pursue or discard an idea. If we pursue it, we can use further gestures to change its appearance without, once again, being committed to a final version. Often it is only after many explorations of this nature that a finished product is created.

Gestures are therefore the meat and potatoes of conceptualization. In them, anatomy, proportion and action all combine in quick fashion to give the artist a peek at whether the direction chosen is worthwhile. It is probably true that many designs are the result of accidental lines that crop up in gesture drawings. Without this spontaneity, we are confined to copying only that which we already have done or seen. If you think about it, doing a fully rendered drawing each time means most probably that the information was in a relatively final form in your mind before you even began. That greatly reduces the chances for innovation. The eraser should not be the tool for creating new ideas. Gestures can be used for any form of art, from

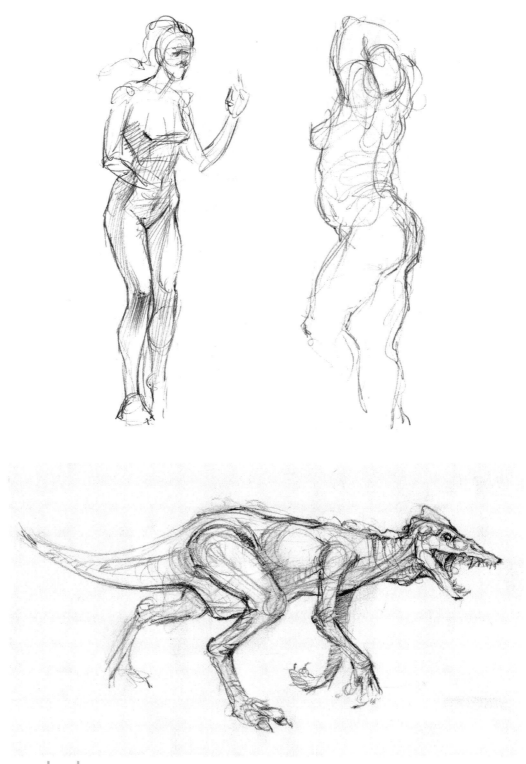

Figure 4-1

Different types of gesture drawings.

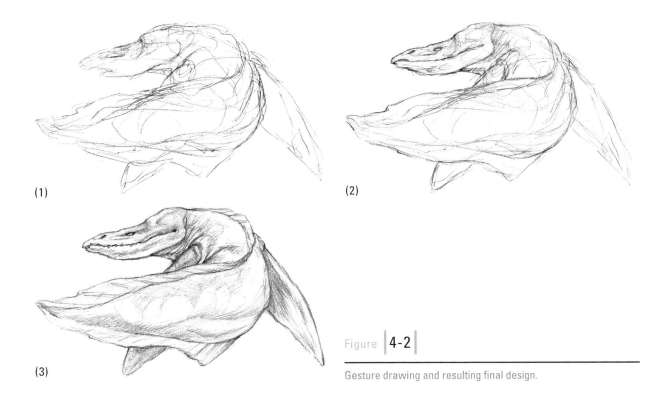

(1)

(2)

(3)

Figure | **4-2** |

Gesture drawing and resulting final design.

realism to cartoon. Because they often contain unpredictable and spontaneous line and form, gestures are a rich source for deriving new ideas by simply allowing the accidental to evolve along with the intended visual idea.

Another aspect of gesture drawings is that they require the artist to gain some real knowledge of anatomy when dealing with character design. This is because much of what is seen in gesture drawing is derived, in part, from anatomic sources. Rib cages, spines, limbs, and so forth direct the artist's line into certain forms and proportions based on real beings. Some examples of drawing using gestures are shown below. In these, we show how the initial line impulse can be developed into a more developed gesture, and finally into a moderately finished sketch.

Figure | **4-3** |

Gesture drawing, then semideveloped rough.

Figure | 4-4 |

Gestures emphasizing skeletal components (e.g., rib cage and pelvis).

Gesture drawings are to a great extent continuous motion exercises. Part of this is due to the need for speed, and part is due to the constant feedback loop from eye to hand. If the latter is interrupted too often, the drawing begins to become disassociated parts, and the energy of the pose is lost. In a gesture, we establish the basis for constructing the anatomy of the particular character by linear signals that hint at specific body forms. In this, some knowledge of anatomy is necessary, and the student is advised to study both human and animal anatomy sources as much as possible.

When creating a character, some of our preliminary drawing might come from our imagination and some from actual living sources. Each has its place in the process. The real source drawings contain verifiable proportion, anatomy, and surface markings that are useful for later doing visualizations from our imagination. Once enough of the actual source study (as in life drawing, drawing at the zoo and so on) has accumulated, the ability to render from the imagination becomes easier and more valid. After covering gesture drawing and anatomy, we talk about how simple units we call *modules* come into this equation. The first part of the process, however, is always a gesture, at least in some form.

Briefly, certain aspects of anatomy generally impact character design. Two anatomic aspects of humans and animals that should be noted are the *axial and appendicular skeletons.* For our purposes, the axial skeleton refers to the rib cage, spine, and pelvis (and skull in some systems), whereas the appendicular skeleton refers to the arms and legs. It is easy to see why this system is used. The center of the body (spine, ribs, pelvis) is where the mobile parts of the anatomy are attached. Although there is some flexibility in the spine and rib cage, for all practicality it does not have the motion range of the arms and legs. The attachment points for the limbs are ball and socket joints, providing a wide arc of movement. Gestures frequently refer, in shorthand version, to these anatomic parts.

Chapter Eight continues looking in more detail at the anatomic issues for vertebrate and some invertebrate animals. A number of excellent anatomy books for humans and animals are available and should be used as an integral part of the artist's library.

Gestures ultimately involve several factors visually. First is the line of action, which refers to an imaginary line that runs through the main thrust (line) of activity in the pose. Some poses really don't have a significant

THE MEASURE OF A (WO)MAN

At this point, we need to take a small detour and very briefly explore the relative sizes and shapes of the axial and appendicular skeletal units. In Chapter Eight, we examine these anatomic elements in more detail. In terms of scale, the human skull is roughly the same height as the pelvis, and it is two-thirds the height of the rib cage. The scapula and clavicle (wing bone and collarbone) are roughly the same length as the head. The spine curves in a double "s", starting forward with the neck (seven cervical vertebrae), curving back along the ribs (twelve thoracic vertebrae), and ending in a final curve going back (five lumbar or base vertebrae) and gently forward again in the sacrum at the back of the pelvis. Generically, the upper arm (humerus) is one and a half heads long; the lower arm (ulna and radius) is somewhat shorter than the average 13-inch humerus length. For the legs, the upper leg (femur) is the longest bone in the body, about 18 inches. The lower leg bones (tibia and fibula) are about 15 inches in length. Midpoint height-wise for a male is at the root of the genitals, whereas for a female it is just above that. Widest point for a male is at the shoulders; for a woman, widest point is a couple of inches above the hip joint. In both sexes, the upper leg inclines inward toward centerline from the hip joint, with this being more pronounced in a woman because of her wider pelvis. The female pelvis is wider and shallower, and inclines forward relatively at the top, forcing the lumbar (lower back) curve to be more pronounced. Male clavicles and upper arms are usually longer than their female counterparts as well. This places the elbow and the hand for the female somewhat higher on the standing figure.

line of action; others have main and sublines of action. Second, gestures contain skeletal hints: the axial and appendicular skeletal forms in extreme simplification. Third, gestures refer to some muscular contours and internal masses of muscle (and other tissue) with simple curved lines. And fourth, there are more randomly selected lines that aid in fleshing out the items listed or in emphasizing the pose or gestural feel.

The Shape's the Thing: Modular Drawing

The second method for constructing character and creature designs (and many other visual designs as well) is modular drawing. *Modular drawing refers to drawing simple shapes or forms and uniting them with a few lines to produce a simplified rendering of the object desired.* This

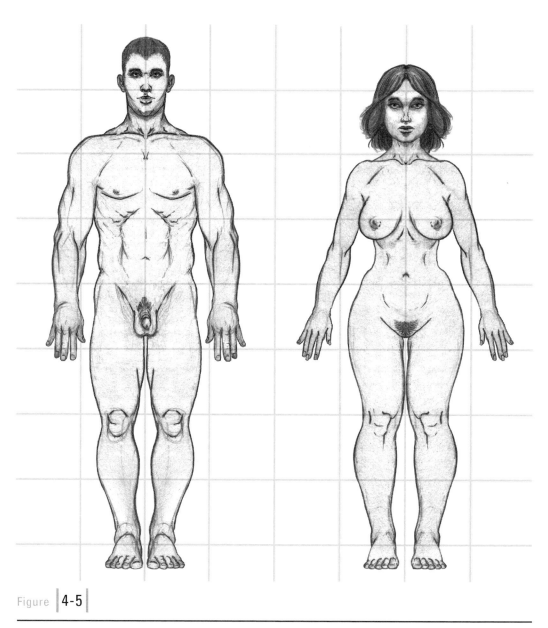

Figure **4-5**

Chart showing relative human proportions.

technique is useful, as is gesture drawing, for creating any type of drawn object. It finds particular success in stylized or cartoon imagery, precisely because they have already dispensed with some of the detail found in more realistic renderings. In this technique, ovals, circles, cylinders, and other simple forms are manipulated and combined to form simple versions of the character desired.

There are really two realms that utilize modular drawing to a large degree. The foremost is cartooning and the second is what we call *stylized*. The two overlap and in fact blur a great deal into one another. *Stylization refers to the modification of realism to emphasize a particular mode or visual feel.* In general, this means some reduction of information from literally recording na-

Figure | 4-6 |

Gestures showing line of action, skeletal components, contours, and muscles.

ture in order to make certain elements stand out. These elements are themselves modified to one degree or another according to the dictates of the style. In cartooning, the reduction of information is more extreme; in fact, very little that could be termed realism exists any longer.

As you can see, any departure from strict realism can be thought of as stylized in the sense that any loss of visual information forces us to look at what is left in a more focused way. When something isn't there, you look at what *is* there. *When we stylize, we deliberately simplify (reduce information) and modify the remaining information. Cartooning is merely a more extreme form of stylization.* To confuse the issue, what is thought of as straight realism can, in a sense, be stylized, because *what* the artist puts in the image forces the viewer's attention to certain areas or groupings of visual information. Although it may look real, an image that is new or different in and of itself can be felt as style. For our purposes here, we will still treat this latter area as realism (with a twist). Some further examples of stylization and cartooning follow. In these, we have given a step-by-step development to show how modular drawing can be used to derive images.

We now have two important tools in developing a character. By using gesture and modular drawing techniques, an almost infinite number of possibilities for character design can be constructed. Gestures often start an idea and then are refined with modular concepts. Sometimes a modular drawing gets a bit gestural, with extra information being tacked on or the forms changed as the artist sees a new idea forming.

You can see that the "modules" often refer to anatomic units or simply masses dominated by anatomic units (e.g., torsos, rib cages). This plays into the gesture fairly readily. Modules themselves can have parts deleted, changed, or added onto. The game goes both ways. When cartooning, modules dominate because the final product is so simple. The more realistic the image, the more information is needed, and therefore there is more use of gestural line. You might call this a kind of hybrid drawing attack. Use

Figure **4-7**

Modules used to form the basis for sketches.

Figure **4-8**

Simple cartoon characters.

Figure | 4-9 |

Step-by-step demonstration of cartoons built with gesture and modules.

a little of this, add a little of that, and presto, an image emerges. This is rather like cooking where "recipes" are changed in almost an identical manner.

In terms of specific categories of body parts more often used in stylized or realistic characters, apropos of our discussion of anatomy above, the shapes that form the needed modules are often a truncated flattened egg for the rib cage; a tilted box with the lower "floor" smaller than the top for the pelvis; a kind of football shoulder pad unit for the shoulders; a slightly curved cylinder for the neck; an egg shape with an "ice-cream" scoop at the back for the head; wedges for the feet; tapered cylinders for the arm and legs units; and finally a wedge/fan form for the hand.

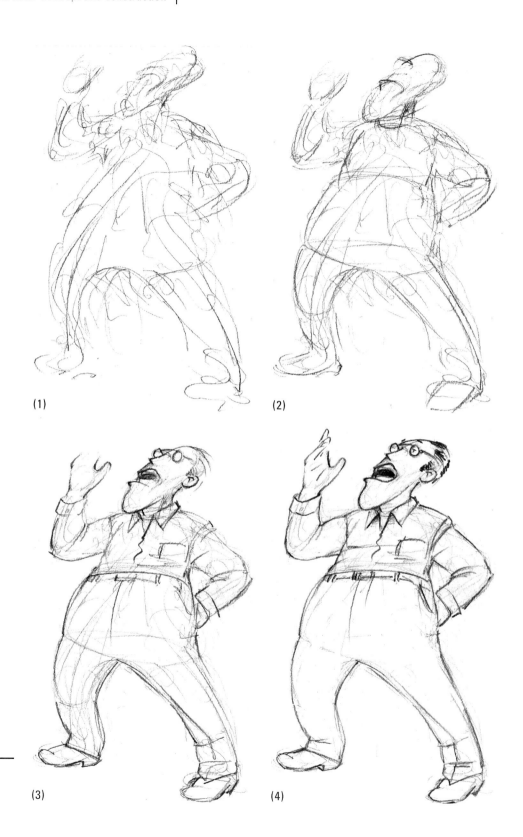

(1)

(2)

Figure **4-10**

Gesture drawing with
modules added as it
develops.

(3)

(4)

Figure | **4-11** |

Body parts represented by modules.

When assembled, they can take on the following generic figure:

This is only the beginning for using these shapes. In this example, we have produced a reasonably realistic humanoid character base. After enlarging just the shoulder and ribcage area, the character takes on a much more heroic aspect.

Conversely, by lengthening the leg, arm, and torso modules, we have a potential NBA star.

By adding a truncated ovoid form to the lower front torso, we get the proverbial beer-bellied character ready for a barroom brawl (with a few details yet to be added of course).

These basic units, which are anatomic analogs, give the artist a series of modifiable shapes that can be manipulated in endless ways to form many proportional figurative options. The illustrations below represent a number of variations of modular construction and variation, using the modules as a resource.

One of the other aspects that immediately becomes apparent in affecting the character while using these forms is the posture. The same forms with different postures take on quite different emotive aspects.

Complementary shapes are those that enhance one another. They may be related in basic form, or there may be a relationship in size (ratio) that provides an effective design solution. Often this means that we pay

Figure | **4-12** |

Modular parts from Figure 4-11 assembled to make a modular, generic figure.

particular attention to varying the scales of elements while still paying attention to the similarities of these same elements to achieve unity in the design.

Our intent is not to give an exhaustive list of all possible variants, but to show a *method* for using these modules. The literature is full of picture-filled how-to books showing how to render specific style or character types. We recommend that the student artist have a wide variety of books available from which to study certain styles and genres. What is most important is that the artist not be a slave to these books. What we are hoping to encourage is an individual approach to using this information. That is why the method and theory are so important. If we can only drive in first gear, our car will have limited means of arriving at its destination. Similarly in art, the more options available to the artist, the more possibilities for new and creative products.

There are other ways that modules can be used. For example, the parts can be inverted (as in Popeye's forearms) or even missing or otherwise modified. This kind of modification is

Figure **4-13**

Assembled Figure 4-12: modified to produce "heroic" look.

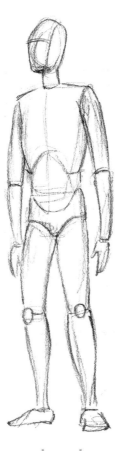

Figure **4-14**

Assembled Figure 4-12 modified to make "NBA" look.

Figure **4-15**

Assembled Figure 4-12 modified with truncated ovoid for pot-bellied beer brawler.

Figure | 4-16 |

Differing types of figures, constructed by modules.

discussed in the chapter on synthesis. For now we simply want to point out new and more exotic variants of assembly.

Realistic characters rely on the similarity between their drawn parts and the real world analogs of those parts. Stylized characters need this no less, except that the similarity can be stretched with some changes, whereas cartoons can take the process into an almost unreadable anatomic matching game.

In the following figure, we take a realistic semimodular character and by a few simple changes arrive at the beginning of a style. Note how the modifications simplify and focus the originally realistic character.

To arrive at what might be termed "cartoon," the process is taken even farther. Look at how the information is simplified even more and in some cases reduced to the barest geometric representation.

Most primers on cartooning build entirely on this simple modular accretion. The artist adds one simple piece after another, and according to the particular cartoon style, arrives in short order at a preliminary version of the cartoon character. Below is such a character built as we have stated.

We have a small sampling of cartoon styles to look at in the next illustration. Look carefully at what the *underlying* modular process is in each. The basic methodology remains the same. Variations on that theme are all that constitute much of the differing styles.

What is readily apparent from going over the modular drawing section after reading the gesture/anatomy section is that gestures and anatomy form the conceptual root of modules. Although we don't always draw the loose gesture in its realistic completeness when cartooning, we still have in mind this knowledge as a source for what we do come up with. With this being said, sample demonstrations of using modules and their variations are shown below, with several different categories of character being used.

Having established the general methodology and given examples that demonstrate different means of character construction, we would direct the artist or student to some more comprehensive charts showing different general types of forms used in making the simpler character genres (cartoon and very stylized). For realistic characters and creatures, the complex possibilities are too numerous to publish in one text.

Figure **4-17**

Varied postures of modular figure showing different emotional states.

Figure **4-18**

Complementary shapes versus "antagonistic" shapes.

Gestures and Modules: A Marriage (or At Least a Long-Term Engagement)

It should be obvious that most artists, at some point, start with something looking very much like a gesture and then proceed to add modular bits and pieces to it, or in fact go in the oppo-

Realistic character and extremely "cartoony" character contrasted.

site order. Depending upon the circumstances or the artist's personal taste, combining elements of both gesture and module in differing amounts can solve a design problem in ways that each method alone cannot. We have found that unless a pure, simple cartoon is being produced, some element of gesture creeps in during the early or late part of the drawing process. This is because certain aspects of pose and action are not easily accounted for with purely modular drawing. Even when including the line of action, some looser signal for the pose usually is necessary, and

(1)

(2)

(3)

(4)

Figure | 4-20 |

Realistic, semimodular character developed in steps showing modification to stylization.

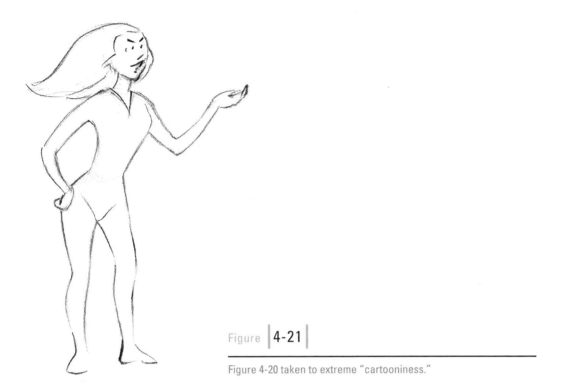

Figure | 4-21 |

Figure 4-20 taken to extreme "cartooniness."

Figure | 4-22 |

Cartoon character built from gesture and modules.

Figure | **4-23** |

Varying cartoon styles, all exhibiting underlying modular construction.

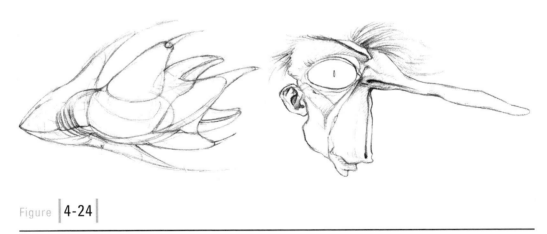

Figure | **4-24** |

Modular-based characters and creatures in varying styles.

this comes in the form of a partial or whole gesture sketch. When the two are overlaid or integrated, each has a strength that it brings to the table.

Gestures are good for organizing action and pose, whereas modules are great for mass, proportion, and directness. Our natural tendency is to resolve a design too early with attention to the details instead of the essential elements of a character (or anything else for that matter), leaving the overall "fit" dissatisfying, because it was only revealed when enough detail had accumulated. By using gestures and modules, we force ourselves to see the overall design (hence the name of the book) of the subject. Below is a sample of how the two techniques might work together to resolve a creature design.

Sketching, Sketching, and More Sketching

Artists take sketchbooks for granted. It's a fact. As students, we often dread them because they feel like "make-work" assignments: do so many pages per week in your sketchbook and turn them in to be reviewed or graded. Professional artists begin to lose interest in the daily formation of ideas in their sketchbook because of life pressures. All in all, sketchbooks can diminish or even vanish from an artist's life. This is not only sad, but a terrible mistake. It is in the sketchbook that quick, spontaneous ideas and observations can be recorded. Only a modest number of these images ever get developed more fully. But because they exist at all, we as artists have an enormous bag of tricks with which to pull the proverbial rabbit out of the hat.

Sketchbooks constitute our personal idea factory, coupled with our own style. Together these give us solutions when the creative well seems dry. Musical composers have an analogous kind of sketchbook, but in their field the sketches are musical notations, minicompositions, or even just chords and musical phrases jotted down when the idea strikes or the ear is stimulated by music or natural sound. Creativity in all fields of endeavor has a similar mode of operation. The "how" of creativity changes only in its means and ends. We have a couple of sketchbook pages included here as generic examples of what variety might crop up in preliminary thought and execution.

It should be getting clearer now that some of the drawings in a sketchbook link to the genesis idea in extremely rough form only, and some are partially or even fully developed from the initial impulse. Some drawings have endless variations, exploring first one mode and then another of an idea's visual options. Others are single forays that go nowhere and are, at least for the moment, abandoned. This does not mean that the drawing left on its own is worthless, but rather that at the time it was drawn, the artist either felt it lacked developmental possibilities or it didn't fit the needs at that time. Sometimes we return to these images later and discover that they hold the key to a solution. Sometimes we rip the page out and hide it in the nearest landfill. There is no "correct" way to use a sketchbook. They are instead a reflection of the artist's personal mode of visual ideation. Our workbook/sketchbook may include more finished work than a student's only because we have a more extensive drawing background and because we are more likely to be able to work over a quick idea more easily because of sheer familiarity with drawing and development. We have seen "student" sketchbooks that would have made some professionals jealous.

Despite having referred to sketchbooks in a relatively brief manner, their importance is at the top of the scale for both developing and professional artists. This is because the sketchbook is where ideas germinate; they are manipulated and given fuller form, they are discarded or set aside for the future, or they are combined with other ideas to form a new creation. With-

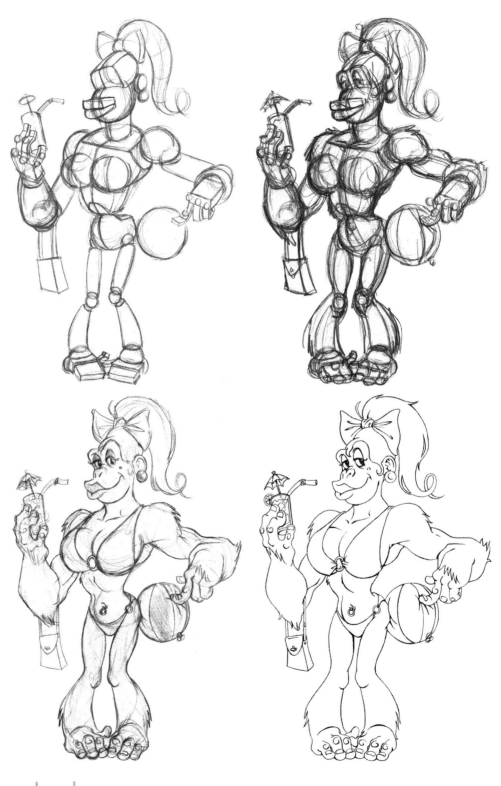

Figure | 4-25 |

Demonstration in steps of modular (shape) and gesture (linear) working together to make a character design.

out this process, we are confined to two modes of operation. One is to depend upon ready-made sources (other art, templates, stock photos, and computer program preloaded images and templates). The other possible avenue is to simply be a production artist. This is the assembly line worker who takes others' material and puts parts or all of it together—creatively less satisfying but necessary nonetheless. You may, in fact, find that the latter mode is your preference. You should, however, still be familiar with the basic processes involved in character design in order to better aid in their completion. No artist should be ignorant of history and technique.

Materials Are Not Immaterial

Before moving to any summary of character design and conceptualization/construction, the student should have a broad grasp of the generally accepted materials used to create preliminary and final character designs. These include both dry and wet media, markers, and computer programs. In our text, we don't pretend to be able to replace methods and media classes with such a limited overview, but we do want to point out both the variety available and some of the usefulness of some of the different mediums. There are excellent texts available for detailed exposition on each of these mediums, such as *Ralph Mayer's Handbook for the Artist*, annually updated to represent the newest information available about a wide variety of materials for the artist, and *Hwommy Klachnurt's Markers for the Right Brain*, which gives a good introduction to the uses and techniques of marker renderings.

Figure | 4-26 |

A couple of sketchbook pages with loose or "early stage" drawings.

The first and foremost item used in character sketching and rendering is the pencil, which a colleague of ours called "12,000 DPI and unlimited undo," which, although humorous, is absolutely true. Versatile, with a wide range of darks and lights available, the venerable pencil (and graphite stick) have been around forever and are probably the best choice for initial sketching and idea formation because of their fluidity and ability to be reworked. Running the gamut from the barely visible H series to the dark and inky B series, pencils can produce an astonishing array of tones and line qualities that would satisfy the most rigorous character design demands.

Charcoal is another versatile medium and has a similar range of hard to soft in its quality parameters. The main difference between graphite and charcoal is the more limited ability to erase and modify charcoal (although it certainly can be modified) and its deeper dark tones (due to the granular structure of the charcoal particles and their multidirectional light scattering properties). Graphite is a powdered substance that is actually, on the microscopic scale, a group of flat little flakes. Graphite reflects light more directly, giving a sheen to the drawing, especially in the darker, higher numbered B series of pencils. Charcoal is great for mood and drama because of its high contrast possibilities.

Ink, including the many colored inks available, is another medium useful to the rendering of character designs. By nature of its more permanent quality, it has the risk of "ruining" a design through some mistake or misapplication, but it has a strong dramatic feel and can be used in both wash format and airbrush to produce soft, velvety tones and colors. With an old-fashioned crow-quill nib or a newer Rapidograph, the artist can explore the wide variety of line and line variation in a bold manner. The older flexible pen points allow a variation in line that the newer chamber-filled ink cartridge pens cannot. Brush and ink are another means of rendering and drawing the characters, with the fluid and mobile line and tone available from brush being able to produce an extremely varied range of qualities.

Markers provide yet another means for designing and rendering character creations. Markers generally are used on specialty paper designated for markers and have a wide range of light and dark grades, along with "blenders" and many color ranges. Because they can come with narrow or wide tipped points, the marker family has the capability of rendering a large range of line, and the figure being created can have direct tone applied quickly and easily because of these varying sized tips. Some larger studios rely on marker renderings because of the quickness of applying line, tone, and color in a single product. They do not, however, replace the erasable pencil for initial sketches.

Other dry media include conte crayons (a kind of pastel-like drawing pencil or stick), also in a broad range of hard to soft grades; pastels, with their rich color and ability to be layered and blended; Crayola crayons, which surprisingly can be used to great advantage in some drawing situations; and oil sticks, a rich but limited drawing medium more suitable to larger renderings.

For color renderings in other media, the artist might consider watercolor, which is quick and light and has a nice transparent quality. Gouache, the opaque water color system, is widely used for rendering in the animation industry, and can produce everything from washes to deep, rich opaque passages in a design. Casein and other related water mediums are rarely used, but acrylics are another popular solution to color rendering, because of their wide range of colors and quick drying time.

Acrylics are water-thinned and have a number of extenders and mediums that produce gloss, matte, texture, and other effects to the finished product. As with all brush-centered media, these require maintenance and training to control and use over a long period of time. Oil paints are ultimately the richest rendering medium available, with a somewhat slower drying time and larger learning curve. With oils, a design can be taken to the finest detail and exotic range of colors and tones. When alkyd resins were introduced some years ago, the drying times for oils were drastically reduced, and now paintings can be completed, still with the full blending capabilities of standard oils, in a couple of days. There are even water-thinned oil paints available now, with molecularly altered linseed oil base that allows thinning and cleaning with water. They lack the luster and full layering of regular oils, but are a decent substitute in a pinch.

Airbrush constitutes a category of its own, requiring substantial equipment and training to produce professional results. Even so, much can be done in airbrush, and it is particularly suited to soft blending and multiple, thin layers. The artist should be aware that airbrush equipment should be used with a respirator or at least fine face mask and exhaust fan due to the dangers from particulates being inhaled into the lungs. There are smaller combinations of markers and compressed air bottles that mimic airbrush and have less maintenance and health issues, but with more limited results.

Other materials are available to the artist but are not commonly used, and they should be explored if there is some special character design rendering problem. The mastery of any of the materials discussed in this section takes time and patience. As we have said elsewhere, practice, practice, and, yes, practice some more. Look at artists you admire and copy their technique. Inquire of teachers, peers, and other artists about techniques, practice methods, and demonstrations. Like any learning process, with careful study and repetition, anyone can progress satisfactorily in a chosen rendering or sketching medium.

SUMMARY

Conceptualization and construction as applied to character design involve several different but related arenas. This chapter looks at how ideas can be generated through observation, memory, and a combination of the two. The importance of drawing skill and technique are emphasized, because only through these can the idea be translated into a visual product. Drawing concepts involve two main modes of assembly: gestural and modular. The first is a looser, more pose-oriented drawing technique used as a kind of brief notation of the object being observed. The second is a system of simplifying body (or inanimate) parts into fundamental shapes that can be modified, assembled, and reassembled into different configurations. Combining the two can make a hybrid technique useful in constructing everything from realistic to simple cartoon character designs. The sketchbook is introduced as a simple and effective means of jotting down ideas quickly, trying out varying options with these visual ideas, and recording live and other pictorial resources. Sketchbooks provide a type of visual diary and resource that the artist may refer to over a professional lifetime. Finally, this chapter discusses the variety of mediums available for quick sketching and more finished rendering of character designs, and some of their merits and weaknesses.

STUDENT SHOWCASE

Landon Armstrong

Student artwork by Landon Armstrong: The Great Hunter. In this character design, we are given some of the particulars about how the basic character is constructed from modules. In addition, along with a model turn-around, we have some sample facial expressions consistent with the construction style chosen by Armstrong. Included in this black and white version are color keys for the model turn-around.

exercises

1. Take some sketchbook character ideas and first develop them as a cartoon, then as a somewhat more realistic stylized character, and finally as a realistic character.

2. Practice with a simple character idea using interchangeable modular forms to vary the look.

3. Using some gesture drawings from life, transform one or more into stylized and/or realistic characters.

4. Draw daily from life using quick gesture observations of various people in a variety of settings.

5. Draw animals from life in pet shops, zoos, home situations, and so on. Do these in gestural form.

6. Make a list of written ideas that might inspire or generate visual character or creature concepts.

7. Using the list in exercise 6, create, from early gestures/modules to final product, three different characters and creatures. See how the visual developed from the written ideas.

in review

1. What does conceptualization refer to in relation to character development?

2. What are gestural drawings?

3. What are modular drawings?

4. How can gestural and modular drawings work together in character design?

5. What are some anatomic issues that relate to character development?

6. What are sketchbooks used for?

7. What is the basic difference between cartoon, stylized and realistic characters, and creature designs?

8. How does basic drawing technique influence the designing of characters and creatures?

synthesis: two and two makes five

objectives

Gain an understanding of the meaning of synthesis and its typology.

Discover how synthesis functions as a design process and its practical application.

Learn the relationship of synthesis to character design.

Observe actual examples of character design being created using synthetic means.

introduction

Although teachers and artists often make use of the word synthesis in relationship to the creative process, it remains a bit like the grapes of Aesop's fox, seemingly clearly visible but just out of reach. *The American Heritage Illustrated Encyclopedic Dictionary* defines synthesis as "The combining of separate elements or substances to form a coherent whole." This chapter looks at the process of synthesis in more detail and unravels the process into a more understandable methodology. While doing so, we give examples both in progress and in finished form that demonstrate what we mean at every step.

Our journey in the "synthetic" world starts with understanding just what separate elements are and what the act of combining them actually means in character design. Practically speaking, most artists in time pressure don't think in purely academic terms about the project in which they are involved. But being aware that such means exist and having practiced them in an academic setting with professional feedback makes problem solving much easier later in industry settings. Our first stop is to define and look at more closely the concept of *separate elements.*

Separatus Elementus: The Alchemy of Art

When we speak of separate elements, we are referring to a whole constellation of items that relate, in the context of this book, to character design. These are the parts assembled to make a character. They are best dealt with when broken down into categories:

- Anatomy (general)
- Like species anatomy
- Differing animal species anatomy
- Robotic or mechanical elements
- Plant elements
- Inanimate elements (natural)
- Surface texture (three dimensional)
- Surface pattern or markings (two-dimensional)
- Color
- Scale (general)
- Relative ratios of parts (scale)
- Costume (historic/thematic limitations)
- Props
- Gender
- Other (including stylistic synthesis)

These comprise the main categories that artists encounter when creating a character. You'll notice that we avoid talking about the context of the story line directly. It affects all of the elements but in and of itself is not an element. We give an explanation of the relationship of character design to the story context in Chapter One. What we are concentrating on now are the *particular pieces that can be assembled, mixed, taken apart, and modified to produce various options in a character creation. Synthesis in character design is the process in which these different elements are united and edited to produce new designs.*

Let's talk about each of the elements outlined above and give some idea of what they are and how they are used in character design. First, here are a few words about general design theory. In design, there is a principle that changes in designs are made one at a time, because any single change rearranges the totality of the design by making all of the elements function in a visually new arrangement. The brain takes in this new array in a completely different way than the original, because all relationships within the design have been altered by the addition, modification, or deletion of any element. In other words, you have a new design. Change two items, and the change is exponential. That is why we can't change too much at one time, because there is no predicting how profound the *total* transformation will be.

The first *element* is anatomy. To begin with, anatomic elements always play a dominant role for synthesis in character design. The reason is obvious. Anatomy defines shape. Changing the shape of any element is a major visual shift. By providing a new option anatomically, the artist has in a very real sense reinvented the character (humanoid, sentient creature, or just plain dumb creature). Without going into the implications for motion and physical viability, any modification or substitution of anatomy provides both a shape change and a possible function change.

Within the realm of anatomy, there are two general types of *substitution* available. (This does not cover any artificial or nonliving elements). What we mean by this is actually taking a body part (from bone/musculature to entire limb, tail, or head) and replacing an already existing body part on the original character. This is somewhat different from *modifying* a particular piece of anatomy, which is discussed later. The following are examples of substitution in anatomy. Some involve *like species anatomic substitution* and others *differing species anatomic substitution.*

The results can be either extremely interesting or comically impractical. A set of elephant legs on a gnu makes for interesting locomotion, to say the least. Notwithstanding the relative impossibility of anchoring the musculature of such enormous trunk-like structures to a smaller main body, it does make for at least an interesting thumbnail/rough design look. There are ways around the impossible in fantasy.

The real issue is the design itself and whether the synthesis of these two differing sources actually makes for something *visually compelling*. An endless stream of substitution ideas comes to mind when this method is contemplated; butterfly wings on a flea, giraffe neck on a dachshund, a colorful baboon snout on an English bank clerk. Each of these is a substitution. Another, sometimes amusing (or horrifying) type of substitution is to simply move body parts around on the original body, or moving some parts around and simply removing others. Having legs where your arms should be and vice versa can accomplish the synthesis task in unexpected ways. This method is particularly useful in the horror genre.

Things to consider: Is the substitution physically at least plausible? Can the new character actually function in any real sense (or does it need to) with these substitutions? Does the marriage of the new part to the original larger body make for interesting and dynamic design or does it merely abruptly interrupt the original configuration to no real visual or functional purpose?

Modifying a body part means changing one or more of its descriptive attributes. This fancy phrase reduces to this: change of scale, number (of parts), ratio, surface texture, pattern, and/or color. Furthermore, *additions and deletions* to the part can be made. For example, a paw can reduce the number of toes, or a head can add a pair of eyes (or several pairs). Large scale additions

Figure | 5-1 |

A frightening display of anatomic substitutions and mutations.

and deletions refer to such things as adding octopus tentacles to your character's head, or removing a pig's legs and making it aquatic.

Changing ratio is a term referring to the relative sizes of subparts in a larger unit. For us, this means something like having an ordinary arm suddenly possessing a huge biceps muscle, or even

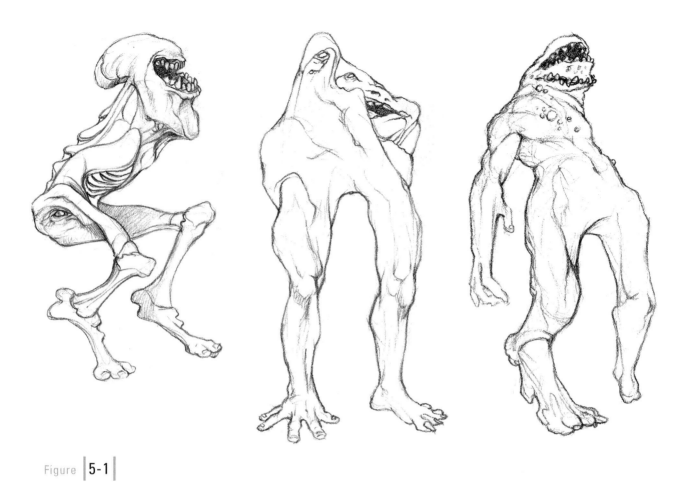

Figure | 5-1 |

(continued from page 122).

within the bicep itself, having the upper half lengthened compared to the lower half. A staggering variety of ratio changes is possible. It is here that most artists do a great deal of "fiddling" without ever really realizing *what* they are doing. They are changing the scales ratios between different subunits of a larger entity. This larger entity can be anything from a head to a toe. It just needs to have smaller parts that can be adjusted in scale relative to the larger unit.

The other modifiers are more obvious. As an example of texture, scales can be added to an arm (some might call this a substitution). Color can change, as in a rat becoming bright green or oysters having flaming red shells. Patterns can be shifted to interesting ends: A tiger might have spots instead of stripes; conversely, a leopard could now sport stripes instead of spots. (Again, this can be a subtle form of substitution; we won't quibble about the semantics here).

We can reaffirm now that there are two main types of synthesis in character design. One is *substitution.* The other is *modification* (which includes addition and deletion). Parts and pieces of these larger parts can be replaced, interchanged, or modified in some specific way to alter the

Figure | 5-2 |

Even more anatomic substitutions.

appearance and function of the character. (As an aside, this methodology obviously applies to such things as costume, architecture, and natural elements as well.) The two overlap each other, and each has any number of ways and means of accomplishing its task. Whole-scale multipart substitution (as in taking half of one creature and half of another to make a new creature) is merely a larger version of the same game. We can now move to some of the other elements listed at the beginning of the chapter and see how they integrate into this system of change.

Robotic elements are conspicuous today within the fantasy and gaming industries. They reflect a growing preoccupation with technology and its effect on our lives. Machine/live creature hybrid characters are commonplace, and probably one of the most widely used forms of synthetic character design. Androids or humans with *internal* additions of computer chips or nanotechnology start the list. These characters rarely show in any overt visual way their synthetic qualities. The

Figure 5-3

Functional and dysfunctional substitutions.

Figure | 5-4 |

Aquapig and tentacled chimp.

idea of synthesis in these characters is deduced from their *behavior*. Although of some value to us as artists, in reality this is more an acting or script issue.

What we are interested in with robotic/machine elements is the look they provide. Quite frankly, the "coolness" of human (or animal)/machine hybrids lies in its odd, but fascinating mix of biomorphic (living form) elements with hydraulics, motors, electronic enhancements, and otherwise machine-oriented parts (e.g., technology = emotional remoteness ; living entity = warm, intimate). These sources can be completely unlike or mimic one another, but

Figure | 5-5 |

Critter scale shifts.

together they force the brain into an odd sort of dance between what is expected and what is perceived. This jolt is what provides the excitement of the design.

The addition of mechanical or related parts to any living creature can be broadly divided into three categories. First is the addition of computing power to the brain of the character. This may or may not be visible. In this instance, the implied change may be in concert with other more overtly visible changes, for example, the enhancement of sensory organs as related to new computer inserts. (We'll dodge the issue of nanotechnology for the time being; for anyone interested, the changes wrought with micro-scale modification may not be able to be obvious to the naked eye at all.) Eyes might have to be reconfigured to handle the new "brain-power." Tongues might have extended length and surface area, and so on.

A second category is a change in the general movement and locomotion of the character. Here we can visualize pistons, hydraulic systems, cables, and similar elements being added to and substituting for normal body tissue. In this instance, the ability of the character to move is changed or enhanced. Running, jumping, climbing, wrestling, or any other movement capability is subject to modification. Visually this provides a great deal of fun for the artist as the rendering of both biomorphic and mechanical

Figure | **5-6** |

Never-before-photographed piebald tiger.

| NOTE |

In fact, this is a general principle of synthetic design: *The mixing of two differing visual sources into a single design relies on both prior visual expectations and the surprise of new visual results from the synthesis for its success.* We play off of the spectators' expectations and then grab their attention with something unexpected. Of course, this doesn't guarantee success. It could just as well provide disaster. The other ingredient to success is whether the elements chosen actually enhance one another or just seem desperately out of synch. This is where resemblance in shape, size, color, texture, and so forth can play a role. Too much mimicry and you have barely crawled out of the original visual concept. Too great a change and the brain has trouble understanding the design as a united entity. The key is to find some common ground in at least some of the new parts chosen in relation to the original design. There are, to be sure, some designs that defy this common-sense logic. In their case (and in all cases really) it is a matter of testing before trial audiences. Ultimately, it is there that the worth of the design will be determined.

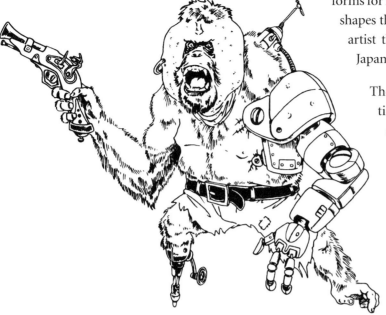

forms for movement involves large and fascinating shapes that lend themselves to great design. One artist that comes to mind immediately is the Japanese illustrator Surabaya.

The third category includes simple additions to or substitutions on a living character. This might include such things as electronic scanning eyes; biomechanical arms, hands, legs, or feet; an extra limb or two; or even internal additions (filters, processors, extra mechanical organs, and so on). Items not related to specific body parts can also be added: jet-packs for travel, water condensers for desert planets—the possibilities are endless.

Figure **5-7**

M.O.P.—Mechanized orangutan pirate.

Another realm for exploration is the unusual combination of plant forms with animal characters. (This brings up plant characters, which is discussed briefly in Chapter Three.) Remember, as we look through these successive categories, elements from *any* of them can be used in combination with any others. Plant forms can be used with mechanical additions and an animal or humanoid character. In the specific category of plant forms as possible character synthesis solutions, many options present themselves. Some of these options are intriguing, and some are comical. A doglike character that has the capability of photosynthesis because of a cluster of leaves along its back certainly bears a second glance. Branches sprouting from a head might make us stare in disbelief or laugh out loud, depending on how they are handled.

Because most plants (like tired students) move slowly, locomotion does not present itself as a high priority in using plant sources for synthetic design. Plants are more suited for strength, structural modification, and metabolic types of design functions.

If we go through the same options outlined for general synthetic principles, we could substitute plant parts, add plant parts, or modify existing anatomic areas with similar plant parts. The process remains the same: substitution, addition (deletion), and modifica-

Figure **5-8**

Svelte robot.

tion. Depending on what you are working with, one or the other or several of these options can be chosen. With plants and the plant kingdom in general, the functional difference between realms of animals and plants in such things as skeletons, locomotion, surfaces, and so on mean drastic functional design problems for the artist. Of course, this has never stopped creative minds from combining the two, and many designers simply don't care about the impossibilities that they have raised in their characters. The famous 1951 science fiction movie *The Thing from Outer Space* (starring James Arness of television's "Gunsmoke" fame) had as its main antagonist a plant biped from another planet (and not a very nice one at that).

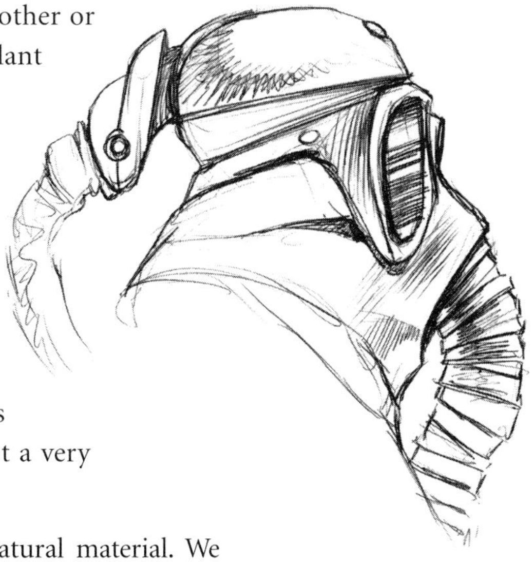

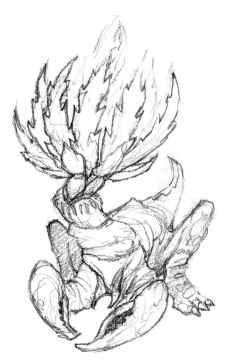

The next arena for character synthesis involves inanimate natural material. We chiefly think of such things as rock in its many forms, or even liquids or gases (some science fiction stories come to mind of intelligent fields of interstellar gas). Inclusion of any of these items produces much the same set of problems and possibilities as with the categories we have previously examined. As ever, things to be considered include locomotion, motion in general, metabolism, and so on. A diamond-studded carnivore or an undersea creature that is part inflatable gas bag (reminiscent of some politicians we know) seem not too unreasonable, but it takes some thinking to combine granite outcroppings with a large, grazing herbivore. Obvious issues are mobility and flexibility. The challenge would be to find ways in which this seemingly contradictory combination could work. This is where Chapter Four, with its emphasis on using the sketchbook and working out ideas in multiple preliminary concept pieces, is valuable and completes what we are talking about in this chapter on synthesis. The most direct area to be confronted with this synthetic solution is the nature of combining living and nonliving materials together in viable ways that are also visually interesting. One of the 12 principles of animation laid out by the Disney animators was appeal, and we can't forget this important point as character design decisions are made.

Moving into a somewhat different realm of synthesis resources, we should now consider surface texture, surface pattern or markings, and color. These present themselves as both independent qualities and inherent properties of certain elements that might be used in a synthetic solution. What this means is that the artist/designer, in trying to conjure up a new character, can turn to what really amount to abstract categories such as designers normally manipulate. Color, actual physical texture, pattern, and markings are part of the foundation of design. When designing, borrowing a color or texture from another source is an obvious

Figure **5-9**

Biomechanical attributes.

Figure **5-10**

Plant + animal = weird!

type of synthetic solution. In this instance, many examples come readily to mind. It is probably the easiest means of modification (other than scale) of an existing design.

When adding, substituting, or trading any of these elements, some thought should be given to "reasonableness," that is, whether the color or pattern is being added just because the artist can't think of any worthwhile changes. As in fashion, mix and match works sometimes, and sometimes it falls with a thud. Here, as always, it is whether the new element *enhances* the design. Deleting one of these elements is also a possibility. An alligator with the skin of an eel (in a sense a deletion) or an albino hummingbird can be relatively subtle but effective design changes.

Actual physical surface texture, as in the bumps on an iguana or the fur of a yak, present technical problems for the artist in execution. These are probably more easily solved in three-dimensional programs through texture mapping. Nevertheless, in preliminary concept work, a symbol for the texture must be found that relays in an effective way what the texture actually is like. Changes in this element are like all other synthesis, where addition, substitution, deletion, and modification are the tools.

We have already touched to a certain extent on scale and ration as elements to be used in synthesis. To reiterate, a change of scale or the relative sizes of parts of a character can be an effective technique for creating a new character design. Scale change has the virtue and vice of being so obvious that some changes must be done carefully, so as not to provoke an unwanted response. A savage barbarian with a pin-head probably won't evoke much fear from his/her opponents. Voluptuous babes have curves; frankly speaking, they get the attention.

Various amounts of change should be explored before settling on a final version. Subtle differences in scale and ratio (as with all element modifications) can make the difference between success and a near-miss. This is where extensive preliminary work is so valuable, as we have emphasized before.

Costumes and props are elements often overlooked by beginning designers. Just a simple change of costume can send a character into an entirely new feel. Changing props can help in this process as well.

Costumes are role symbols for the viewer. They also help place the character in historical and cultural contexts. One of the subtexts for this synthetic change is how costume can modify how we perceive the gender of the character. Costumes are often gender-specific, and a simple alteration or substitution can bring interesting (or odd) results in the feel of the character vis-à-vis their gender.

Costumes otherwise normally give us cues as to what the character does, its qualities as a being, and, as stated above, where and when it lives. It is obvious that being able to render cloth, metal, leather, and a host of other materials is vital. Here the practice sketch or study is king. A

Figure **5-11**

Bipedal "plantoid."

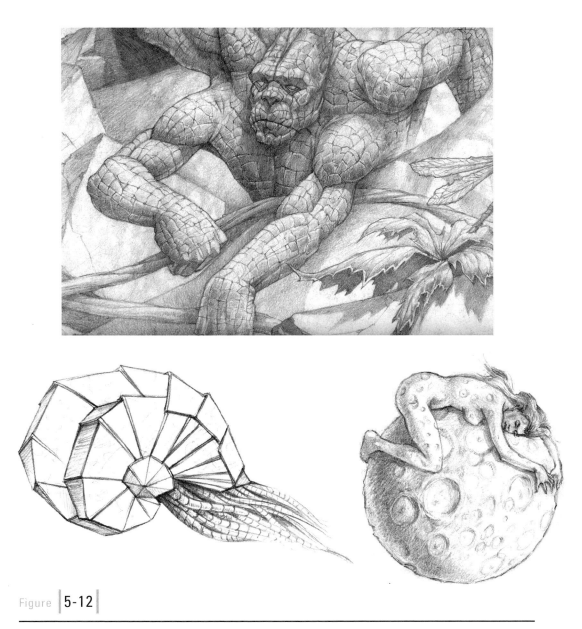

Figure | 5-12 |

Animate + inanimate synthesis.

study of historical costumes and props along with contemporary overviews will aid the artist in design potential. Costumes are discussed at more length in Chapter Three, but it bears reminding of their crucial role in character development.

Lastly, style, as in actual drawing style, can be used as a tool or element in character synthesis. Here we might note that different studios, artists, and cultures have characteristic "styles" that they lend to their characters (as well as backgrounds and other elements). By trading a little of one style with another, or simply substituting or modifying so as to incorporate a stylistic

Figure **5-13**

Eel-skin 'gator.

change in part or all of a character, the artist can produce a new result without actually having to reconfigure any of the elements already extant. A word of caution: This can be a legal quagmire. Borrowing styles too perfectly can result in an occasional "cease and desist" letter from the legal department of a studio. Individual artists are sensitive to the

Figure **5-14**

Dangerous curves!

Figure **5-15**

Costuming contexts.

Figure | 5-16 |

Gender-bending.

Figure | 5-17 |

A veritable plethora of synthesized critters.

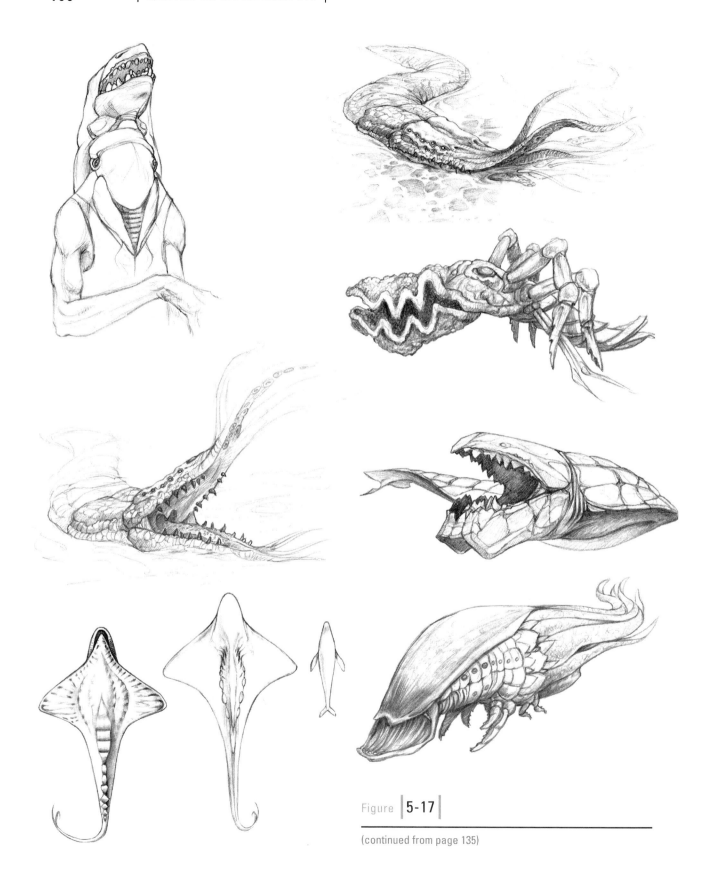

Figure | 5-17 |

(continued from page 135)

STUDENT SHOWCASE

Ramon Hippolito

Student artwork by Ramon Hippolito: synthetic elephantine creatures. Hippolito shows us a fascinating series of possible solutions to a hybrid animal design problem. In some, the more elephant-like parts of the anatomy dominate; in others, a more ape-like or boar-like form comes to the fore. In each design, Hippolito seeks to find the best combination of shapes in an overall design.

uniqueness and personal ownership of their own stylistic innovations, and these should be respected. It does not mean that some aspects of style derived from these sources can't be used. By all means, explore whether or not a Japanese manga style of art work can be introduced to romance novel covers. Just take care and use common sense. If in doubt, inquire at the source.

The following are more examples of synthesis, including some before and after images and some variations explored at the sketch level.

SUMMARY

Chapter Five deals with the subject of synthesis as it relates to character design, showing how the combination of new elements can change and even completely create a new character. The various elements possible for synthesis are many; this chapter covers the major categories most likely to be encountered by an artist and gives some examples of possible work modes and solutions. Synthesis is one of the most powerful tools in the artist's arsenal and can take a character design from ordinary to appealing by subtle changes in the character's elements.

exercises

1. Take several images from your character design sketchbooks and modify them by addition of an element and then by deletion of an element.

2. Produce a synthetic solution by changing the ratio of the scale of individual parts of the character design. Try several versions.

3. Mix species in several character designs. Pay attention to authentic anatomic observation.

4. Add robotic elements to a character design. Try to preserve the ability to move and function like the original (although enhanced) character.

5. With a costumed character, change or exchange the costume so that the character itself remains the same but its feel becomes profoundly different.

6. Modify or substitute surface markings, patterns, and texture in a character design.

7. Change the color of a character design.

8. Modify the anatomy of a character to produce a new design.

in review

1. What is the definition of synthesis?

2. What is an element in design synthesis?

3. Name 5 to 10 elements covered in this chapter.

4. What signals do costumes and props give the viewer?

5. What are the major types of synthesis for artists?

Stylin'

objectives

Gain an introduction to the concept of style as it applies to character design.

Learn about visual design for characters and its subsystems: shape, line, surface, symmetry, repetition/variation, and contrast/affinity.

Learn about genre, appeal, and rendering as applicable to creating character-based visual art.

Gain an introduction to conceptual design for characters.

Learn about how color relates to character design.

Acquire a basic understanding of materials usage and methodology for developing and refining character art.

Gain an introduction to the model sheet as a character reference tool.

It Ain't about Fashion

The term *style* is bandied about in our daily culture in its relationship to "being fashionable" and in reference to items ranging from hair to shoes to clothes and even to the manner in which food is prepared. For our character design purposes, style does not refer to whether or not our creations are the niftiest things since sliced bread, but it does refer to the "look" of the character and the visual manner by which it has been described.

As artists, ours is a visual medium, and the appearance of our characters determines and is determined by stylistic choice. While design theory can provide an overarching plethora of challenges to creators, the core concepts of character style can be broken down into handy subject areas that will let us successfully tackle the possible complexities of creature design. These aforementioned groups and fundamental design concepts are visual design, rendering, genre, and appeal. Lest we lose our way down the trail to good character design, this chapter provides definitions of these critical terms and their related components.

Visual design, for lack of a better moniker, refers to the fundamental precepts of design theory that can be applied to character making. The "subsystems" of character design that have been isolated for character design purposes are:

- Shape
- Line
- Surface
- Symmetry
- Repetition
- Variation
- Contrast/affinity

Shape of Things to Come

An initial method for creating a basic simplified structure on which to base a character illustration is through the use of shape. It is also an effective tool for developing character recognition (as through the silhouette of a figure). For example, the protagonist (or other good guys) in a story are circular, spherical, or utilize a circular motif somehow within the noticeable realm of their construction or visual aspect. We are forced to eventually recognize that circular = protagonist. In contrast (another important design factor in and of itself), a designer might then be led to delineate related villainous characters with a triangular/pyramidal motif, suggesting hard angles vs. the soft curves of the heroic characters. In the following examples, you can observe how shapes can be used as a basic construction form that translates directly into a character's visual aspect.

A designer can also mix shapes as part of a character design basis. Perhaps, based on the aforementioned shape relationships, a character who displays a combination of angular (bad) and curved (good) forms, would represent a neutral character. We may also mix our shapes

EVIL + GOOD = NEUTRAL

Figure | 6-1 |

Characters shape up using shapes.

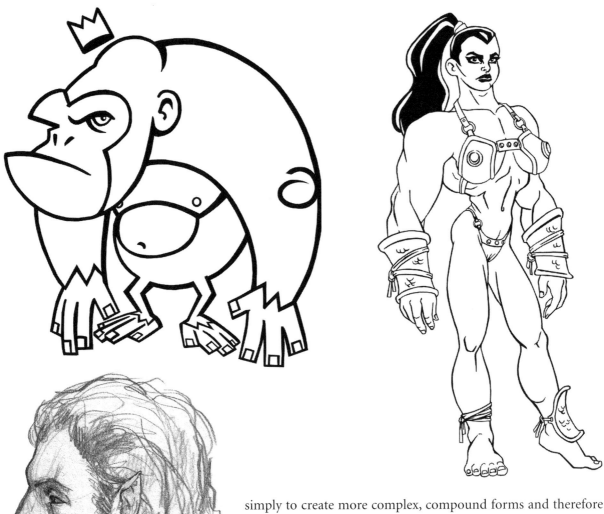

Figure | 6-2 |

Character line-work line-up.

simply to create more complex, compound forms and therefore expand visual possibilities of design.

Let the Blandishment Fit the Line

Line, as a design element and drawing convention, is a key player in developing stylistic variations for character creation and rendering. It's typical with character design that the project tends to generate a suggestion generally or specifically of the look of the character or creature, particularly in a situation with 2D animation. For instance, a particular studio may specialize in types of characters that are drawn with a heavy, thick trap-line; a squiggly line; a realistic type of line rendering for characters; or some linear form that's more simplistic. These are issues with 2D animation and, once again, relate back to an artist's skill in drawing.

The ability to create appropriate line-work and to delineate characterization that is within the structure of design is paramount. Good line-work in character design tends to play curved lines off of straight lines and show a variation in line quality. These kinds of line-work issues also affect a character design for illustration. For example, the style of art for comic books is usually based on the inherent drawing methods of a particular artist, generating the look of that comic book. Early traditional printing methods created the need for comic book drawings to rely on a heavy trap-line: a black outline that defines the edges of the characters to allow for simple coloration. Now, with a lot of comic books being digitally (often over a scanned pencil drawing) and traditionally painted, the advances in reproduction technology allow more generous feasibility in regard to such methods.

Comic book characters require a design that is repeatable over a series of panels as sequential art, just as 2D animation characters require a form that is repeatable as they are being drawn frame after frame to create an animation sequence. This kind of production requires the skill to maintain tight line quality and character volumes.

In clean-up for traditional animation, rough pencil animation is redefined to put the characters "on model" (i.e., making them match the model sheets) along with sharpening up and cleaning the line-work. Clean-up is another area that requires good drawing skills. The character designer (or the individual seeking that job) must be able to draw in a wide range of styles, developing various "looks" for characters (whether "cartoony" or realistic) in a variety of mediums. Character creators need to be able to work in various facets of diverse industries where character design is done.

Surface Tension

When we discuss "surface" as an element of character design, we mean the visual look of the exterior of the character (e.g., skin, fur, bark), and how we represent texture and the implication of

Figure | 6-3 |

Hirsute hobgoblin. Metallically coifed: "cartoony" and realistic.

the related material from which the surface is formed. In other words, does the surface look like scaly hide or polished metal? This element is related to both rendering and observational skill.

Associated with the concept of surface are tonal value and color as conditional elements. Both of these qualities are defined by how the viewer perceives the way light reacts with the surface from which it is reflected or absorbed. Tonal value is the effect of surface modeling through light and shadow on a 3D form. Value creates the effect of dimensionality and emphasizes the texture by contrast, such as in the highlighted folds and dark furrows of wrinkled hide. Strong highlights, visible reflections, and a virtually texture-less surface can suggest shiny metal or plastic. Thorough observations of organic surfaces or textures (scales, horn, hair) and inorganic surfaces or textures (stone, metal, rubber) will yield an understanding of the effects of tone and texture for the artist.

The portion of the visual spectrum of light reflected from a subject determines the color of its surface. Dark tonal values and heavy texture create a darker shade of surface hue, whereas strong light brightens and lightens the color.

Value rendering methods (like hatching, crosshatching, and scribbling with a drawing tool) in and of themselves suggest texture even without creating a representational description of the subject. The relative rendering style of a character illustration—cartoony or realistic—determines the way a surface is described. For instance, a furry monster's head wearing a metal helmet depicted realistically may be represented by detailed drawing with the following attributes:

- Blended tonal values based on lighting from a specific imagined source.

- Fur texture patterned after comparative anatomic reference; that is, the artist observed some particular animal fur and noted how it grows out from the cranium, the nature of its thickness, and how it lays. Coarse, stiff hair that sticks out in clumps would be drawn with a heavy line.

A cartoony critter's cranium requires a different stylistic look and may display the following illustrative attributes:

- Adjustments in line weight or designated areas of black to suggest light and dark contrast on the surface

- Texture of fur suggested by simple lines that develop a symbolic pattern-type solution to hair

A major component to creating an effective character surface rendering is to develop a method for drawing or modeling surfaces that are recognizable to the viewer and work in the context of the character's look.

Striking a Match (or Mismatch)

What is symmetry? The *American Heritage Dictionary* (Fourth Edition) defines symmetry as follows:

1. Exact correspondence of form and configuration on opposite sides of a dividing line or plane or about a center or axis.

2. An arrangement with balanced or harmonious proportions.

Both of these descriptions apply to how we develop the relative dimensions of a character to create visual interest in the viewer, not to mention good design.

We, as human beings, think of ourselves as being symmetrical in structure—two arms, two eyes, two nostrils, two legs—along with other parts evenly centered or distributed upon the centralized head and trunk. All of these parts are exactly proportional and exactly the same size in relationship to each other, right? Wrong! In fact, human bodies and those of other animal forms typically have dominant anatomic parts that are elements of a set (a pair, for instance). These aforementioned parts might be longer, stronger, bigger, or even hairier than their opposing counterpart. Here's an example of what we mean: Try putting your two index fingers side by side, as evenly comparable as possible. You will notice a variation in the shape of the nails, the manner in which the skin wrinkles at your knuckles, and perhaps a minute yet noticeable, difference in the finger length and width. The differences are by no means tremendous, but they do exist. Usually, a dominant anatomic element gets more use (as in right hand vs. left hand) and therefore increases in muscle tone and mass.

Figure **6-4**

Lopsided? Just a hunch; backed by observation.

This phenomenon is asymmetry, or the lack of symmetry. Asymmetry can be a wonderful tool for the character or creature designer. It allows visual variation in the anatomic proportion of a character and therefore adds visual interest. Lopsidedness in a dimensional form (2D or 3D) causes changes in visual or physical direction in the character's form. Asymmetry suggests a spatial shift away from vertical and horizontal coordinates. Spatial changes cause more work for the eye and therefore stimulate visual curiosity.

Rob D'Arc, puppet designer and sculptor, has recently discussed asymmetry related to character design in an issue of *The Puppetry Journal*. He has mentioned vertical, horizontal, and (what we call) oblique divisions of humanoid facial features that define the basis for creating visual imbalance in each case. This method works equally well with the figure itself as the subject of the process.

In an upcoming illustration, we see that character heads have been physically divided in half from top to bottom (vertical), side to side (horizontal), and at a diagonal (or oblique angle). Having created these divisions, or "equators," each half of the head/features can then be modified in an opposing manner via scale, proportion, and shape.

A character's form may also be twisted dimensionally on a z-axis or equator to create asymmetry. Visualize an imaginary line running from the character's head to his or her feet and the body, head, and so on turned in a spiral around that line.

Figure | 6-5 |

Stretched to the limit with asymmetry.

Related to asymmetrical distortion, visual interest in character design must occur "in the round," that is, a character should display spatial changes of structure that make him or her appear interesting no matter which view is presented. This philosophy applies to both 2D and 3D character solutions. This concept relates to character posing and more importantly to character structure and detail. The addition, as appropriate, of a mane, spines, or a fin down a creature's back makes for a more attention-grabbing dorsal view.

Repeated Repetitions and Variable Variations

Repetition is a type of design relationship in which elements (like shape or line) are used over and over to create a unity of form. The idea of repetition in character design is to be complementary as opposed to being simply redundant. A character design may make use of repeated shapes to develop and overall look. As we have seen in the application of shape in character design, repetition may also be grossly or subtly related to structural form. A fat character's face may be made up of repeated oval or circular shapes to suggest the round, meaty forms. A robot might be constructed of box-like components (head, chest, feet) and bristling with dozens of round rivets, creating a visual theme. Parallel lines or grids could form speakers or exhaust vents for such a mechanical man.

Scale, color, size, direction, and other elements can be repetitive.

Another important concept in visual design and style is variation. Variation occurs when set elements that make up a character are modified over a series of preliminary sketches in the development of the design to change the look of the character. Typical modifications might be changes in orientation, in the distance between parts, or in the scale and placement of these elements. For instance, if we take an average human-type character's face, we may vary the symmetry by making one eye larger than another or by moving the eyes closer together. An ovoid nose could be placed with its long axis up and down or side to side, or the nose could be placed higher or lower on the face, or the entire set of facial features could be moved up and down the long axis. These are kinds of variations that can help define the look of a character.

Figure | 6-6 |

Twist and shout: an example of asymmetry through axial rotation.

One of These Things Is Not Like the Other

Contrast and affinity, as defined in the book *The Visual Story* by Bruce Block, relate to how visual elements are different or alike, thereby creating different impacts on the viewer. By its nature, contrast in line or shape within the design of a character can make it visually more interesting. Playing curved lines off of straight lines or angled forms off of round forms within the structure of a character adds a dynamic feeling to that character.

Affinity suggests, like symmetry, sameness or direct relation in elements of the character. This is important for suggesting cohesiveness in a design. A character, for instance, may have a variety of colors that are all within the red end of the spectrum, with all related equipment, surroundings, and so on having that kind of sameness of hue. Once again, that kind of association can be made with warm (or cool) colors and that individual character.

Figure | 6-7 |

Back to back: not so exciting and exciting dorsal designs.

Conceptually Speaking

Preliminary character and creature designs typically evolve into what we call *concept art* in the industry. Concept art consists of more developed character renderings (beyond initial sketches) that give the producer, directors, or other artists working on a film, game, comic book, or animation project an idea of what visual possibilities for a character exist. It's at this

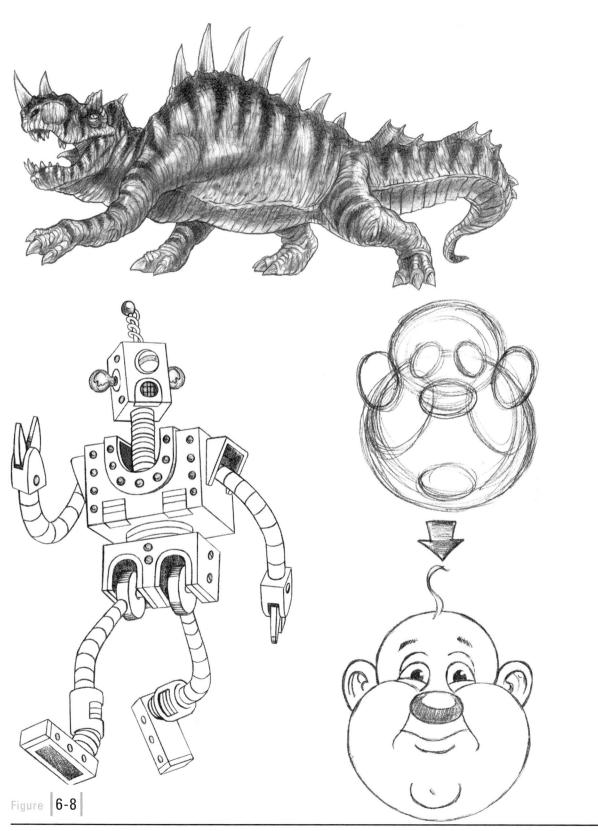

Figure | 6-8 |

Repetition of character elements again and again and again.

Figure | 6-9 |

Facial fiddling as variation.

point that the initial idea of a character is fully developed to a point where it can be looked at and decisions can be made about the need to further modify the character, change the design, or modify the materials used to render the character. Concept renderings are often relatively quick and many times involve the use of color. Once again, this process is subject to variations based on the individual artist's style and the project. Pencil, marker, water-based paints, pen and ink, and even digital illustration are media that concept artists use. Initial concept sketches may be further developed and refined, perhaps to commit them to more advanced digital illustrations. Full acrylic or oil paintings might be used to describe a character or creature.

Past the concept art stage, different artistic directions may be taken with the character design. One choice is to leave the design at the concept art stage and to make use of that. For instance, much of Ralph McQuarrie's initial designs for the original *Star Wars* trilogy found their way more or less directly into final film designs. Depending on the nature of what the next production step will be, the concept art, in and of itself, might be sufficient for preproduction needs.

Whether black and white or color, concept art is important in the visual effects industry and may be produced to previsualize make-up effects, to show the design for an animatronic puppet or a stop-motion creature, or perhaps to show designs for complex monster suits and elaborate costumes. All of these creations benefit from a concept rendering. If the final character concept is going to be developed as a 2D animation design, then it is necessary to observe the parameters of character needs in that industry. For 2D animation, a character will be drawn thousands of times to generate the number of frames necessary to create an animated film, so simplicity is of the essence.

Figure | 6-10 |

Cool character conceptualization.

PLEASE TAKE NOTE!

Draw, Draw, Draw...Well!

We should re-interject a key point here—Drawing skill is paramount in character and creature design. The ability to understand how to describe complex forms in space using a pencil or other medium directly translates to the ability to simplify anatomy for animation, to render realistic creatures that will become large-scale puppets for the cinema, or to visualize special make-up effects and so on. The ability to draw realistically in this sense helps in creating dimensional renderings of characters or creatures.

To create good concept art reference for sculpted characters, for example, one needs to be able to describe in detail the color, texture, and details of anatomy that act as a guide for building that sculptural anatomy. Preliminary artwork for traditional puppet-making might include an illustration that depicts how puppets work mechanically, where joints are, and so on. The preliminary work also should emphasize the dimensionality of the characters' exaggerated sculptural features that project to the audience. This is paramount for reference in the final creation of puppet anatomy.

Roy G. Biv and Associates

Color testing for character designs is also of value, assuming the final output of the project is in color, of course! Digital coloring of artwork using some type of photo-manipulation program is quite handy in this situation, because modification to hue, value, and chroma balance by the mere click of a button allows the artist to quickly see many variants in color schemes. Traditionally, markers and colored inks have been used to put together color tests of characters.

Color as a component is important in that it can suggest themes or emotions: a red, white, and blue costume of a superhero can suggest American patriotism; a black hat on a cowboy can suggest that he's evil. The challenge is to make associations that are interesting and original, even when still playing to the stereotypes. For instance, by itself, orange relates to neither good nor evil; but suppose that every time an evil character appeared on the screen in a motion picture, there was an orange tint to the lighting or some article of clothing worn by the villain or villains that was orange. The viewers would begin to subliminally associate orange with evil.

Certainly, warm/cool colors and bright/dark colors could suggest different emotional states of characters or even cause different emotional states in the viewer. For example, a horror character would be typically better suited to displaying dark, subdued, cooler colors: hues that might suggest coldness, cruelty, night-time—things of that nature. There are certain color associations like this that are developed within the human psyche and are based on previous relationships and views of life and nature.

General Genre

Another element of style that is important to consider in character design is genre. By that we mean not only a classification of whatever medium the character is being produced for, but also the look of the character by virtue of the type of storytelling medium in which the character will be included, that is, the story, the mood, and related elements that are part of a classification of genre.

We can look at general genres and those that are more specific to other visual design elements such as rendering. A generic genre, for instance, could be that of the horror variety. Typically, horror themes include evil monsters, death, darkness, and the like, and tend to require characters that reflect such themes in the sense of how they might be rendered or lit (perhaps in pen and ink, in dark tones, or in a sort of film noir lighting). Our choice of type of character can also be typical: monsters, the undead, ghosts, bats, rats, and things of those sorts. These are traditional types of basic character forms that we might associate with horror as a genre. Unless we are trying to create some sort of visual or conceptual contrast, we would not add any kind of comedic references to a character design scenario for horror, and we would not add a silly look to the characters or render those characters in a manner that is the antithesis of the genre.

Figure | 6-11 |

Demonic diva: deliciously, yet dastardly displayed.

Comic book, or comic strip, characters are affected by their ultimate output format, and budgetary concerns can be related to these issues. A comic book company may publish predominantly black-and-white comic books, so the ability to develop a character design that not only functions in its role but also works visually in black and white is an important and specific consideration.

Like a Banana, You Need Appeal

What is the definition of appeal as it applies to character design? Without consulting the dictionary on this topic, I believe that the readership will agree to say that appeal suggests our disposition on the relative attractiveness of a person, place, thing, or idea.

PLEASE TAKE NOTE!

Form Follows Function

Sometimes characters and their designs have to be modified to fit a specific final medium for which they're created, for example, the character of Sally in Tim Burton's stop-motion film *The Nightmare Before Christmas*. Anyone who has seen the film or any of Burton's designs for that film will notice that several of the characters, including Sally, have very long, spindly limbs. This presents a problem when translating that style to a stop-motion puppet, because these puppets have an internal metal-jointed ball-and-socket skeleton to support them. Those joints must be made small enough to fit within the foam rubber body of the puppet, but they must also be able to fully support the puppet's weight. In the original drawings of Sally by Tim Burton, she did not wear the baggy socks that she is seen sporting in the film. The socks were added to cover Sally's bare ankle joints because the puppet builders could not create a functional joint that could fit inside such a tiny ankle.

Remember that form follows function: design and style must be predicated on the character's intended function, be that a stop-motion puppet, football team mascot, or breakfast cereal sponsor.

Physical attraction (often with the intention of mating) can occur between humans, based on visual appearance (a gorgeous woman or a handsome man). A baby may become stimulated by viewing objects sporting interesting shapes and bright colors. People may be drawn together based on a common attraction to an abstract idea like politics or religion. While these ideas on appeal are certainly viable, the concept, as applicable to character design purposes, is slightly askew of the previously noted tenets.

During the early decades of the twentieth century, 2D animation was an art still in relative infancy, but rapidly moving forward as a practical entertainment medium for the motion picture industry. Walt Disney was a huge proponent of the idea that animated "actors" were as capable of storytelling as their real-life counterparts. Based on this precept, he pushed his animators to master the medium and infuse it with a naturalism that would capture the audience's attention and imagination. Unfortunately, early animators had no guide for animation development, making it up as they went along and solving problems as they occurred. For the first time in animation history, a functional set of foundational rules for 2D animation was created when Disney Studios' "Nine Old Men" (the original team of studio animators/directors) sat down to codify a group of regulations through which good animation could be achieved. These rules are known as "The Twelve Principles of Animation," one of which is "appeal."

Appeal, in the aforementioned context, refers to whether or not the visual aspect of a character will garner audience attention or sympathy, and whether or not the look is viable in regard to the character's nature. This means that the character's appearance should be striking enough in some way to stimulate and maintain viewer interest (cute, sexy, hideous), and should appropriately belie the character's underlying nature in some way (heroic, evil, studious). Even an attractive villain may be predisposed to frowns, snarls, or violent behavior; along with possible physical attributes that thus brand them, without depending on grotesque stereotyping. A beautiful but nasty demon lady might be an example of such a character.

Renderiffic

The next key element of the overarching concept of style is rendering. For our purposes, rendering means the method by which the determined concept of a character (a mental or written idea) becomes transformed into some type of visual art. Depending on the needs of the project and the idea, this concept of rendering will vary. Once the idea has been committed to paper, then the designer can move on to other art materials or methods to continue the rendering.

We're all a little rough around the edges and may be able to use some refinement, but we're not talking about wrinkly clothes or a 5-o'clock shadow here. In this case, refinement refers to the artistic process by which preliminary artwork is cleaned up, "tweaked," and otherwise developed into what will become its final visual form. In this section of the chapter, refinement is discussed as the modification of early drawings through a process to develop more fully rendered images.

To recap the drawing and visualization process: The designer first thinks of an idea for a character or creature (researching in areas relative to its design) and then commits to making images on a page, that is, converting mental ideas onto paper by drawing. The typical first step is the thumbnail, or small preliminary rough sketch. One issue that comes to mind, even at this early point in the conceptualization process, is when should refinement begin and how far does that refinement go to create the final character design? One answer is that the artist can take the rendering to any level based on the artist's own skill and desire. Ultimately, as we are playing in the field of character design and inventing our own artwork, this concept is a normal way of looking at character image creation.

On the other side of the coin, companies or individuals hire artists to develop these characters or creatures for a specific reason. In this case, the parameters of the industry project will ultimately create a direction for the character artist and define the actual refinement needs for particular character design.

As previously discussed, the final character product is going to determine how the character designer proceeds with the creation. For instance, if a character designer is creating a character or characters for an animation production company that is going to create a 2D animated feature film, we will ultimately see the need for clean, simplified character model sheets rendered tightly in pencil or ink.

Perhaps a character designer gets a job illustrating a one-panel cartoon in a magazine like *The New Yorker* or *Playboy*. If so, a variety of various cartoon styles may be applicable: comic-book realism, photo-realism, or characters captured by a few strokes of ink from a brush.

Along with these stylistic possibilities comes rendering variety: the use of basic pen-and-ink drawing, color cartoons fully painted in watercolor or gouache, or even cartoons created through mixed media. The rendering, thematic, and stylistic choices here, not to mention the level of relative refinement, rest on the nature and look of the magazine itself. Because magazines like *The New Yorker* and animation studios like Walt Disney or Pixar use and create artwork that has a specific look, character designers and cartoonists must familiarize themselves with the nature of the artwork used or produced by those companies. This becomes an issue of design compatibility between the artist and the production company.

Before moving forward into the nuts and bolts of character refinement, let's talk about a critical concept in the production of good character design: solid drawing. One of the 12 Principles of Animation, solid drawing refers to the concept that an animator's (or character designer's) drawing talent, ability to look at real-life objects and living entities, and ability to translate that to a 2D page in a manner that is plausible is a critical factor in creating successful drawings that are paramount to successful design.

It is also important to touch on practical applications of character design and the skill sets needed, hence the importance of drawing. Because character designers often have to create technical drawings like model sheets in which continuity in character images and posing is absolutely necessary, the understanding of how to maintain consistent scale and volumes is absolutely essential for developing plausible character images.

In life drawing, we refine our quick gesture sketches that capture the essence of a pose into more realistic renderings by first developing volumes of forms to essentially flesh out the anatomy. This may include scribbling or rendering shapes that begin to suggest dimensionality. Often, artists will substitute geometric solids, the modular forms that we've discussed, over a sketch in order to develop solidity, that is, a solid structure, to the character. The trick is to be able to maintain those volumes. As a character moves or is drawn in different poses, the character's head or, for example, potbelly remains the same mass, the same circumference; with the addition of foreshortening as a factor. Part of this issue of understanding volume is rooted in a good core understanding of human anatomy. By doing life drawing exercises and observing the human form and the forms of animals, we can gain cognizance of the scale and mass and shape of body parts as they relate to each other.

A method that's often used to create scale reference for animation character's model sheets is to use a known volume (for instance, the head) or a circle that represents the circumference of the cranium of a character's head as a unit of measure. Animation characters are often measured by how many heads high they are. Characters are often given specific shape elements or modular elements by which they are constructed. A key to their construction that may be provided as an addition to the model sheets can give the character artist known size values of body parts that can be measured so consistency of volume can be met by physically measuring those parts and making sure that they maintain those measurements at all times. Model sheets are discussed later.

At this point, let's segue back into some of the practical application matters of refining character artwork; that is, going from a preliminary drawing to a final rendering. One of the first things that the authors do as part of their instruction in a character design class is to get a variety of student input on their own individual processes for getting character ideas on paper, and then moving them forward to some kind of final character design image. We have, through students, our own experience, and that of our colleagues, synthesized some common procedural tools that most everybody, whether amateur or professional, uses when refining their character design studies. Please understand that this is but a brief glimpse at the steps toward creating finished character artwork. Search your local bookstore and library for many fine books on drawing, painting, and digital coloring that can expand your knowledge of art production related to character design.

Step Up to the Drawing Board

For Step 1, we need to pull the idea for our character out of the old brain box, mix that with a generous helping of research, and then prepare to disgorge the whole mess onto paper. In this case, we are referring to thumbnails or other initial, preparatory drawings. It's important at this early conceptual stage to keep drawings rough because the artist is essentially brainstorming on paper. Many times a character creator will get great ideas at

Figure | 6-12 |

Character thumbnail on dubious substrate with photocopy of same.

odd hours or odd places, and find themselves sketching ideas out on anything from lined note paper, restaurant napkins, to the back of a discarded envelope from a water department bill. Many is the time we have gotten strange looks pulling out wads of napkins and other crumpled, odd chunks of paper and tossing them onto the photocopier to preserve our studies via such reproductions.

At this point, we've actually meandered into Step 2, which involves developing the format and composition for the study that will eventually be built into the final rendering. One method is to take our thumbnail sketches and create a scale for our drawing by enlarging or reducing on the photocopier. If someone has created a character sketch in a sketchbook or on other art paper that is the correct scale, it may not be necessary to make such a modification. One thing the designer can also do via the photocopier, or by scanning sketches into a digital environment and using a photo-manipulation program, is to enlarge, reduce, cut and paste, or move around parts of an initial character study, adding props and experimenting with variations of the character before committing to a cut-and-pasted or otherwise proposed final layout that is ready for more complete rendering.

This process was very popular with one of our colleagues who did a lot of character paintings and illustrations. He would take his original sketches of a variety of characters and props that would appear within the painting and then photocopy them, enlarging and reducing to various sizes. He would then cut out character elements and props, tape them to a board, and adjust their arrangement until he created the variation and composition that he wanted. At that point, he would lay a piece of tracing paper over the entire taped-up composition and retrace it as the next stage in his refinement process. For a smaller painting, he could simply re-photocopy the pasted-up board to achieve a uniform reproduction as a basis to paint from.

At this point, we've actually moved into the next possible step in the series, Step 3, in which we take a reproduction of a rough drawing or enlargement of a thumbnail in which we have adjusted scale and composition, and then use a piece of tracing paper over that drawing on a light table, and carefully and lightly retrace it with a relatively hard pencil, like a B or HB.

Step 4 is to refine the tracing paper drawing by adjusting and correcting lines, and checking volume, scale, and anatomy, fixing any of the rough mistakes that came from the initial drawing or thumbnail.

Step 5 involves transferring this cleaned-up line drawing to a substrate or environment where we will create the final rendering. The traditional choice that we'll call Step 5, "A" solution, would be to coat the back of the drawing with graphite so that we can transfer it to illustration board, art paper, gessoed masonite, or the like that will serve as the final support for our traditional rendering. Next, place the graphite-covered back of the tracing paper drawing against the substrate surface, and then carefully redraw over the pencil lines with a red ballpoint pen, exerting enough pressure to transfer the graphite on the back of the tracing paper to the final substrate. The reason for using a red ballpoint pen is that it makes an excellent stylus and the red ink shows you where you've been in the process of retracing. The "B" solution to this process would be to scan the cleaned-up tracing paper drawing into a digital environment where one can further manipulate line quality and add color or other visual effects via a photo-manipulation or "computer paint" program to create a final design. While the capabilities of creating in a digital environment are monumental, the ability to successfully work in a traditional medium (like pencil or watercolor) provides the artistic springboard for taking the plunge into electronic art forms.

Blueprint for (Avoiding) Disaster

Of all the possible permutations of visual art that can be created in any form to visualize and define the look of a character, the model sheet is by far the most important of these conceptualizations. The model sheet is the visual blueprint for the character; fully describing the character's physical appearance, common costume, typical actions, emotions, and even physical scale. These technical renderings provide references for artists and animators who need to understand the full visual nature and expressiveness of a given character or creature.

Figure | 6-13 |

Outlining the photocopy: if DaVinci had had a
lightbox, he would have traced, too.

Figure | 6-14 |

Character measures applied
to previous drawing.

Figure | 6-15 |

Solution "A" transfer and digital black-and-white
clean-up (Solution "B") gives final "look."

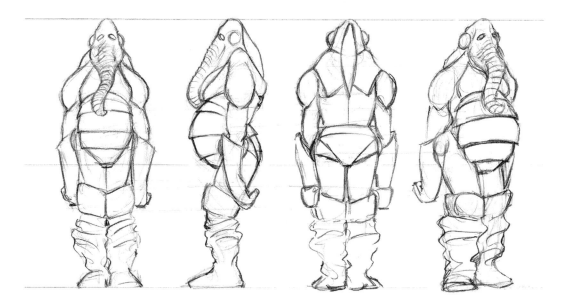

Figure | 6-16 |

To every pose, turn, turn, turn in a turn-around.

The model sheet acts as a continuity tool, making sure that all artists who draw, sculpt, or model the character will be using the same pictorial reference and that the character will be "on model" (i.e., conforming to the official look of the character). These blueprints are always approved by the director or artistic leads before being disbursed to other artists working on a character-related project in an industry setting.

A key factor in creating good model sheets is good drawing skill on the part of the character artist. The ability for this artist to keep the character on model—maintaining continuity in line quality, scale, volume, and style—is paramount to a successful model sheet. Remember, model sheets are technical diagrams of characters.

Several styles of model sheets exist and serve a variety of visualizations. These types are as follows, broken down into the most basic categories:

- "Turn-around"
- Action pose sheet
- Expression sheet
- Construction (variant)

The character turn-around model sheet is so-named because it describes a series of views of the character in rotation, as if the character was standing on a turntable and rotated to accommodate a variety of positions. It is the most visually comprehensive and widely used of all the model sheet

Figure | 6-17 |

An action-packed action sheet.

Figure | 6-18 |

Expressive expressions expressed here.

types. The turn-around is meant to give a full physical description of the character's appearance. Three to five views of the character are typical for the sheet and include front, 3/4 front, profile, 3/4 rear, and rear. Views are often referred to as "points" and a "4-point turn-around" is a model sheet showing four positions of the character drawn on the sheet (usually front, 3/4 front, profile, and rear).

The turn-around views are to-scale and proportional, and all views are typically arranged side-by-side on one sheet. Long-bodied, tailed, winged, or otherwise oddly configured critters may have turn-around poses that are separated over several diagrammatic pages.

The action pose sheet (or sheets) is rather self-explanatory: a series of on-model, full-figure drawings that depict the character in a variety of poses depicting actions appropriate to the individual, which may include anything from martial arts stances to book-reading. These poses may also show emotional states related to the depicted actions.

The expression sheet is a model sheet (being subsidiary to the turn-around and action pose sheet) depicting the character's emotions through a series of different on-model drawings of facial expressions. These drawings are typically head-and-shoulders or face-only views of the character.

Last, but not least, is the construction variant of the aforementioned model sheets. This style of model sheet is a variation of the turn-around, action pose, or expression sheet wherein modular construction, referential measurement systems, and text-based construction notes may be included on the model sheet to aid the animator or character artist in "building" the character accurately and on

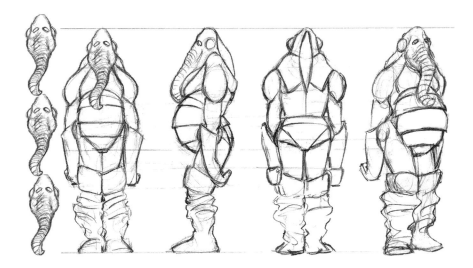

Figure **6-19**

Heads measure up in this model sheet variant.

model. A common example of this variation is the introduction of a scale diagram wherein a character's dimensions (height most often) is calculated by using the character's head (top to bottom) as a unit of measurement (e.g., Jingo the flying chimp is 4½ heads tall).

Researching the internet or books regarding the art of 2D-animated films are good resources for finding examples of model sheets and their variations.

Speaking of such, you've now been given a "heads up" on model sheet design.

SUMMARY

Style as applied to character design involves several interrelated subsystems that allow the character designer to create the "look" of the character. These subsystems are shape, line, surface, symmetry, repetition, variation, and contrast/affinity. These subsystems combine as key components of the character's visual creation.

This chapter defines conceptual art and addresses the importance of such visual development in character design. Conceptual art is often the foundation for more finished work; the groundwork of such "tweaking" and finishing is discussed in a probable sequence of development.

Also discussed is the importance of the model sheet as blueprint for understanding the visual design of characters in the round. The model sheet is an important tool for character designers and comes in a variety of incarnations, which include the turn-around, action pose sheet, and expression sheet. Variations of these sheets may include visual or text information on modular construction of the character or related measurement/proportional information.

STUDENT SHOWCASE

Garza, Armstrong, Thayn, and Hippolito

Garza, Armstrong, Thayn, and Hippolito give us various versions of model sheets and related visuals for various character designs. Garza's Bennington eventually becomes a computer modeled character. Armstrong shows his "monster" creature in a variety of poses and gives a basic structural model. Thayn and Hippolito show examples of model sheet turnarounds in differing styles.

ARMSTRONG

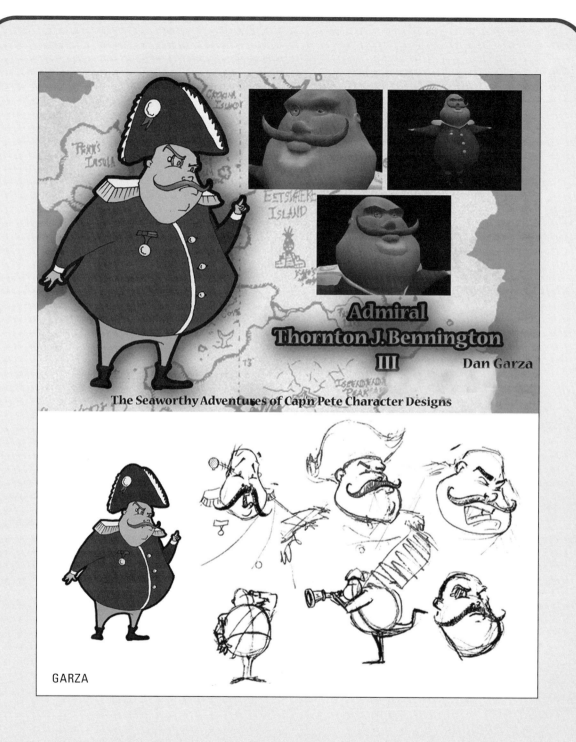

Admiral
Thornton J. Bennington
III
Dan Garza

The Seaworthy Adventures of Cap'n Pete Character Designs

GARZA

THAYN

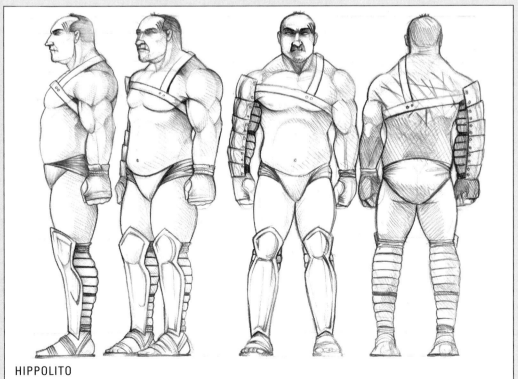

HIPPOLITO

exercises

1. Develop designs for two characters: one good and one evil. Describe each character's form through variations of a single, different shape (e.g., circle, trapezoid).

2. Draw a character's head as symmetrical and asymmetrical design solutions.

3. Make a series of photocopies of a black-and-white character drawing and try creating a series of color variations of the character using traditional media.

4. Draw a character that you have created as it would appear if designed for a particular genre "look" or industry style. How would the character come across done as a manga-type individual? Or, what if the character was designed to appear in a Disney 2D animated film?

5. Draw a character realistically in graphite. Retrace the character on tracing paper, simplify its detail, and ink the drawing so the character is defined by a heavy traplines. Compare and contrast to see which rendering variation seems to be the most effective.

6. Design a 4-point turn-around, action pose sheet, and expression sheet for a character from your imagination. Try variations of "realistic" and "cartoony" styles.

7. Design a 4-point turn-around, action pose sheet, and expression sheet for a character based on a historical personage.

8. Create a construction variant of one of the model sheets you designed for Exercise 7.

in review

1. What is the definition of "style" as it applies to character design?

2. What are the names of the subsystems of visual design described in this chapter?

3. What is "concept art?"

4. Why is drawing/rendering skill important for character designers?

5. What are the aforementioned five possible steps to refining a character drawing and preparing it for a final rendering?

6. What is the definition of a model sheet?

7. What is an example of a model sheet category?

notes

PROFILE

matthew mocarski

Matthew Mocarski has worked in many mediums, including comic books, television, and video games. Matt has always had an affinity for art that dates back to the 1st grade. His professional career began in 1997 after graduating from the Art Institute of Phoenix with a degree in Computer Animation. After a brief stint developing intellectual properties for Myers Entertainment Group, Matt moved to Portland, Oregon where he became a Lead Storyboard Artist on the Emmy Award-winning animated series, *The PJs*. Matt has also worked in the video game field working as an artist on such AAA titles as *Legacy of Kain: Soul Reaver* and *Soul Reaver 2*. He is currently working as a Senior 3D Artist at Blizzard Entertainment on the record-breaking *World of Warcraft*. This year Matt returned to his first love, comics, where his latest creation, Corporate Ninja, will

debut. He currently resides in Southern California with his girlfriend and 4 cats.

How did you get started doing character design work professionally? ``I think I was very fortunate as to how my career developed. I was lucky enough to work at companies where you had to wear multiple hats. Sure, my title may have been Storyboard Artist or Environment Artist, but if there was something extra that needed to be designed (and there always was), anyone could step up to bat. One day, I was asked if I wanted to take a shot at designing some characters. I had always done my own designs at home, but when I proved I was capable of doing it in a professional environment, more and more work came my way. It's as simple as that.''

What are the most important skills required by a character designer? ``It's hard to nail it down in words. You just need to have a good eye. A good sense of shape, form and color are important too. I think the research you do on your character is invaluable. If you nail down everything you can possible know about them (where they're from, what they like to do, what they're favorite food is, etc.) you can incorporate it into your design, making it all the richer. A good designer will know their character front, back, inside out, and right-side up. Don't think you can skimp on secondary characters either. It's just as important for them as it is for the main cast. Don't give any of your characters the short end of the stick. They'll thank you in the end.''

Does the approach to creating character designs for a variety of mediums (video games, comic books, animation) differ? If so, how? ``The fundamentals are the same but you do

Terrance Yee

Effective character interaction, as seen in these illustrations, is the key to visual storytelling.

Shown here are examples of synthesis using the comparative anatomy of extant and extinct animals to create

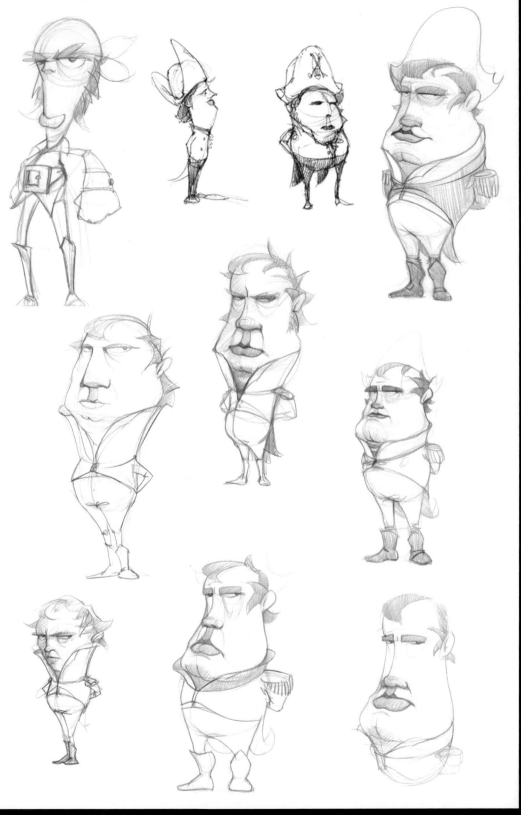

The first step in creating a character is to explore various designs through the
concept sketch, as seen with this cartoony pirate captain.

David Dawson

These images show the final 3D pirate model derived from the previous sketches. Notice the
similarities and differences between the concepts and the final character creation.

David Dawson

Terrance Yee

Tamara Ramsay

Digital painting and image

This series of illustrations shows the developmental steps in creating a character image: pencil sketch, inked line drawing, and digital painting (student work).

Pure exploration of physical structure, color, and texture can yield intriguing character design results.

Prehistoric creatures and mechanical contrivances are amongst the numerous visual resources available to the character designer.

Steve Missal

Steve Missal

Matt Mocarski

Background design is an important yet often neglected skill for the character creator. An appropriate milieu enhances characterization, as seen in these images.

Danny Beck

Color, lighting and facial expression combine to create a threatening, if not evil, look to this character portrait.

Bold outlines and bright, fanciful colors enhance the lyrical feeling of fantasy represented by this faerie female.

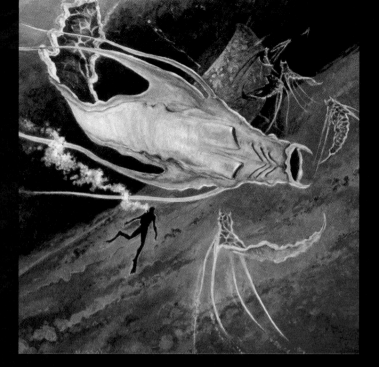

The mystery of the unknown and the exploration of physical scale create intrigue in these creature-based illustrations.

Past artistic styles and production methods are resources that can aid in the development of character designs.

WOLFIE

R. STEINHILBER
30. V. MMIV

Robert Steinhilber

The multitude of variations in the physical appearance of human beings, including such things as hair color, posture, and clothing styles, are wonderful fodder for character design ideas.

Gorilla gone ape! Dynamic poses, expressions, and figures that break the boundaries of their environment help to create visually stimulating character imagery.

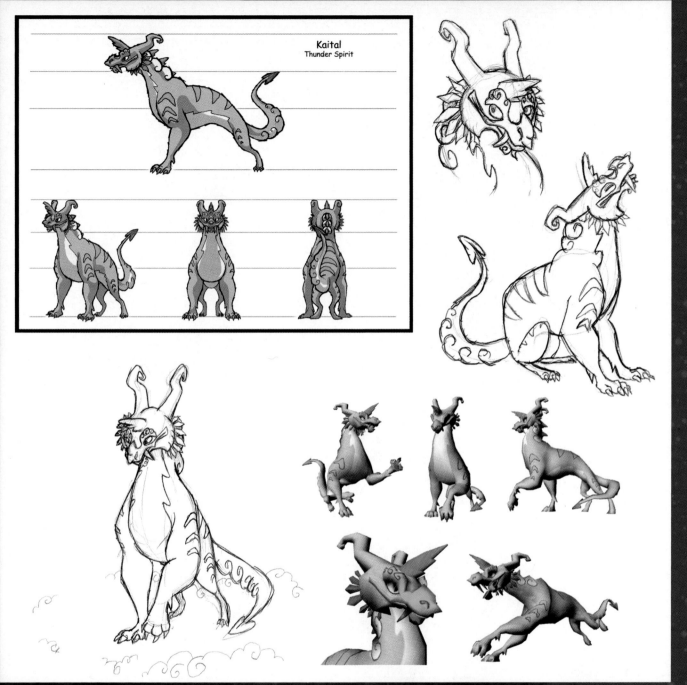

Kaital
Thunder Spirit

Character concept sketches, a model sheet and 3D action poses provide a visual blueprint for this fantasy creature's look and characterization (student work).

Darcie Banfield

Landon Armstrong

The Seaworthy Adventures of Cap'n Pete Character Designs

Admiral
Thornton J. Bennington
III

Dan Garza
outtapez@hotmail.com

Dan Garza

These examples of student work remind us that character designs evolve in concert with storylines, surroundings and visual development.

CONCEPT SKETCH

David Dawson

COMPLETED 3D MODEL

Here are examples of
pre-visualization and a
final 3D model for a
videogame character.

Darcie Banfield

This in-progress color character drawing shows areas of development from rough graphite sketch to finished colored pencil illustration (student work).

Cameron Forsley

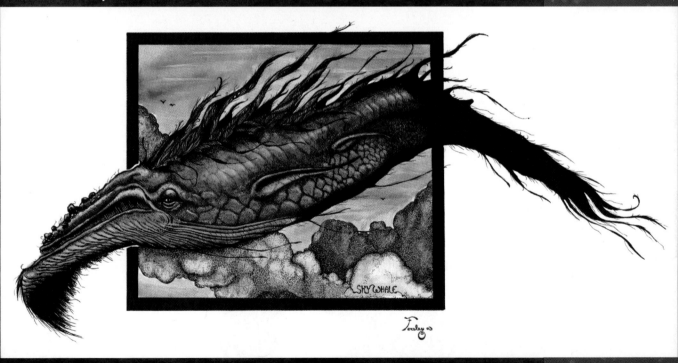

The unexpected juxtaposition of disparate character elements or environmental contexts, as
seen with this flying whale creature, can be attention-grabbing.

A human/crab hybrid character is complemented by its role as an appropriately-garbed, scurvy pirate.

**Character equipment and accoutrements provide
visual interest and aid in characterization.**

have to take which medium you're designing for into careful consideration. In comics, your characters don't have an established voice to define their personality. The reader determines who that character is and how they speak through the character's design. So, a designer in comics would need to incorporate the character's `voice' into the design more than with animation. Well, it's still important with animation, but you don't have the option to use it as crutch when designing for comics. In games, the player may very well be staring at the back of the character for the majority of the time they play. Therefore, there would need to spend a little more focus on the back side of your character. It wouldn't make sense to spend a lot of time designing something that the player would only see maybe 10% of the time, would it? There's also a whole technical side to design these days. If your technology can only afford to render a given number polygons, you'll have to consider sacrificing a few details from your character. *Which* details are up the designer, but the details you keep better get more bang for the buck. Otherwise it's just a waste."

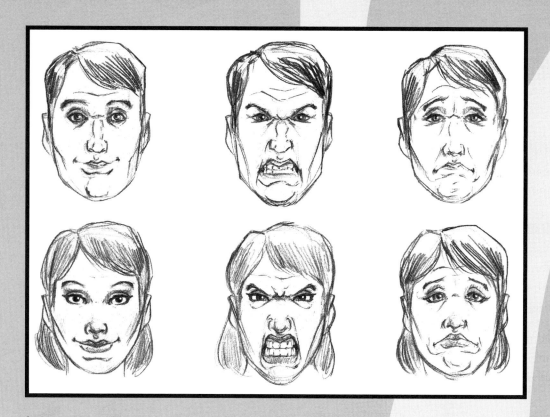

expression and emotion or vice versa

objectives

Learn the importance of expression and emotion in character design.

Be introduced to how the face and body produce emotional signals.

See how the line of action relates to expression and its use in gesture drawing.

Learn about hands and expression.

Learn about posing, silhouettes, readability, and character expression.

Be introduced to lighting and emotion.

Be introduced to some basic animal expression signals.

Find out some cultural and universal signs of expression types of expression categorized.

Explore the connection between motivation, role, and expression.

View examples of how dance, sports, and other visual arenas can be used for designing expression.

introduction

Emotion and expression give characters a dimension of appeal that connects them to an audience. Even characters or creatures that are simple or just dangerous on an animal level still possess some quality to which our own emotional world relates. The remote, neutral feel of a robot is actually a sort of emotional state. Lack of something is, in fact, still *something.* The job of the artist is to understand what sort of visual cues to give these creations to lend them expressiveness.

Emotion is relayed in a variety of ways by living beings. When we say to express emotion, the word *expression* has two fundamental meanings. One is the *means* by which emotion, meaning and other information is communicated. This includes gesture, tone, words, and other communicative tools. The second general sense of the word is a gesture, thought, facial expression, or other that is itself an emotion or feeling. It is an act or mode that communicates an emotional state. So what we explore here are the types of emotions or feeling states that are possible (and appropriate for the circumstance) and the means by which they are communicated.

As artists, we want to find how to shape and move the physical parts of the character or creature creation to make it assume its proper emotional role. Does it have weird facial gestures? Do the hands or paws clench or assume interesting poses? How does its pose reveal its mental state? What kinds of emotional states are possible? There are a great many issues to think about when applying expression to a character.

The Power of Emotion (sob. . . sniff. . .)

If you and I were watching a movie in which basically all that happened was the moving of things or people from one place to another without any apparent reason, the people expressionless and the movement random, both of us would probably endure this for maybe 15 minutes and then demand our money back from the box office. We would be bored senseless. Human beings need to experience the world by feeling. The sensibility of being here is not one of artificial mechanics, but rather one of how beings interact and affect one another. Animals are not exempt from this need. More primitive animals certainly rely on instinct but still are driven by the will to *survive*. That isn't just loose change, as they say. Survival plays an enormous motivating role in all beings. As animals evolve into higher forms, the complexity of feeling states gets larger and larger, until we finally encounter the tremendously rich emotional world of human beings.

Humans (and this would be extended to other sentient beings) live lives driven by needs and desires that produce harmony and conflict. We label people (and of course, characters) according to what their motives and displayed emotions seem to tell us. The pleasure of creating characters and creatures is that they fulfill emotional roles that the audience will respond to. Villains are just as important (and often more interesting than other characters) as heroes. Minor characters flesh out a narrative, bringing depth to an otherwise simplistic plot. Tragic characters remind us of the fragility of life, while those that overcome great obstacles give us the urge to walk out of a theater and conquer our own problems. Without judging any of this, the artist has an immense amount of visual information to use to apply to character and creature design because of this complexity. We have talked about appeal, the basic premise for success in artistic creation. If the audience is yawning or irritable with your product, then you as a designer have little chance for success in industry-driven character design. Just the mere need to make a living and pay the rent should motivate designers to examine their creations closely.

Of chief interest to the artist is, of course, how something *looks*. There is definitely the "cool" aspect of design. The difference between a mundane solution and an inspired one is often just a few minor changes in the details. When we discussed conceptualization and synthesis, we referred to ways and means of trying out different parts of solutions using various artistic tools. As an artist combines different elements, trying first one combination and then another, the success of the expressive component of the character varies as the parts are manipulated. One configuration ultimately will give just the right feel, and then

Figure | 7-1 |

Villain and hero face to face with expressive countenances.

the designer is off and running. If you want a really nasty villain, it does bear thinking about that the audience will not root for the hero if the villain is weak or flat emotionally. The expressive success of the whole enterprise does, in fact, depend upon the interchange of emotion between characters. Even in stand-alone designs, there is an implied environment or "otherness" with which the character or creature is in relation. So a part mightily influences the whole. Expression is a fundamental ingredient to the business of character design.

Body, Face, and Head: Expressive Tools

Humans and related character types have certain intrinsic body signals for emotional expression. Body posture (including arms and hands), head posture and movement, and facial expressions all are used to convey emotional information. There seem to be two kinds of understandable body expression. The first is hard-wired into the brain and involves basic instincts, survival modes, reproduction, and the like. The second type of expression is culturally modified. A certain gesture in the United States, such as the okay sign with finger and thumb, means something quite negative in Brazil. People from Vermont or New Hampshire are fairly quiet physically in their responses, whereas an Italian from Venice might use a great many hand, face, and arm gestures to make a point.

Humans spend a lot of time "reading" each other's voice tones, facial expressions, and body poses for clues to emotional state, motive, and future actions. In character and creature design, our job is to identify, learn, and use these signals (except for sound, the province of animation, voice-overs or live action). Certain of these seem to be more recognized as universal in nature. When confronted with a stressful or stimulating circumstance, the face of a human reacts with generally the same muscular contractions. These pull the features into different alignments that are instantly understood by an onlooker. Some of these more common facial expressions follow in the next illustration.

These can be used as a chart or guide for general adaptation to human or human-like characters. Some other facial expressions, in simplified form, are found in the next illustration. These are often variants of the major emotional states, and sometimes are more culturally influenced. In eighteenth century Japan, for example, crossing the eyes in the characters of artwork signified intense emotion, a signal we would find oddly out of place in our society. Below are more examples of facial expression in Western society and their commonly associated emotional states.

What constitutes a simple grin in the Western world can be a sign of embarrassment or even polite disgust,

Figure **7-2**

Italian hand gestures, perhaps a fellow talking at a cafe.

Figure | 7-3 |

Common facial expressions: man and woman.

depending upon where one finds oneself. Without expounding too much further on the cultural differences, the likelihood is that you as an artist will use the symbols most associated with your own culture. Because we are immersed in a standard Western industrialized country, the symbols most often used for facial expression are the ones encountered above.

Facial Primer

The face portrays emotional states far more subtly than the body, although gestures and stance are important to the overall reading of emotional states. It is in the muscular pushing, squeezing, and pulling of the facial muscles that we develop the range of emotional visual triggers that most observers are familiar with. Charles Darwin very wonderfully demonstrated that much of what we read as emotional states are related to primal physical needs and states. Many subtle variants of these (listed below) are ultimately tied to some fairly simple origins. Tears, violent expiration, screaming, frowning, squinting, laughing, retching, snarling and baring of

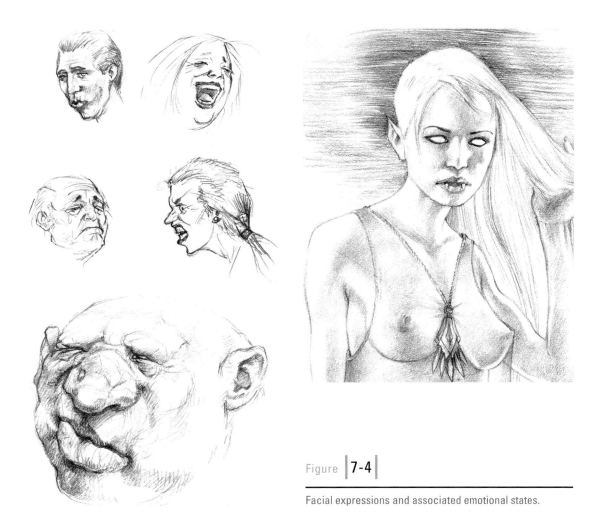

Figure | 7-4 |

Facial expressions and associated emotional states.

teeth, blood circulation, sweating, breathing, hair bristling, and raised eyebrows form the fundamental instruments of signaling emotional states.

In infancy we acquire the ability to shed tears when the eye is in need of moisture, usually during coughing, screaming, or similar intense states. Later, during extreme stress (as in grieving, overwhelming happiness, and so on), we associatively activate the tear ducts in a similar manner, and will still use them when the original more violent acts like coughing are present. By violent expiration we mean sneezing, yawning, shouting, throwing up, loud laughter, and coughing. This forces the mouth to open widely and the eyes to squint or shut entirely to avoid damaging their blood vessels. Laughing uses short bursts of sound that are the opposite of longer distress sounds like moaning. Besides communicating a lighter state, it requires the eyes to at least squint for protection (in real laughter, hence the "tell" when the *eyes do not laugh with the mouth*). Smiles are smaller versions of laughter, the end or beginning of such states. Showing the teeth is an animal gesture, because the teeth are used only for attack, cutting, and chewing, and therefore when revealed are a threat gesture. Pulling the lips back with bared teeth results in a grimace that may signal contempt or similar emotion. Snarling is a smaller version of baring the teeth, using only part of the mouth, and conveys a variety of negative emotive states (contempt, defiance, rejection). By sharing the dangerous quality of teeth-baring but without the full display, a person can give a variety of somewhat threatening signals. Retching produces a raised upper lip, slightly open mouth, and loose tongue; these used without intent to vomit give the sense of disgust or rejection. The eyes often squint and the brow may furrow. Frowns and squints accompany screaming and shouting, and so when displayed without the mouth and sound, give the early signal of suspicion, concentration, or displeasure. Yawns also force the eye to squint, and are associated with boredom, tiredness, and sleep. Screams and shouts are distress, anger, and fear signals, and use both the squared open mouth and the raised upper lip, with some contractile motion around the eyes to raise the lip. We pout as a small version of a scream; the motion is the same, but smaller. Eyebrows are raised towards center, and the mouth is downturned.

Darwin also referred to direct action of the nervous system: heart pounding, blushing, sweating, redness, paleness, and trembling. Other random muscular activity may also be used when

Figure | 7-5 |

Characters with range of facial expressions each.

dealing with the need for relief. The first group is more or less involuntary and relates to rage, embarrassment, fear, and horror—basic physical states that require immediate response. Below are some characters with facial expression applied, showing the potential range of the character's personality.

Word Games

A list of types of emotional states could be broken into subtle variations, and as a word trigger, each can give an artist a slightly different twist on a character development. For convenience, we have organized them into common related groups. Anger (including hate), fear, love, pride, desire, apathy, sadness, envy, happiness, sentiment, cynicism, lust, slyness, conceit, surprise, disgust, and courage are included. Here are some major categories and words related to them. Note how each gives a slightly different twist on the feel of the category.

- **Anger**: wrath, rage, enraged, ire, snarl, hate, shriek, scream, yell, howl, fury, vex, gall, rile, annoy, chafe, ruffle, acrimony, bitter, provoke, hostile, madden, displease, indignation, pique, bile, nettle, ill temper, inflame

- **Sadness**: teary-eyed, melancholy, depression, mope, blubber, crying, sob, dejection, despair, low, blue, grim, hurt, joyless, crushed, pitiful, serious, desolate, distressed, pessimistic, melancholy, miserable, grievous, grief, troubled, inconsolable, heavyhearted, downcast

- **Fear**: terror, worry, horror, horrified, shaking, dread, phobia, dire, awful, aghast, scream, shriek, howl, yell, quaking, affright, cowardice, nightmare, shudder, nervous, dreadful, appalling, tremulous, distressing, alarm, panic, anxiety, tremble, quake, threat, foreboding, apprehension, eerie, timid, shocking, skittish, alarmed, terrible, ghastly, shocking

- **Happiness**: thrilled, excited, laughter, giggle, boisterous, chuckle, fit, glad, lucky, elated, joyful, joyous, content, gleeful, pleased, tickled, blissful, cheerful, pleased, pleasant, gratified, rhapsodic, exultant, jubilant, fortunate, mirth, gaiety, comfort, delight, ecstasy, jolly, felicity, pleasure, beatitude, merriment, exuberance, satisfaction, harmony, giddy

- **Desire**: yen, itch, urge, hunger, pining, craving, thirst, longing, need, wish, want, eager

- **Envy**: jealous, greed, spite, resentment, begrudge, malevolence, covet

- **Lust**: desire, lewd, crave, lechery, passion, carnality, sexuality, covet, yen for, hunger, leer

- **Cynicism**: scoffer, skeptic, pessimist, fault, derisive, sardonic, scornful, sneering, sarcastic, bitterness

- **Apathy**: numb, lethargy, coolness, lassitude, unconcern, impassive, inattention, unresponsive, emotionless, boredom, dull, dejection, tire, weary, tedium, doldrums, jaded, uninterested, monotony, discontented

- **Conceit**: pride, vanity, ego, bragging, self-love, braggadocio, vain, boastful, smug, stuck-up, puffed-up, strutting, bombastic, haughty, upper-class, elite, self-absorbed, icy

- **Sly**: crafty, foxy, smart, shrewdness, tricky, conniving, mischievous, artful, plotting, Machiavellian

- **Courage**: guts, bravery, nerve, spunk, valor, daring, mettle, boldness, fortitude, derring-do, heroic, fearless, strong hearted, intrepid, stout, brazen

- **Surprise**: astonishment, stun, amaze, astound, nonplus, revelation, wonderment, startle, stagger, stupefy, confound, bombshell, dumbfound, incredulity, boggle

- **Disgust**: repel, appall, offend, revolt, sicken, dislike, abhorrent, sickening, despicable, nauseating, reprehensible, repugnant, horrid, loathing, distaste, repulsion, detest, aversion, abominable, antipathy, hatred

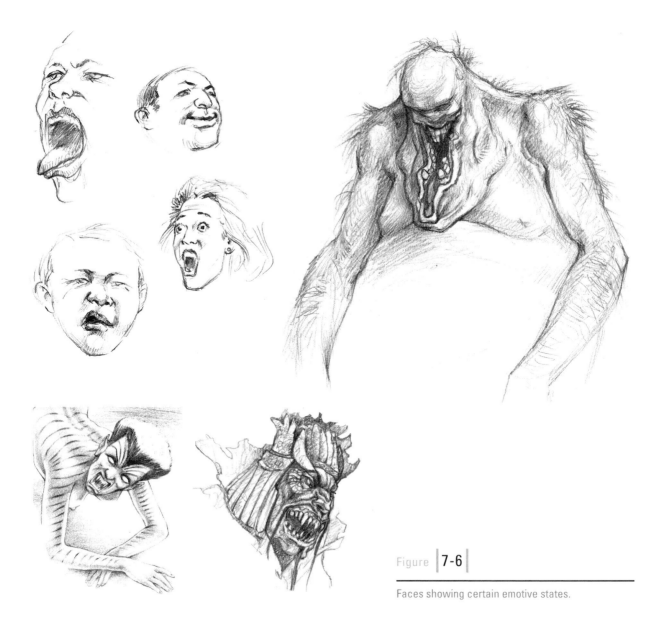

Figure | 7-6

Faces showing certain emotive states.

Other words that are connected to facial expression include actions and states such as:

- Blinking
- Puckering
- Sneezing
- Licking
- Squinting

- Grimacing
- Gaping
- Wide-eyed
- Heavy-lidded
- Choking

- Whistling
- Blowing
- Kissing
- Winking

- Flapping
- Pinched
- Frozen
- Blank

And the list could certainly go on.

There are states that could have their own categories, such as:

- Anticipation
- Pondering
- Questioning
- Reasoning
- Recalling
- Reflection
- Mistrust
- Meditative
- Listening
- Bitterness
- Stubbornness
- Sleepy
- Skepticism

- Tormented
- Tired
- Zealous
- Idiocy
- Hopelessness
- Aggressiveness
- Craziness
- Contempt
- Impudence
- Kindness
- Defiance
- Shame
- Coyness

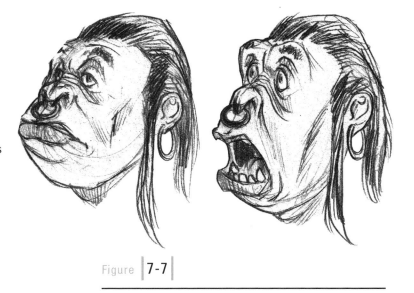

Figure | 7-7 |

Character without and with expression.

See if you can construct lists and appearances for these terms. An entire volume could be dedicated to this one type of analysis alone.

With these emotional categories and their application to facial expression, the artist now has a valuable tool to produce more effective character designs. Applied to some sample character designs, it becomes obvious how this enhances the effectiveness of the creation.

Bodies, Poses, and Darn Good Character Design

The character's range now is extended, its appeal enlarged, and all through the use of simple facial expression. In addition to the face, we include body posture and pose in this list of modifying characteristics. Line of action was described in our first book, *Exploring Drawing for Animation,* as "a kind of imaginary axis (line aligned with length or width of form) that

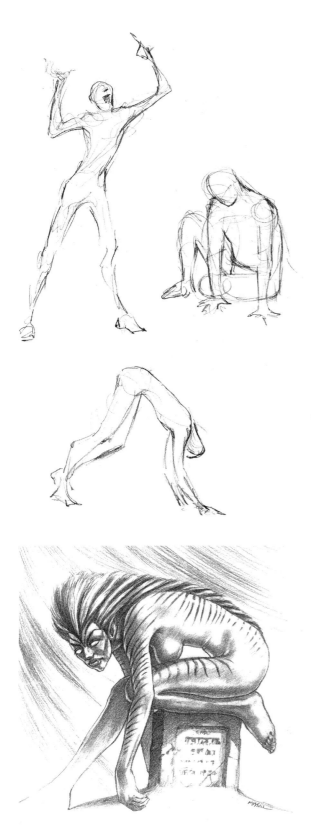

moves along the direction of the action and major form(s) of the object in question." In other words, the dynamic thrust of the larger body pose plus fairly obvious actions (minor lines of action) of the remaining arms and legs (and sometimes head or tail or wings). Expressive poses are dependent to a great extent upon the line of action and subgestures of the character or creature design. Further examination reveals that there are types of poses that have certain shared qualities. We mentioned in our earlier book that there are *open, semiopen, and closed poses.*

These are larger categories that involve how much the arms and legs are contained near the central axial body (torso). If the appendicular (arms, legs, and head, and maybe tail and wings) body parts are jutting out from the torso to any extent, the pose can be considered open or semiopen. If the appendicular parts are overlapping and perhaps folded into the torso, then the pose would be considered closed. For open poses, a looser gestural drawing is preferred. Its linearity dovetails nicely with the longer lines of the pose. In a more closed pose, modular forms with some gestural lines work better, because a closed pose is visually a set of combined shapes.

Now to complicate matters: Open poses can be *static or active.* Even closed poses have this capability. What do we mean by static or active? To a great extent, this quality depends upon the direction of the major line of action. In addition, the general gesture of the arms, legs, and head (and tail and wings) can be considered as important dynamic signals.

A pose with the major line of action parallel to true vertical or horizontal usually, but not always, is thought of as less dynamic, that is, somewhat static. This is due to the visual habit pattern we have as human beings of considering things in relationship to gravity's pull and

Figure **7-8**

Open, semi-open, and closed poses.

the horizon line. If something is constrained to vertical or horizontal, then our re-action is that it is not "free" or dynamic in its pose or movement. It is bound by its physical context.

It is quite possible to have a "static" pose with active components. An example of this would be a preacher standing straight at the pulpit with outstretched arms, gesticulating while making a point.

Body posing is, in its own way, as complex emotionally as facial expression. Interviewers are taught to look for certain body pose characteristics as signs of nervousness, arrogance, falsehood, and so on. Within cultural norms, all of us have learned the skill of "reading" body postures. Some are linked to *survival issues, some to emotional needs, and others to simple communication.* Dominance, submission, fear, rejection, courtship: these are some of the survival modes known well within a species. The emotional types are discussed earlier in this chapter. Communication on a mundane level is self-explanatory. Some examples of each category are shown below.

Looking back at the emotional categories we gave in some detail along with various similar word signals, we can now make the overlap between just applying those to facial expression to now using the body as a means of expressing them as well. The total character or creature will be involved in expressing an emotional state. In addition, now we can see that some postures, facial expressions, and gestures are less emotionally charged, used primarily for communicating practical matters or less important information. In terms of design, these may play a smaller role, but should be recognized nonetheless.

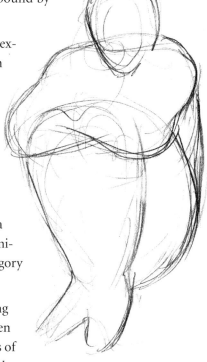

Figure | 7-9 |

Closed pose further showing combined larger shapes.

All this again brings up the issue of *silhouettes*. Within the animation and character design disciplines, the silhouette (simple filled outline of the figure) is important for the following reason. If we cannot understand the basic identity of the character or read their fundamental emotional state through means of the silhouette alone, then we are unlikely to have the larger appeal and impact on an audience. The audience might not be able to differentiate one similar character from another or mistake their intent. Clear, identifiable use of larger forms therefore becomes more obviously important. This all links to understanding how you have built your character from the ground up. Our basic premise of larger things first, smaller things later certainly works here. The emotional states can often be read or at least implied with the clever use of the silhouette.

All Hands on Deck!

A final piece of this puzzle is the hand. Human hands are an integral part of our communication. Some cultures, as we have indicated, place a greater or lesser emphasis on the use of hands when speaking or signaling. We have all experienced talking on the telephone while busily flapping our

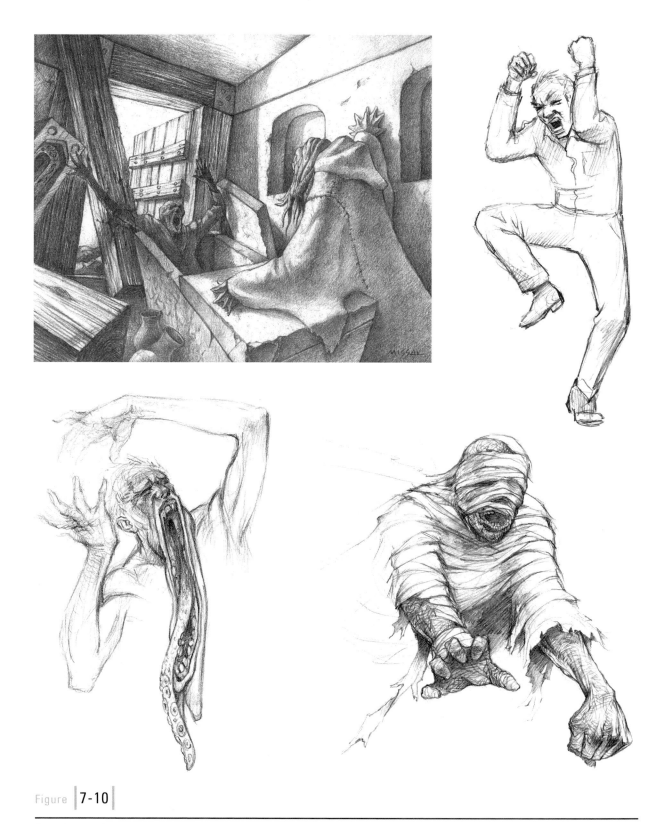

Figure | **7-10** |

Arms, legs, and head gesture aiding emotive state signal.

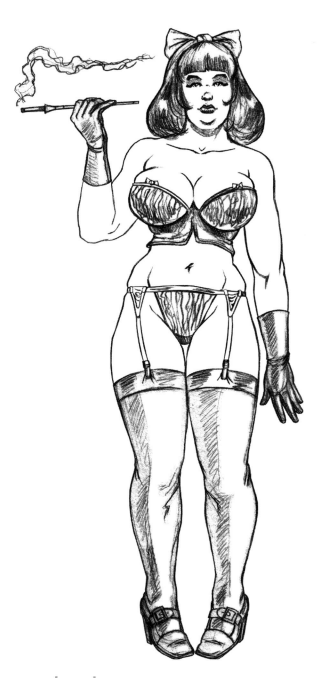

Figure **7-11**

Vertical pose with restrained emotional feel.

Figure **7-12**

Preacher with outstretched arms preaching.

Figure | 7-13 |

Body postures relating to various emotional states.

Figure | 7-14 |

Silhouettes showing emotional/dynamic states.

hands as though the person on the other end of the line could see us. With certain technology now, this too is possible, although not necessarily such a grand idea. You might want to look in a mirror before sending your mug over the airwaves. This particular mode is quite culture specific, for reasons we are not wholly sure about. Perhaps early signaling and needs of that particular region reinforced certain gestures as practical over others. Whatever the reason, we have become familiar with many culture's gestures through mass media and entertainment. Their use with certain character designs can enhance (or confuse) the creative possibilities of that character. Animals in general don't share this trait, mostly because outside of primates and related species they simply don't have the physical or intellectual tools available. We have drawn some representative hand gestures to demonstrate their wide variety and possible use. Invitation, rejection, insult, reinforcement, and a myriad of other subtle and not so subtle feelings can be conveyed with hand gestures.

Often hand gestures are inseparable from arm or body position in terms of expression. The arm and hand and sometimes body unite in a total expression, as in this hand/arm/shoulder/head pose below.

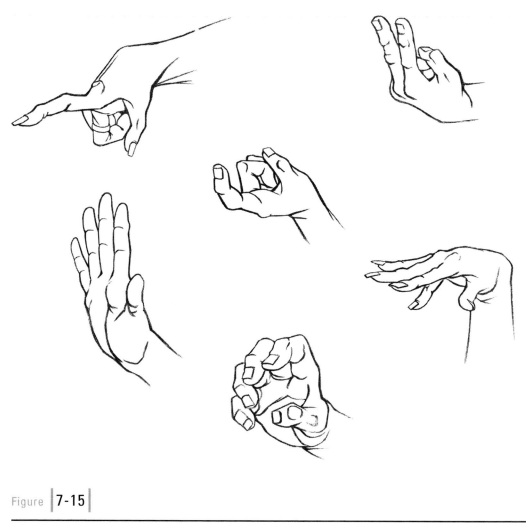

Figure | 7-15 |

Representative hand gestures.

Understanding What You Are Seeing and Seeing to Understand

Readability is an important factor now as we become familiar with different body/face/hand options in expression. It does no good to construct a character and then place the emotive content out of sight. Other than characters or creatures that have limited emotional ranges, the need to actually "get" what they are communicating is of utmost importance to the designer.

As in our comments on the silhouette, the general prescription is to produce work that is clear and understandable from the outset. This comes in two packages. The character design itself must be clear enough and readable to communicate a basic sense of what the designer wanted and how it fits into its context. Then the posing and camera shots must present the character (or creature) in such a way as to give the information to the audience without any ambiguity (unless that is what is intended). We have drawn a couple of options for each to demonstrate our point.

Figure | 7-16 |

Arm/hand/shoulder/head combination for pose with expression.

Something to be considered is just what audience you are aiming at. Bad grammar aside, a group of 90-year-olds from Iowa will not respond to the same information that stimulates a group of teenagers from Los Angeles. And even there, one cultural group might not fully understand what another comprehends. Characters are, to a great extent, audience oriented. The emotional world of an adolescent girl from Boise will be somewhat far removed from a grandmother in Brooklyn. Each will demand her own variety of emotional entertainment. And we do mean entertainment. Human beings like to indulge in vicarious emotional play. If we did not, there would be no demand for most of the movies, games, and other products aimed at the human populace worldwide. We would go about our business in a drone-like way and march in obscurity to our ends. The reality is that there is gossip around the water dispenser at the office, political intrigue in a university, scandal and mayhem in sports, and we love it. Newspapers are by and large involved with "news" that is also entertainment. You don't see headlines about rescuing kittens very often.

Figure | 7-17 |

Character, camera shot, posing as combination to make emotive state: two examples.

Lighting: Emotionally Speaking

Although our overview would not be complete without considering the effect of lighting on the emotional content of a character, this subject is also part of scenic design and other related technical fields. What we do emphasize here is strictly how the rendering of a figure in monochrome or color should take into account the light sources, and how this affects the feel and mood of the character (or creature). This is a problem in technique and how much to do. Underdone studies can be deadly, but at some point a neutral look at the character or creature demands no light, just simple observation of the forms, textures, colors, proportions, and other elements of the designs.

There are several types of lighting. These include diffuse, single top source, single oblique source, single bottom source, multiple light sources, backlighting, and spotlighting. Spotlighting is different from single top or oblique lighting because of the localized nature of the light. The other would be more like room or outdoor lighting. We have taken a couple of designs and displayed them in different lighting situations to show how the mood can be affected by this tool. Obvious differences are in the amount of pooling of shadow and the starkness of contrast. Diffuse or multiple light sources can reduce contrast to such a degree that the features or details of a character or creature can be obscured. This should be considered when displaying the final product.

It can be readily seen that there is a kind of scale of contrast that determines greatly how we "read" an object. This is true whether the object is a character or an architectural setting. Darker, higher contrast settings clearly are "darker" in emotional tone, moodier, more somber, or sinister, depending upon other information. Lighter, less "contrasty" lighting produces a less moody feel, more likely to involve happier events. Great mischief and violence can occur in well-lit contexts and with low-contrast character lighting, so we have to be careful to remind ourselves that there are many more elements propelling character expression than just lighting. The use of value (light/dark scales) is paramount in the final "look" of the character of creature. Without controlling the contrast and its component values, the artist may find his or her best design efforts lacking impact. It is a powerful tool and cannot be underestimated. We suggest examining many samples of static art and animation or live action to see how lighting and value systems enhance (or detract from) a character or creature.

Motive and Role: Why and Who?

The role a character plays in a plot is, more times than not, pretty clear. If everyone's role was ambiguous, no one would have a clue why events were happening, and certainly no heroes to root for or villains to hiss. We talk about this at some length in Chapter Three. At this point, we would like to reinforce that the expressive part of character design, whether in the actual physical make-up of the character or with how it moves or is displayed, is an integral part of the design process. Remember that ultimately the character will most likely be in some sort of plot, script, or action scenario. The same holds true for creature design. For most characters, this means giving the cues to the audience that will allow them to understand and be involved

Figure | 7-18 |

Different lighting affecting emotional state of characters.

with the roles they are playing. Often the roles are simple protagonist or antagonist ones (good guys and bad guys). Sometimes they are more subtle or complicated. Costumes, expression, props, and body and facial types all lend a hand in focusing this information.

Figure | **7-19** |

Further examples of lighting and expression for characters and creatures.

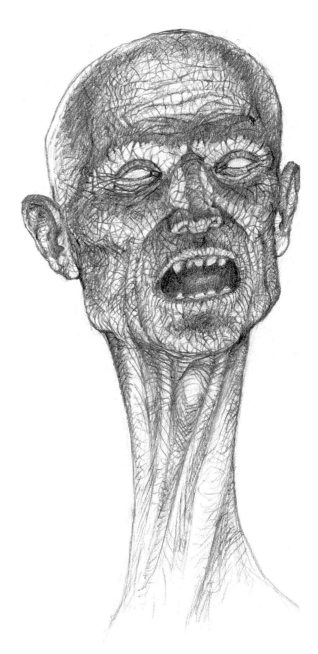

Figure | **7-19** |

Continued from page 195

STUDENT SHOWCASE

Cesar Tafoya

Student artwork by Cesar Tafoya: sample comic (sequential art) page. Here the emotive content is paramount in how we understand the character. Use of varied facial expressions, body postures, and camera angles along with other contextual information give us an intense emotional ride. We are completely engaged with the fate of the falling figure.

Contextual signals (lighting, architectural settings, landscapes) and story inertia give more information for the viewer. By story inertia we mean the accumulated plot devices and information that help the audience build a more and more complete picture of each character. Cultural signals such as dresses, hats, and so forth reinforce a particular role for a character. The point to remember here is that *expression is a product of a character's role, motivation, physical type, and cultural accessories.*

SUMMARY

In this chapter, we deal with the related subjects of emotion and expression, and how they relate to character and creature design. We discuss how emotion was communicated by expression, and how the physical types, facial expressions, poses, gestures, and lighting affect the expression of the emotional state. Different categories of emotion are outlined, and some observations on facial expression and body poses are illustrated by example. Cultural influences and universal signals are also addressed, and the nature of role and motive reviewed. How lighting affects the final design is also considered. We conclude that expression is a function of a character's role, motivation, physical type, and cultural add-ons.

exercises

1. Show several sketches in which hands are the primary factor in expression.

2. Produce a series of self-portrait sketches that demonstrate common emotive states.

3. Invent a new emotional look (or emotive expression) for an alien being. How would it be different than a human emotive state?

4. Draw from life: postures of people around you that demonstrate various emotional states.

in review

1. What is the definition of an emotive state for a human being?

2. What are examples of 10 to 15 emotive states for humans?

3. How does character design link with posing to communicate emotion?

4. How can lighting manipulate our emotional response to a character and scene?

5. How does the physical context of a scene affect the emotional content?

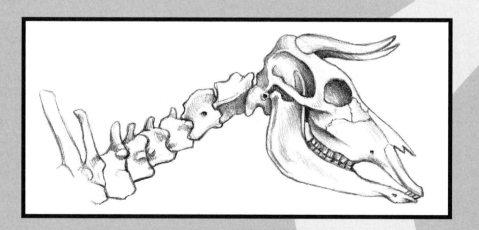

anatomic correctness

Look at general anatomic considerations in more detail.

Understand basic body and head construction for humans and some animals.

Be introduced to basic anatomic terms.

introduction

All living things are essentially defined by their anatomy, that is, their biological structure. At least a moderate understanding of anatomy, both human and nonhuman, is necessary to design viable and interesting characters and creatures. No one should be expected to be a professional anatomist, but complete ignorance leads to both weak design and unbelievable circumstances for the character or creature. By applying this with at least some accuracy (with artist's license to "fiddle with") an artist can create both authentic and appealing characters and animals.

Fortunately, anatomy is fascinating and learnable. Vertebrate animals (those with backbones) share many common features, and once you understand the basic configuration, many synthetic design possibilities become apparent. Even invertebrates, with some clearly otherworldly looks to them, are useful and fun to meld with design constructions. Artists have, for many years, been conversant with the basic anatomy of many living things, and have successfully applied this knowledge to the invention of many wonderful character and creature designs. This chapter is devoted to some basic anatomy, and does not pretend to replace the many wonderful texts available that give more detailed information. However, as an overview, and as a useful quick resource, we have outlined some of the more common anatomic considerations that you might need to be familiar with. Chapter Nine, Locomotion, gives the basic picture of living things and their anatomic/locomotive capabilities. The two subjects are interdependent, as you will see.

General Anatomy: Bones and Things

Living things are assembled from a sort of biomorphic collection of anatomic parts, rather like a child's assembly game kit. "Bio" refers to living and "morphic" refers to shape—living shapes. Underlying similar species are shared body parts, as in the mammalian design, wherein humans, dogs and antelopes all have basically the same bone and muscle blueprint, with some additions, deletions, and modifications. In fact, animals with skeletons have common ancestors, which accounts for the similarity in design. Even fish have much of what we as humans have anatomically. Other species, such as spiders, snails, sea anemones, and jellyfish are quite different from us, but within their own group have many characteristics in common. Some animals are endowed with endoskeletons (internal) and others have exoskeletons (external), while others dispense with any rigid structures almost altogether. Here are some general anatomic types and how they compare to one another.

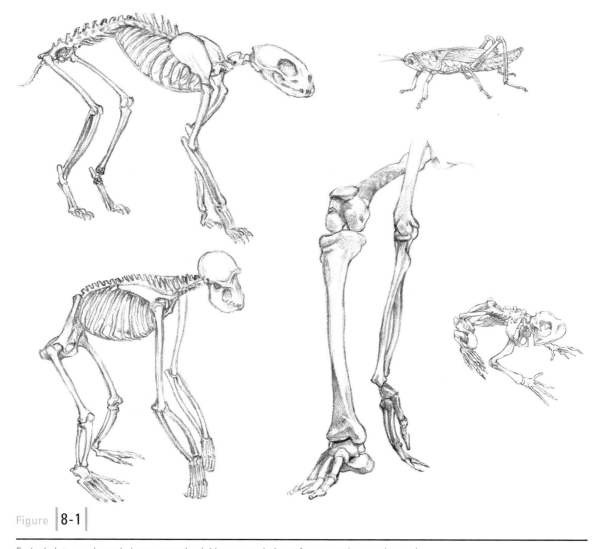

Figure | 8-1 |

Endoskeleton and exoskeleton examples (chimpanzee, bobcat, frog, grasshopper, human).

Spinal Taps

Artists are like architects in that they need to understand the underlying framework before building the overlying structures. For vertebrate animals, that is, mammals, reptiles, birds, fish, and amphibians, the skeleton provides this framework and is critical to understanding the movement of any species (and ultimately, a character or creature design). Even general configuration is dependent upon the skeletal framework. Animals that have skeletons are equipped with a central structure on which the rest of the skeleton is assembled: the spine.

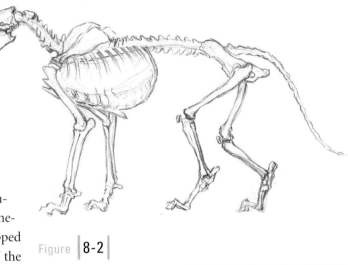

Figure **8-2**

Vertebrate skeleton example: lion.

Animals with spines come in several forms. Those that walk and run on legs are called *quadrupeds* (four-legged) and *bipeds* (two-legged). Quadrupeds and bipeds share some basic skeletal formats. Even birds and bats have most of these structures, although in highly modified form. In order to move over the ground, held down by gravity, animals have evolved a remarkable system of bony structures to fulfill this task. The spine, which encases the spinal cord, provides a central, stabilizing core for the attachment of limbs, head, and tail. To accomplish this, two major structures have emerged to provide attachment and stability for the *appendicular* (arms, legs, and head) parts (the rib cage, pelvis, spine, and head are referred to as the *axial* skeleton). One is the pelvis. The other is the shoulder girdle (sternum, clavicles, and scapulae). Although varying in form according to need.

The pelvis is built as a rear-end piece to the spine, flaring out and having two sockets to accommodate the hind limbs. It encircles and protects the reproductive and excretory parts of the body, and the hindmost parts of the viscera. Constructed of pieces that fuse to form a whole, the pelvis is essential for stability and strength in a land-based quadruped or biped. A tail may flare out from the end of the spine, often as a balancing tool or even for self-protection.

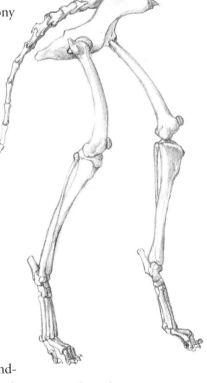

Humans still have a vestigial tail, the coccyx, at the end of the spine. Depending upon how the pelvis is built, the legs are placed at different angles to the body and so provide different amounts of vertical support. Some ancient carnivorous reptiles in the Permian era (just prior to the dinosaurs) experimented

Figure **8-3**

Animal skeleton with tail (dog).

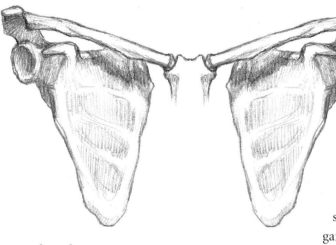

Figure **8-4**

Shoulder girdle of a human.

with a joint at the pelvis (and at the front) that had the leg directly underneath the body, rather than flaring out slightly. It seemed to work quite well. We inherited the other format for pelvic design.

The main difference between four-legged and two-legged pelvises is in the basic overall shape. For creatures standing upright, the need for horizontal streamlining vanishes. Instead, because of their vertical placement, the organs require a more bowl-shaped bony structure to hold them securely. Four-legged animals are geared to motion with all limbs, and so, with the spine more or less parallel to the ground, their pelvises also configure horizontally. This allows their limbs to move freely for walking or running while still providing support to a horizontally inclined skeletal system. Reptiles have a pelvis that juts forward with extended ischium and pubis bones.

At the front or top of the spine are two sets of bones and a third central bone that form the shoulder girdle and breastbone. These are the forward or uppermost part of the limb support. With the ribs providing the remainder of the protection of the internal organs, the scapulae, clavicles, and sternum form the structural basis for supporting weight (if a quadruped) or for lifting and throwing (if a biped). Many quadrupeds dispense with the clavicles. This shoulder unit is also the core for flying animals (birds and bats). Gliding animals also use these structures. At the ends of the scapulae are sockets for the fore or upper limbs. It becomes apparent immediately that this end is somewhat weaker in overall bone structure.

The advantage is that it is like independent suspension. Each side can move on its own, providing a greater amount of distance and direction for the fore or upper body. For humans, this allows a wide variety of activity that would otherwise be impossible. To compensate for the structural weakness, the vertebrae in quadrupeds often have elongated spines for extra muscle attachment as a support. Birds and bats have an enlarged scapula with a keel for fastening strong flying muscles.

Figure **8-5**

Bird keel attached to sternum (side view).

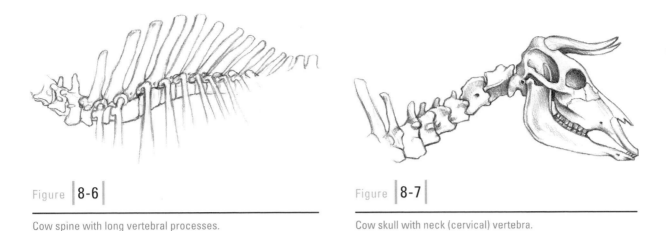

Figure | 8-6 |

Cow spine with long vertebral processes.

Figure | 8-7 |

Cow skull with neck (cervical) vertebra.

Elongated vertebral spines occur often at the pelvic vertebrae for the structural support as well.

Although the vertebrae usually are somewhat smaller toward the front and top of the thorax (rib cage), in quadrupeds they remain quite robust to accommodate the strain of supporting the animal's weight on the ground. The neck vertebrae of a lion or cow are robust, allowing stability of the massive skull.

In mammals, the rib cage has been reduced to just occupying the thorax, leaving the lumbar (base) vertebrae without any ribs; reptiles and amphibians still retain ribs back through the lower vertebrae. The ribs can provide some support to the shoulder girdle, despite their seeming fragility, but they also are something of an impediment to movement. The pelvises and ribs of quadrupedal carnivores and herbivores (meat eaters and plant eaters) are laterally flattened, partly to allow the forward and backward motion of the limbs. Carnivores also have laterally flattened abdomens, whereas herbivores have more rounded abdomens to accommodate their larger digestive needs.

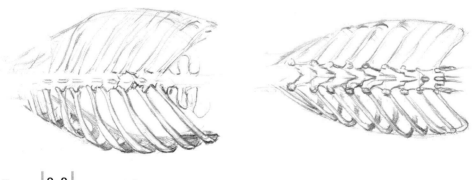

Figure | 8-8 |

Cow rib cage and lion rib cage (herbivore and carnivore examples).

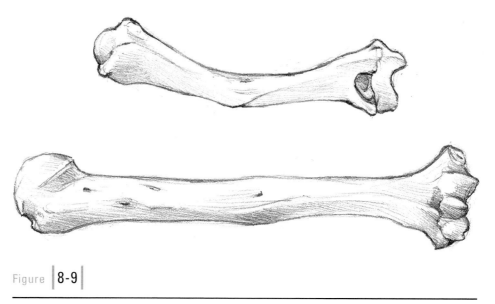

Figure | 8-9 |

Humerus of a human and a dog.

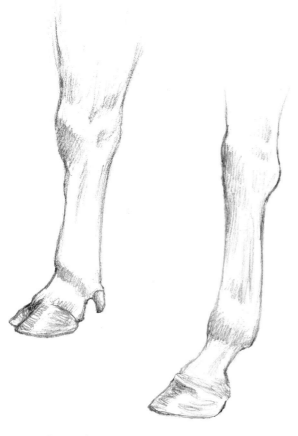

Figure | 8-10 |

Cow and horse lower leg and "foot."

Comparing the limbs of quadrupeds and bipeds can be very instructive. For humans and primates (and bears to a certain degree, because they are plantigrade, with the foot flat to the ground), the humerus, or upper arm bone, is longer. With digitigrade (walking on the toes) animals, the humerus becomes much shorter to allow both the bend of the leg and the motion necessary for moving on all fours. The faster the animal, the shorter the humerus and the longer the total limb in general.

After the humerus comes the lower limb bones—the radius and ulna. In an animal like the horse, the lower "arm" bones, the radius and ulna, have fused to provide extra strength. For bipeds, the two can move around one another to give the hands multiple options; in a dog, they cross in normal conditions, and in most herbivores they fuse, as we noted above. The hands of humans are not designed for weight bearing at all. Primates still have the ability to use their hands for some locomotion, and quadrupeds, both carnivorous and herbivorous, have highly modified forefeet for support and movement. The unguligrade (horses and ruminants) have evolved feet based upon reduced numbers of digits. The horse runs on a single toe, with some of the metacarpal bones fused to form a solid support above. Other unguligrades have similar bony fusions in their lower legs to support their bodies.

Hind legs for a biped have quite long upper leg bones (femurs). In humans, this is the longest bone in the body. From the wide flaring ilium of horses and humans comes the pronounced hip landmark of these types of creatures. Below, at the joint of the femur, the upper hind leg bone projects out and then immediately downward. For humans and primates, this is fundamentally more vertical, whereas in quadrupeds, the femur projects somewhat forward. This again is to allow the digitigrade (toe walking) form of locomotion.

In quadrupeds, the lower limb bones have special development. Whereas humans, primates, and carnivores still have distinct and separate tibia and fibula, herbivores have almost no fibula development, its structure having partly or wholly fused to the tibia, allowing a massive tibia to support their weight. These bones in quadrupeds flare backward and are at an angle to the ground, while the feet flare forward between 40 and 55 degrees. It must be remembered that the foot is elevated off the ground, with only the toe(s) touching. Along with the lower or hind leg in the diagram, we show the hind and front legs in a generic quadruped and biped diagram.

Figure **8-11**

Human and cow femur: verticality.

Again, humans and carnivores have clearly longer femurs in ratio to the other leg bones, compared to herbivores in general. All mammals show limbs vertical to the ground when viewed from front or back (anterior or posterior). Reptiles and amphibians have limbs that jut out more laterally. The movement derived from a lateral placement of limbs is addressed in the section on locomotion.

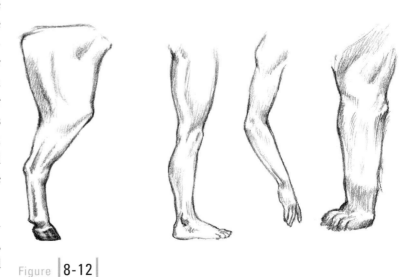

Heads for most vertebrates are relatively large compared to their bodies, and this weight has to be accounted for when standing or moving. Balance is a real issue. The neck vertebrae are often more massive in quadrupeds to

Figure **8-12**

Limbs of cow, human, lion.

anchor and hold a reasonably weighty head. Think of bison, elephants, bears, and horses. All require fairly strong necks to support considerable heads. The head acts as a mass that must be compensated for when in motion. Again, this also means the vertebral spines just before the cervical (neck) area often are longer or stronger to accommodate the musculature necessary to support the head. Walking birds thrust the head forward and back as a counterweight while moving. Even humans do this to a certain extent. Sometimes the motion is from side to side, in concert with, but not always, a lateral spinal motion. This can be seen in canids, cattle, and elephants. The motion may also be vertical. When running or trotting, the head may rock in motion with the rhythm of the cadence or be held still, as in a charging tiger or bear.

Tails are a counterbalance tool *par excellance*. From the time animals first emerged on land, tails proved to be an excellent method for keeping the equilibrium of the total body both in stasis and motion. The reason is obvious. Both weight and position allow the tail to act as a compensatory mechanism for the animal. Those animals that are flat to the earth still use the tail in this manner. Dinosaurs were reconstructed with jutting, horizontal tails when it was realized that the way the vertebrae locked together would not allow for the older, ground dragging images we may have seen in earlier reconstructions. A cheetah uses its tail both for balance and to help it execute quick turns when pursuing prey.

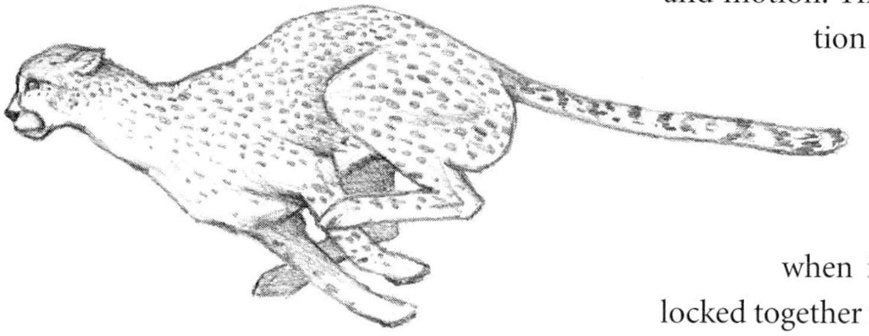

Figure 8-13

Cheetah tail used for balance in running.

Tails range from slender, delicate, and expressive extensions of the housecat to a cursory bob on a lynx.

The tail, an extension of the spinal structure, is also useful for communication and pest maintenance.

Reptiles and amphibians share the same basic design but with modified leg positioning. Rather than having the weight borne underneath as with other quadrupeds, reptiles and amphibians thrust the legs out to the side more, giving a waddling type of gait as opposed to the gaits we are used to in, say, a horse. Interestingly, a crocodile has both a more erect gait and a flatter, more lizard-like motion, depending upon speed

Figure 8-14

Tails of animals: platypus, wolf, lizard, housecat, jackrabbit.

Figure **8-15**

Alligator splay-legged stance; turtle with carapace.

and need. The feet in reptiles and amphibians in general splay out in a more sprawling manner, giving a different grip to the ground. Turtles and tortoises have developed a carapace to which the bones of the body have been attached. This protective device enormously changes their appearance and locomotion. The lack of flexibility is compensated for by the safety provided by this structure.

Bipeds are a chief factor for character design, because they resemble us, and we are fascinated with ourselves. Most conversations people have are really monologues about themselves or their opinions. When we pass a window or mirror, we can't help looking at ourselves. Like any species, its own kind is its core experience.

Figure **8-16**

Gorilla with large abdomen for herbivorous diet.

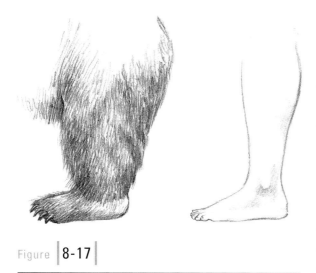

Figure | 8-17 |

Plantigrade diagram: bear and human legs.

Therefore, character design is, in some ways, a narcissistic exercise.

Spinal columns for bipeds are more massive at the lumbar, or base section, because the sign has, to a great degree, centered on beings not unlike humans. Weight of the entire being is balanced vertically. From the side, the graceful "s" curve of the spine reflects the flexibility and mobility of the spinal column. Rib cages flatten from anterior (front) to posterior (back), a refinement workable from a couple of points of view. One, the organs should not be in a protruding structure that can be more vulnerable to attack or injury, and two, the carriage and motion of the upper torso is less obstructed with a flattened form. We can both see and use our hands directly below our downward eye view because of this adaptation. Some primates still retain a heavier, almost quadruped look, because much of their locomotion is still four-limbed. Gorillas, with their mass and herbivorous diet, require a large digestive tract as well, giving them a greater frontal mass in the abdomen.

Bipedal structure uses the same (although vertically placed) skeletal plan as the quadrupeds, except in the legs and feet, where the planting of the foot in a flat position on the ground gives certain design advantages to a standard bone model (shown in Figure 8-17). The plantigrade (flat-footed) posture gives a considerably different feel to the legs (and arms).

The bones of the foot are designed for weight bearing, flexibility, and a kind of spring support. Several connecting muscles act as a kind of spring/arch between front and back of the foot, having some give under the weight of the total body mass. Under the foot is a pad of fat that acts as a cushion. The heel (calcaneus and talus area) connects to the back of the leg via the Achilles tendon, and this tendon is vital to locomotion, acting as a mechanism to store energy when stretched, releasing it later during a stride. More on this later. Above the talus, the tibia rides and moves more or less directly upward (with some in-leaning), with the fully separate fibula acting as almost a flying buttress support to the central bone. Although the ankle can pivot left/right to some degree, its general flex is hinge-like, designed for forward motion.

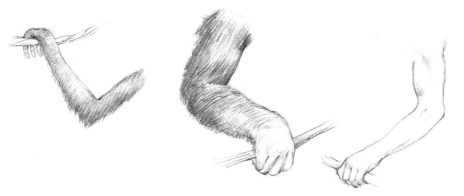

Figure | 8-18 |

Spider monkey arm; gorilla arm; human arm.

Because the arms are free from weight bearing, their mass is considerably diminished in humans. The shoulder girdle is smaller, and the general sense of the limbs is gracile, articulate, and mobile. Other primate arms still show the adaptation for *arboreal* (tree) dwelling (colubus and spider monkeys, for example) or ground locomotion (chimps and gorillas). The humerus and lower arm bones are more nearly the same length, and the wrist (carpal) and hand bones are smaller and constructed for grasping, not weight bearing.

The apes have longer and more robust arms than humans for use in locomotion in trees and on the ground. Monkeys share this feature, especially in the length of the upper limb. One could certainly picture a character with arms that were excessively long, yet placed on an upright, obvious humanoid biped.

The basic posture of primates versus humans tells this tale in another way:

This overview of basic biped and quadruped anatomy gives a general picture of how the parts are put together and their general size and configuration. Characters and creatures relate strongly to vertebrate animal structure. Swimming, flying, and crawling animals have somewhat different properties.

Figure | 8-19 |

Human-like character with extremely long arms.

Birds, Bats, and Flying Bricks

Anatomically, birds share a great deal of the skeletal structure with other vertebrates. Their skeletons have been highly modified to allow flight (as have bats, which we also cover briefly). One of the chief changes, obvious visually, is the alteration of the upper arm (front leg) into a superstructure that becomes a wing. In birds, this retains its basic humerus (albeit short and robust), elongated radius, and ulna configuration, with the fingers modified greatly into a tapering format. The bones of the hands support the primary feathers, while the secondaries are supported by the radius and ulna.

The clavicles have fused into a bone called a *furcula* (wishbone). By addition of muscle (anchored to an enlarged breastbone or sternum) and a covering of highly specialized feathers, the animal

Figure | 8-20 |

Basic posture of primate (gorilla) versus human.

Figure | 8-21 |

Bird wing bone structure with feathers.

has the ability to fly. To save weight, its bones are hollow, with tiny struts inside giving structural strength. The differences in proportion and size of the wings and bodies relate to the different niches each bird occupies in the ecosystem. Some are active predators of other birds and modest sized animals, while others are consumers of small meals of insects and similar taste treats. The greatly enlarged breastbone has a keel for the attachment of the large flight muscles. The hind legs show the relationship (now deeply suspected by anatomists) to dinosaurs. Unlike humans, birds walk *digitigrade* (on their toes) and have the general zig-zag leg look that we associate with this type of locomotion.

Bats are a somewhat different solution to the same problem, namely, getting airborne. Being a mammal, their lineage is different from that of birds. In fact, because of their tiny and fragile skeletons, the fossil record has only a modest record of their entry into the world. The assumption is that bats evolved from a gliding ancestor of some kind. Looking at a bat skeleton, we see that the arms are greatly elongated, especially the fingers, to accommodate a membrane used for flight. Rather than having the larger arm bones take the brunt of structural underpinning (as in birds), bats evolved a more spread-out frame of the first through the fifth phalanges to stretch the membrane into a flying mechanism. In addition, this membrane stretches to the hind legs and even between them. Their pelvises are fused to provide a solid anchor at the base of the skeleton. We look more closely at this anatomy later in the chapter.

Some animals of differing species have evolved gliding as a means of locomotion, but the basic underlying skeletal configuration remains the same as for other related species. Most gliders "fly" over short distances only. A few larger flying/gliding birds such as vultures and hawks can glide over much longer distances. Squirrels, lemurs, and lizards are among those employing this method of locomotion.

Fishes, Crickets, Wallabies, and Wannabes

Before getting to the muscles and specifics of the head (which, although not intimately involved in locomotion, does need coverage in anatomic considerations), we need to look at creatures that have less familiar structures and how they use them for movement. These can broadly be classified as follows: ground insects; flying insects; birds; bats; gliders (any kind); snakes; fish; sea mammals; lizards, salamanders and larger reptiles; some worms; miscellaneous sea animals (starfish, anemones, jellyfish, oysters); hopping animals (kangaroos, some mice, birds). These are briefly charted at the beginning of this chapter. Without making this a comparative anatomy biology text, a brief examination of these follows. It's actually easier to group the animals by how they move rather than by structure alone.

Swimmers would include fish, sea mammals and reptiles, jellyfish, squid and octopi, and various less familiar sea animals. Although other animals can swim, those mentioned are specialized for life in water. Their structures have been modified to function smoothly in a water environment. The most obvious sorting of this group would be to separate those with backbones from those without. Fish, sea mammals, and sea reptiles have backbones. Some sea mammals have been so extremely modified as to closely resemble, in shape, their distant fish cousins.

Fish are cold-blooded animals that have been around for many millions of years. After the development of the spine from the primitive notochord in some early, primitive sea dwellers, early fish experimented with different

Figure | **8-22** |

Bird leg showing digitigrade nature.

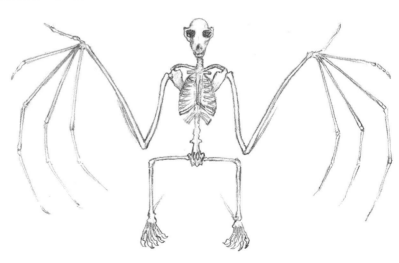

Figure | **8-23** |

Bat skeletal structure.

surfaces, fins, tails, head shapes, and surfaces in a number of combinations. Today we have some pretty fancy fish around, and these certainly give us many ideas for anatomic or decorative character and creature touches.

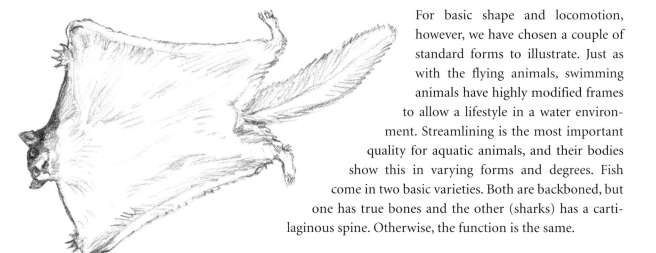

Figure **8-24**

Flying squirrel.

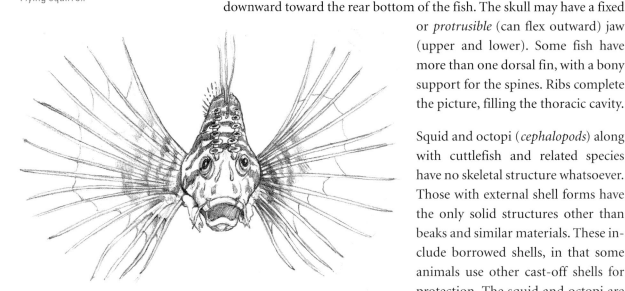

Figure **8-25**

Lionfish.

For basic shape and locomotion, however, we have chosen a couple of standard forms to illustrate. Just as with the flying animals, swimming animals have highly modified frames to allow a lifestyle in a water environment. Streamlining is the most important quality for aquatic animals, and their bodies show this in varying forms and degrees. Fish come in two basic varieties. Both are backboned, but one has true bones and the other (sharks) has a cartilaginous spine. Otherwise, the function is the same.

Looking at the following diagram, we see the spine, *caudal* (tail) fin, *dorsal* (top) fin with bony spines for support, abdominal pelvic girdle, front (pectoral) fins involved in maneuvering and locomotion, and sometimes a thoracic pelvis girdle instead of pelvis. A *ventral* fin projects downward toward the rear bottom of the fish. The skull may have a fixed or *protrusible* (can flex outward) jaw (upper and lower). Some fish have more than one dorsal fin, with a bony support for the spines. Ribs complete the picture, filling the thoracic cavity.

Squid and octopi (*cephalopods*) along with cuttlefish and related species have no skeletal structure whatsoever. Those with external shell forms have the only solid structures other than beaks and similar materials. These include borrowed shells, in that some animals use other cast-off shells for protection. The squid and octopi are basically a head/tentacle arrangement, with the internal organs within the "upper" housing. The name *cephalopod* literally means "head-foot". Frankly, as a place to borrow for creature design, they are, in a word, wonderful.

Aquatic mammals such as seals, walruses, manatees, whales, dolphins, and porpoises are another excellent resource visually for creature or character design. In these animals, the limbs and general shape have been altered as they evolved for life in water. Their spines and heads still look pretty familiar, but the front limbs and hind limbs have become flippers and the hind limbs have disappeared externally in whales and dolphins, showing up only vestigially inside the animal. Other semiaquatic animals, like beavers and otters, have become both streamlined and specialized in other ways, including flattened tails and reduced external ears.

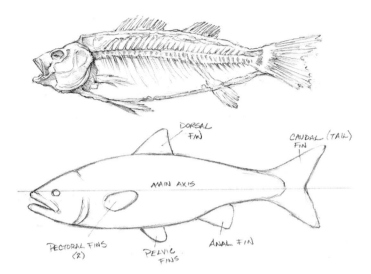

Figure | 8-26 |

Generic fish skeleton and body diagram.

The general shape for true sea mammals has an eerily fish-like feel, except that the excess bony structures for fins and musculature that show up in fish are absent in mammals. The skulls are much different, and within the mammals (and some fish, like basking sharks and manta rays) are striking skull adaptations for such things as plankton feeding (e.g., in some large whale species).

Some animals hop as a primary mode of locomotion. Kangaroo rats, kangaroos and wallabies, birds, some other mice, and humans can hop as a locomotive mode. Structurally, the posture is upright, placing emphasis on the hind limbs for propulsion. The most well known of these animals that hop, the kangaroo, has a large tail and massive hind legs that are extremely well adapted to a hopping mode of locomotion. Old reconstructions of such dinosaurs as tyrannosaurus rex and diplodocus show their tails dragging along behind them, whereas today, we know that the tails were kept straight out behind them as a counterbalance. The interlocking vertebrae and ligament markings show this clearly. Kangaroos also have the tail out behind them while hopping, but they do use it as a kind of "third leg" when at rest, which is different than what the early reptilians did.

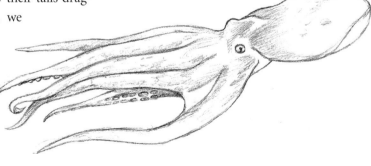

Figure | 8-27 |

Octopus.

Snakes are an interesting example of an extreme but highly successful anatomic adaptation. Although a tiny vestigial hind limb may exist skeletally internally, the snake appears, for all intents and purposes, to be legless. Their skeleton has evolved into a multi-vertebraed and ribbed structure, sometimes with hundreds of vertebrae. Their heads often have the ability to unhinge the lower jaw to accommodate the swallowing of some prey whole. The large constrictors are massively muscled, and can kill and devour fairly large game, including humans. Their locomotion is a serpentine wave sweeping from back to front to propel the animal.

Figure | **8-28** |

Dolphin and otter.

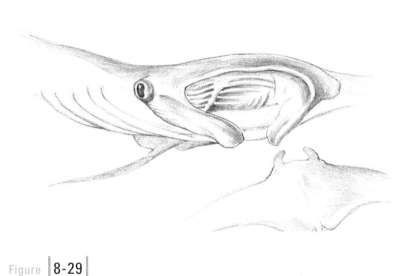

Figure | **8-29** |

Manta ray with unusual filtering mouth parts.

More exotic species (to us) such as jellyfish, starfish, centipedes and spiders have physical structures that rely on quite different strategies for survival and locomotion. Even mussels (shelled creatures in water environments) have a "foot" that can extend out of the shell to anchor and move the creature if need be. Internally located musculature is available to creatures like starfish, who have semi-hard outer bodies. Jellyfish use a cooperative effort among varying cell groups to create a living being, and its semitransparency is a constant source of visual wonder and inspiration to the artist.

External skeletal structures (*exoskeletons*) dominate insects and some arachnids (spiders, mites, centipedes, millipedes). Internal muscle attachments move these animals in varying ways. A head and upper and lower body plan dominate most (but not all) of these smaller animals, much as our bodies follow the same plan. When found in these two groups, the divisions are called the head, thorax, and abdomen. Sometimes a tail extrudes from the back (as in the centipede), or wings attach to the top (like a bee). Insects are a different family from arachnids, and laymen often confuse the two groups. Figure 8-33 is a simple diagram of several generic insects and arachnids. Millipedes have a long, multilegged design that has few counterparts in the rest of the animal kingdom.

Musclebeach

The second part of the equation for anatomy, other than surface, is the *musculature*. Exoskeletons excluded, the musculature of most other animals determines greatly how they appear and bears directly on their movement and locomotion. There are on the order of 600 muscles in a human body, which is similar in general configuration and number to most vertebrate animals. We want to give some general guidelines here for use by the artist, and the most easily used method is by chart or diagram.

Figure | 8-30 |

Kangaroo.

Because of the enormous complexity of tracking the musculature of any animal, we thought we could provide some simple surface musculature samples of certain animals as a way of showing the basic shape modifiers for most vertebrates. The following diagrams are meant to flesh out (literally) the skeletal discussion above. The proportions and general functionality are determined by the skeletal system of the particular animal. There are many excellent human anatomic charts in a variety of books (including our own *Exploring Drawing for Animation*), so here we give as examples two quadrupeds (a cat and a pig) for general reference.

A list of the muscle functions and descriptions follows. Some of these appear in the charts and others are found in more involved anatomy diagrams and books.

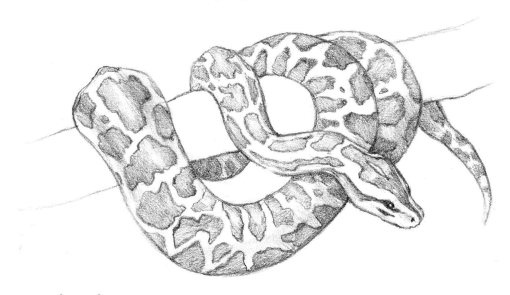

Figure | 8-31 |

Python.

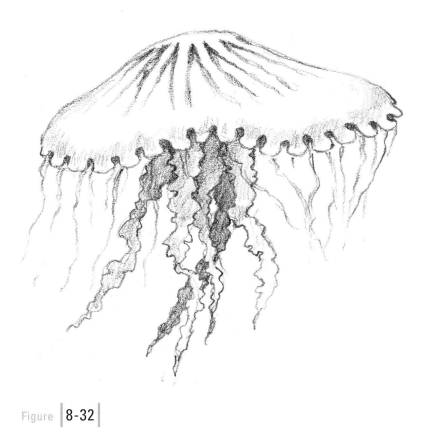

Figure 8-32

Figure | 8-32 |

Jellyfish.

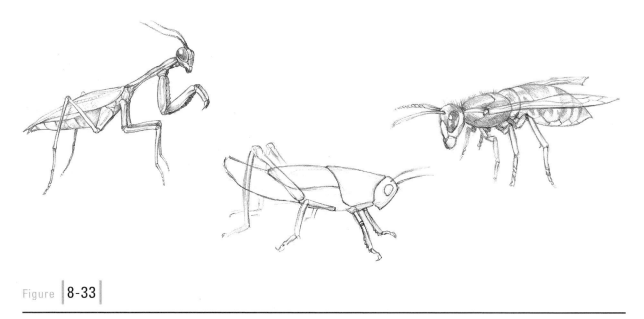

Figure | 8-33 |

Praying mantis, wasp, and generic insect (exoskeleton) example.

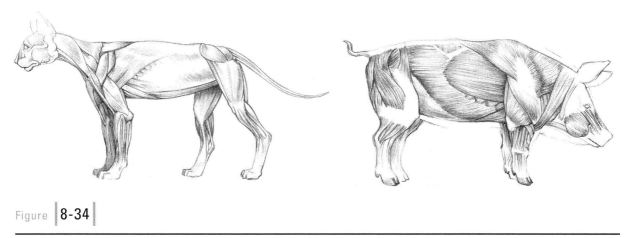

Figure | 8-34 |

Muscle diagrams for housecat and pig.

- *Abductor*: pulls away from midline
- *Adductor*: pulls toward midline
- *Extensor*: straightens
- *Flexor*: bends
- *Levator*: raises
- *Depressor*: lowers
- *Erector*: pulls upright
- *Pronator*: rotates palm of hand downward
- *Rotator*: causes revolving
- *Supinator*: rotates palm of hand upward
- *Tensor*: draws tight

Bundles of smaller, long fibrous tissue, surrounded by different scales of partitioning tissue comprise what we call muscles. Our concern in character and creature design is with skeletal muscles. These are the tissues responsible for movement. Muscles are usually bound to bone by strong tissue called *tendons*. There are some muscles that bind directly to bone (for example, the *subscapularis*). The tissue that surrounds the smaller long bundles of muscle tissue or fibers joins at the end of a muscle to produce a tendon that attaches to bone. Some tendons are narrow, and others are broad and flat (an *aponeurosis*). *Ligaments* are sheets or bands of tough tissue that connect two or more bones (or cartilages). Sometimes ligaments are a support to muscles, organs, or fascia. What we primarily see in the charts are muscles with sometimes the end tendon(s). Muscles, as we pointed out in our earlier book, *Exploring Drawing for Animation*, are arranged as antagonists to each other. That is, after performing an action in one direction, the body needs muscle to return to the original position (or beyond). If this were not so, we could not walk, run, or pick up

(FUSIFORM) OR SPINDLE TENDON

TENDON

(BI-PENNIFORM) TENDON

(PENNIFORM) TENDON

Figure 8-35

Different types of muscle shapes.

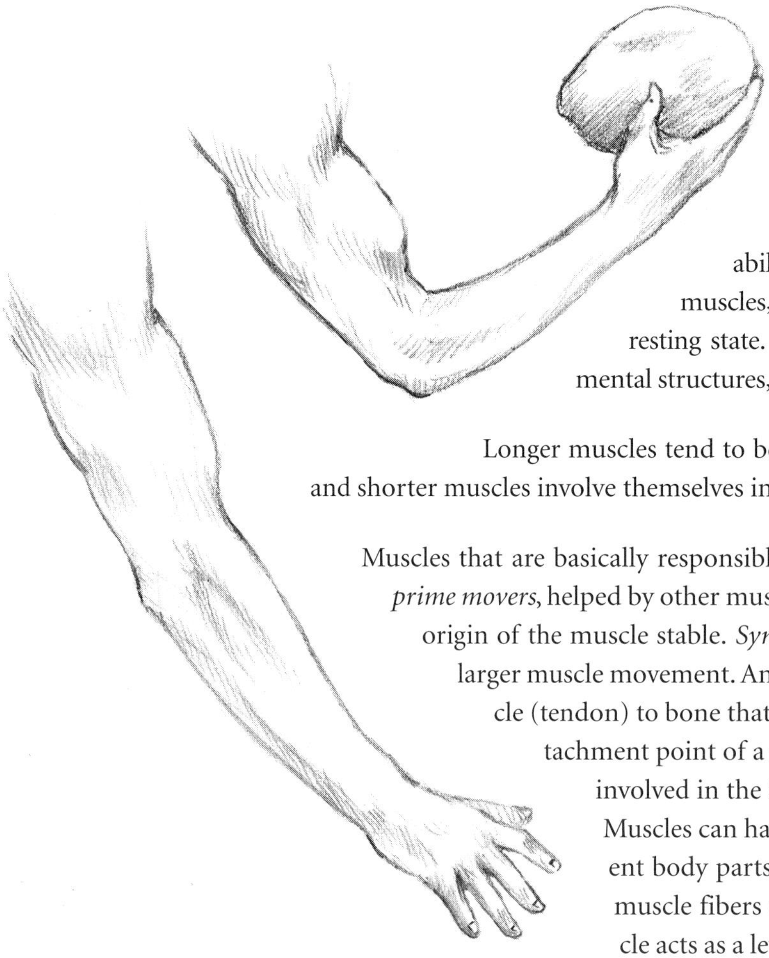

objects, for example. Muscles are arranged so that body parts can move *back and forth*. Our bodies are constantly in a state of *contracting muscular equilibrium*. We call this *muscle tone*. This maintains our posture and ability to produce further actions. Stretched muscles, when relaxed, tend to go back to their resting state. Muscles can have three types of fundamental structures, as in the examples below:

Longer muscles tend to be used in larger, more overt movement, and shorter muscles involve themselves in more small-scale movement.

Muscles that are basically responsible for a particular movement are called *prime movers*, helped by other muscles called *fixation muscles* that keep the origin of the muscle stable. *Synergist* muscles stabilize a joint during a larger muscle movement. An "*origin*" is an attachment point of muscle (tendon) to bone that is relatively still. An "*insertion*" is an attachment point of a muscle that is more moveable. The part involved in the insertion moves, and the origin is fixed. Muscles can have multiple roles, moving several different body parts to varying degrees. Contraction of the muscle fibers (flexion) toward the center of the muscle acts as a lever over (usually) a joint, pulling a body part toward the contracted area via the tendon (using the more "fixed" end as leverage). When flexed, muscles shorten along their long axis, bunching up and

Figure 8-36

Human arm: flexed and unflexed.

"thickening" across the short axis as a result. Different poses, therefore, can have substantially differing looks to a limb or torso area depending upon what the figure is doing.

This simplistic picture of the activity of muscles gives at least a cursory idea of how bodies can move and introduces the idea that in some poses, certain muscles will be flexed, altering their "resting" shape. When inventing in character and especially creature design, these principles should be at least moderately adhered to, giving a realistic mechanism that can be viewed both as a stationary design and as an animation.

Figure | 8-37 |

Realistic creature design.

Head Games

Our final anatomic visit is to the head. The reason we look at this body part is because of the "personality" factor that heads introduce to character and creature design. Of course, some designs don't have heads at all, or minimize their importance. A little anatomic familiarity,

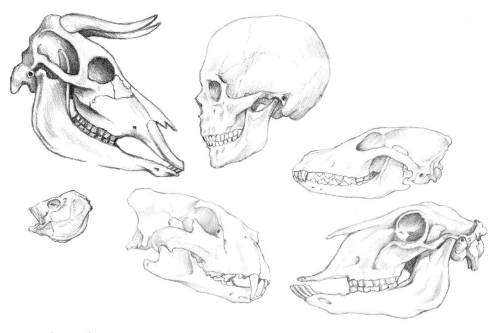

Figure | 8-38 |

Different vertebrate skulls: human, dog, fish, lion, cow, sheep.

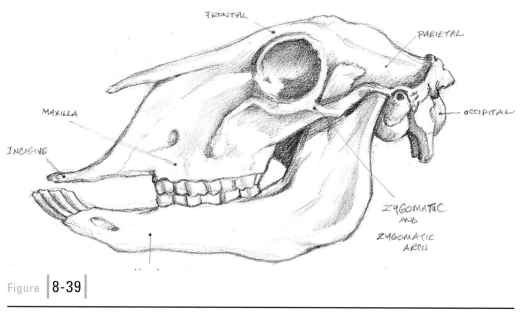

FRONTAL
PARIETAL
OCCIPITAL
MAXILLA
INCISIVE
ZYGOMATIC
AND
ZYGOMATIC
ARCH

Figure 8-39

Sheep skull diagram showing generic vertebrate structures.

though, is a good thing. Heads are where it's at, emotionally speaking. With the exception of some weird, rather alien looking creatures or beings that do not seem to have a head, humans and creatures that are at least distantly like us do have heads, and it is usually with the head that we communicate. Many creatures are so alike one another in a particular population group that it is difficult to differentiate one from another. People are rather odd in this respect. We have almost extreme individuality from one being to another. Couple this with the ability to make head and facial gestures, and we have a highly versatile emotional instrument.

Many animals use their mouths in the same way we use our hands; they pick up things, move things, and generally explore the world around them. Noses sometimes fill this role as well. Think elephant. Animals not only move things with their mouths but attack, defend, warn, chew, and dismember with them as well. We explored earlier how bared teeth are a warning signal. Less "evolved" animals like insects sometimes combine the use of mouthparts and legs to move and explore parts of their small world. Hearing can be missing or extremely acute; some insects are essentially deaf whereas a wild dog can hear things far beyond human capacity. Smell falls into the same analysis: Snakes "smell" with their tongues, ants "'taste/smell" a chemical trail, and humans use noses for the same purpose. Again, we fall into a middle ground here; many animals have the capability of smelling things far more acutely than humans.

To a certain extent, we are somewhat "blind" in this area. Seeing also occurs mostly at heads; the optic nerves most efficiently run to a nearby input/processing system (the brain). Some animals have stereo vision, a nearly 360-degree view (rabbits, for example). Others are like us, with eyes trained forward. Some animals have several more eyes than we do (such as spiders). Some eyes see color, some only black and white, and some see colors we can't (bees). Some eyes in primitive animals see only simple light and dark and perhaps detect motion.

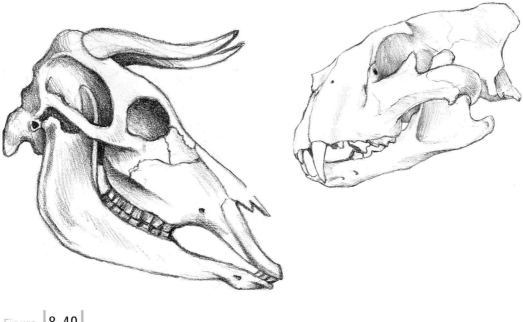

Figure 8-40

Herbivore and carnivore skull comparisons (cow and lion).

Brains tend to inhabit heads; heads are therefore constructed or defended by parts such as to protect this vital organ. Insects don't have much in the way of brains, more a swelling in the neural cord. Our brain may be the most complex thing in the universe, according to some scientific views.

Heads for all vertebrates contain a skull. The skull is the final barrier against harm from the external environment. The portion that houses the brain is considerably larger in proportion to the rest of the skull in humans as compared to all other vertebrate animals. This clearly defines a different shape and proportion for creatures and characters derived from human skull sources versus other animal sources.

The shapes and sizes of skulls of the many types of vertebrate animals show a wide variety of proportions, but there is a basic unified plan for most of these skulls. There are eye sockets and passages for the auditory canal (hearing), as well as a nasal opening and an upper and lower jaw, along with the neurocranium that houses the brain.

Herbivores have longer skulls, complete with quite a bit of dentition for chewing their plant diets. Carnivores have relatively shorter skulls, and omnivores (those that eat basically anything) often have skulls somewhere in between in length.

Animals like rabbits, cattle, and horses have eyes stationed on the side of the head, while carnivores, who need good focused binocular vision to hunt their prey, have eyes more frontally located for this purpose. The zygomatic arch in dogs, cats, and hyenas extends considerably out

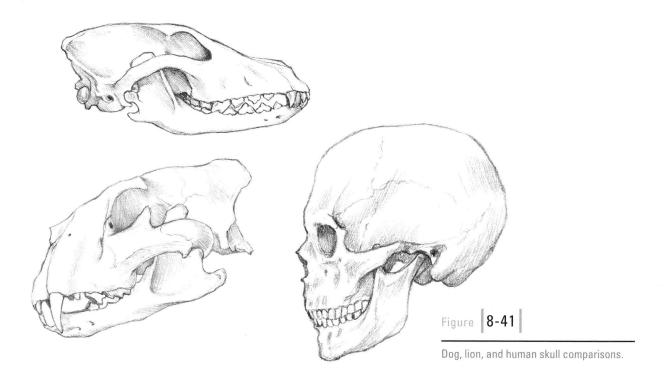

Figure | 8-41 |

Dog, lion, and human skull comparisons.

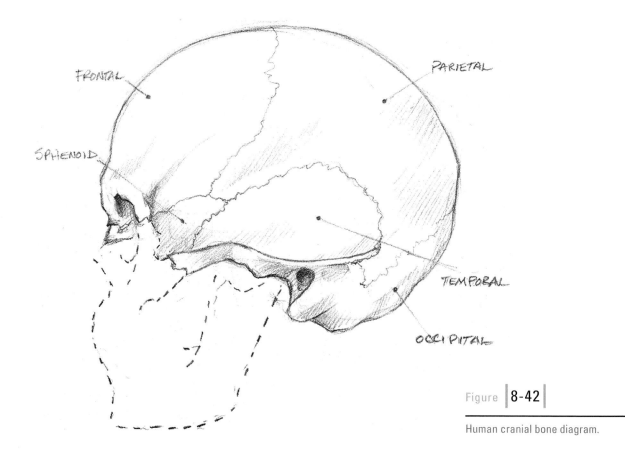

FRONTAL

PARIETAL

SPHENOID

TEMPORAL

OCCIPITAL

Figure | 8-42 |

Human cranial bone diagram.

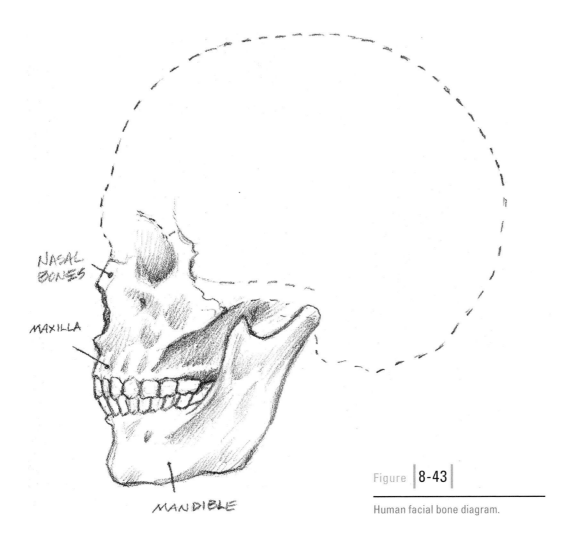

NASAL BONES

MAXILLA

MANDIBLE

Figure |8-43|

Human facial bone diagram.

from the skull horizontally, enlarging their apparent width. Canine species (e.g., dogs, wolves) have far more teeth than feline (cat) species. Their skulls are also (and this includes hyenas as well) much longer than those of the cat family. Humans have the only round neurocranium; other animals have oval shapes for the brain case.

With a number of optional variations, vertebrate animals and humans share basic skull structure on the whole. The cranium contains the brain, and the face has the eyes, nose, and jaw structure. Some animals really don't even have something that resembles a "face." Take a salamander, for example. Their flattened, elongated heads really are more of a whole in a streamlined kind of way. Our *craniums* and faces are more clearly differentiated. A quick look at the parts of the *human* skull will give a basic map for other vertebrate animals.

Our *craniums* are made up of several bones joined together by suture joints. From the rear, we start with the *occipital* at the far rear, which has the joint connection to the upper (*cervical*) spine. Next come the *parietals*, which form the sides up to the top of the *cranium*; then come

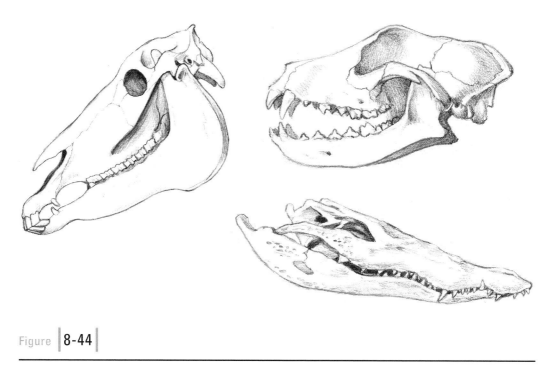

Figure **8-44**

Various common animal skulls (horse, crocodile, wolf).

the *temporals*, which link the *parietals* to the bottom of the skull and the cheekbones. In the front, luckily for us, is the aptly named *frontal* bone. Orbital bony swellings, the *superciliary crests*, help protect the eyes. The *sphenoid* bone fills the gap between *temporal* and *frontal* bones.

Fourteen bones of differing shapes comprise the face (*splanchnocranium*). Of these, only a few are of interest to the artist because of their external nature. These would be the *nasal* bones, which begin the nose structure, the *maxillae* or upper jaw bones, the *mandibula* or lower jaw bone, and the *zygomatics*, or cheekbones, which bridge the gap between orbital regions, upper jaw, and the cranium. The *zygomatic* really consists of three bones, namely, the *zygomatic* proper, the *palatine* bone, which segues up the upper cheek to the outer eye area, and the crest-like structure of the *temporal* bone.

Animals like dogs and horses have much the same basic structure with highly modified individual parts adapted to each animal's lifestyle. With a reduced *neurocranium*, the "'face'" or *splanchnocranial* area is far more prominent, especially with enhanced biting and chewing needs and capabilities. Several representative skulls and views are presented in Figure 8-44 to illustrate some of the more common animals that artists encounter. Of interest to the artist are some variations in bone structure suited to the needs of the particular animal.

We now give several representative illustrations of animal heads, fleshed out, to show how the underlying skeletal structure integrates with the surface tissues to produce differing types of looks. Note that in some animals the tissue overlaying the bone is not necessarily predictable. These views can give an artist some idea of what might be possible with different anatomic origins.

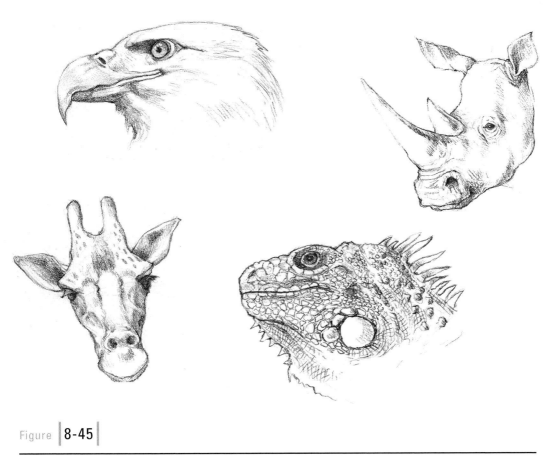

Figure | 8-45 |

Fleshed out vertebrate heads (iguana, bald eagle, giraffe, white rhino).

SUMMARY

To usefully pursue synthesis in designing characters and animals, knowledge of the body parts and their purpose gives a better understanding of how to recombine and modify existing anatomy. Ignorance of these subjects leads to dead, clichéd, and amateuresque design. Vertebrate and invertebrate animals have certain repeated patterns that are the result of their niche function in the biosphere. Humans and other vertebrate animals share a similar substructure, and familiarity with this gives an artist the tools necessary to build authentic designs. Elements of invertebrate creatures also figure into many contemporary entertainment designs, and we can include them as creations unto themselves or combine them (as outlined in Chapter Five) into new and fascinating living designs.

exercises

1. Construct a character or creature that is derived from invertebrate anatomy.

2. Draw several skeletal gestures of horses or lions (or other animals) in various poses; try to match picture resources that you have located.

3. Draw several human skeletal gestures in various poses; match pictorial resources that are from magazines or other sources.

4. Construct a flying animal that does not use its arms for flight; you must invent some new anatomic structure(s) to account for its ability to fly (bones and muscle).

in review

1. What are endoskeletons and exoskeletons?

2. How is an insect subdivided anatomically?

3. In what animal is the head and thorax fused?

4. What is another name for contracting muscular equilibrium?

5. Animals with spines are called _____.

6. Tendons connect what to what in animals?

7. Axial and appendicular skeletons refer to what portions of the body?

notes

come on and do the locomotion with me!

objectives

Discover the relationship between locomotion and its effect on character and creature design.

Find out about bipedal locomotion: locomotion on the hind legs.

Find out about quadruped motion: locomotion on all fours.

Overview flying and swimming animals: anatomy and locomotion.

Examine the movement of insects, snakes, kangaroos and other unusual forms of locomotion (and anatomic issues).

introduction

Developing character and creature design involves many overlapping elements. How they move from one place to another and how they are built both strongly influence the design outcome. Implied and directly observable is the issue of locomotion, that is, how a living thing moves from one place to another (sometimes in several different modes). It is directly observed when we watch some creature fly or run, or watch a character crawl or pull himself over a wall in some dramatic sequence. It is implied by looking at their structure and making assumptions about how that structure allows the creature or character to move. This also hints at limits. There are some things that one character can do that another can't.

Audiences compare the design to their stored expectations and make assumptions about the being's capabilities. The very shapes and parts of the designed character or creature are directly linked to how they move and function. A character or creature design necessarily suggests motion and locomotion (or lack of it) because the body parts are partly for this purpose. We know that this can be augmented by technology (such as jet packs, antigravity boots, and other "gizmos"). But as a designer, we need to start with the core animal blueprint. Animators in particular have the need of learning animal motion, because that is their stock and trade. To this end, we have accumulated a moderate introduction to animal locomotion.

COME ON AND DO THE LOCOMOTION WITH ME!

Put One Foot in Front of the Other

Locomotion means moving from one place to another: the relocating of the entire organism. Animals can also move parts individually without leaving the spot that they occupy, or they can move parts individually while moving from one place to another. Movement for vertebrate animals involves the skeleton, joined by ligaments, being moved by the muscles. Animals without backbones either use musculature or similar systems for contraction and extension to move from place to place; some, like squid, rely on a sort of bio-jet system.

Starting with animals that have backbones, what characteristics do they have in common? In all cases, the centrally located backbone provides a core base from which other forms may be attached and action flow out from. If you consider the wide variety of animals with spines, the means of locomotion are quite varied. Snakes, fish, salamanders, lizards, bison, bears, humans, dogs, birds, and deer all share a basic starting point anatomically, namely, the backbone. In order to move, each has developed a number of methods of both anatomy and motion to solve the problem of how to get from point "A" to point "B." They also can move parts of their bodies while stationary, sometimes in widely differing ways.

Legging It

If the animal has legs and its main means of locomotion is walking or running, what in fact happens when it does this activity? The appendicular (arms and legs) part of the body that touches the ground supports the main body (and in some cases the body may partly touch the ground also), providing the means of "pushing" forward. The total number of feet and hands touching the ground at once during locomotion is less than the full number of appendages available. This means that a dinosaur like a *diplodocus*, moving with heavy strides toward some goal, will have at least one foot off the ground in order to continue moving forward (Figure 9-1).

This keeps the equilibrium of the animal (its balance), and normally, but not always, forces the center of gravity over those legs that are still touching the ground. For some animals, this motion is not possible without additional motions, the bending of the spine either horizontally or vertically (side to side or up and down). Sometimes a combination of these motions is possible.

Dogs often show a side-to-side movement in their spines during leisurely walking. When moving in a walking gait, the three legs in contact with the ground form a stable triangle. This configuration remains basically true for slower motion, even in more highly developed quadrupeds like horses that can have two feet off the ground during a walk cycle.

A *stride* is a part of a pattern that is repeated in what is called a *gait. The gait is the complete pattern of limb movement.* Horses provide the prime example of gait. Horses have about six gaits, namely walk, trot, and gallop, and variations of these, lope, pace, and canter. During running cycles, these animals have all four legs off the ground at some point. Dogs have a variety of gaits as well, and we have included below a couple of diagrams of both dog and horse gaits in profile to illustrate this point.

Figure | 9-1 |

Diplodocus walking: three feet on the ground, one off.

Digitigrade (locomotion on the toes) locomotion forces the femur to be in a more horizontal position, and thus displaces the pelvis likewise. The spine now assumes a greater role than with bipeds, because both front and back of the creature hang, so to speak, from its central axis. Depending upon the gait, the body may, as we indicated earlier, bend left and right or even in the vertical plane to allow for foot strikes. For both four-legged and two-legged animals, each stride moving forward has the kinetic energy of that momentum becoming potential energy and then resumes as kinetic energy when the body falls and the next strides occur. Kinetic energy is stored in the muscles and tendons, especially the Achilles (heel) tendon. When stretched, it is in a potential situation that "unloads" when the muscle becomes shorter in the middle of the stride. This gives aid to the forward and upward momentum of the whole creature, and continues to cycle as long as the creature is walking or running.

In vertebrate animals like cats, pigs, and humans, we discover that differing gaits are linked to changes in velocity and involve patterns that most efficiently produce the speed needed by the

Figure | 9-2 |

Animal running or walking, showing spine flexing.

animal. Hyenas can run quickly, but they have more of a lope than the classic sprint of a cheetah. Similarly, giraffes rock or lope in their maximum speed gait, whereas elephants use an extremely fast sort of walk, really an accelerated version of a normal walk. Camels and giraffes have a unique version of the trot, wherein the animal alternates one side with the other side rather than alternating corner to corner with the legs. This, called a *pace* or *rack*, makes the animal sway side to side as it moves in this gait. A camel's feet and legs are specially built to allow for this motion. This is also an example of a rotary gait, which we deal with below.

Figure **9-3**

Horse gait with three feet touching ground.

Generally speaking, we can think of a quadruped walk as a central axis (the spine) carried between two independent leg systems, almost like two separate people. There is a need to keep the stride equal from front to back to avoid overstepping, and the gait can be alternating legs, as we have seen in a previous diagram. When trotting, the spine is still being carried by two independent systems working (with the exception of camels and giraffes) nonsimultaneously: the legs are not moving all at the same time on the same side. This keeps the center of gravity stable without undue sideways rocking. Trots are energy efficient, whereas the gallop, which we'll look at next, is more energy burning, requiring the animal be thrust into the air for a period of time. However, it is efficient in that the front and back ends do not replicate the other's work.

In a gallop or full sprint, the front and back ends of the animal are supported alternately from each end; if two people were running with a ladder they would find that there would be an inherent inefficiency in the motion, as one would want to thrust and the other pull during the action. Animals avoid this by *not* having the front and back legs do the same type of action.

Gallops or sprints have four separate parts or phases. Part one is when the animal pushes its body forward and into the air using its hind legs. The creature is now transferring to the anticipated front leg portion of the two-part stroke. Part two is the stretch between the back legs and the front legs. The third part is being airborne (for some animals) after the front legs thrust the animal up and forward and curl inward briefly. Part four is when the hind legs strike and the front legs move forward again in anticipation of the next cycle. To further complicate this picture, running gaits (and slower ones for that matter) can be rotary or transverse. That is a mouthful. These terms merely refer to the footfall pattern, which means if the lead feet are (front and rear) on opposite sides, it's a *rotary* gait, and if on the same side, it's a *transverse* gait. The lead foot will merely be the one moving further forward. A dog has a rotary run, whereas a horse has a transverse one. Asymmetrical gaits (like gallops and canters) are so-called because

Figure | 9-4 |

Foot plants and profile diagrams of dog/horse gaits.

the footfalls do not occur at equal time intervals, whereas symmetrical gaits do have such equal time intervals (as in walks and trots).

The point at which all feet are off the ground in a run is sometimes referred to as *suspension*. Horses have a one-suspension gallop (only off the ground once), whereas dogs have a two-suspension sprint or gallop (off the ground twice). Runs are defined by the fact that they induce a suspension. It is through the suspension (being airborne) that the restriction on stride length is overcome and velocity increased. Walks are always a supported gait, that is, one foot is always on the ground.

It has been pointed out that some ungulate (hooved) animals rock while running. Their vertebral spines (the processes that extend up well beyond the spine itself on the backbone) act as a cantilever while running, helping hold up alternate ends (front and back) during front and back footfalls, thus increasing the efficiency of the gallop. During the second phase of a canter or gallop, this action kicks in and allows such an animal a great advantage for conserving energy over long distances. This is further aided by the storage in both the neck ligaments and Achilles tendons of energy, making a gallop less exhausting than one might think. Carnivores expend far more energy in quick sprints, for which they are built the best; they tire easily after a moderate chase. Wildebeest, hartebeest, and other tall-spined ungulates all share in this design and motion. Because the hind legs are fixed in their sockets on the pelvis, the motion allowable for them is limited to the radial arc of their joint/pelvic axis. This means only that moving in an arc from a fixed point is more limited than moving from independent and mobile joint areas, like the shoulders. However, if the front limbs are to move freely, they must be *raised* high enough to allow a greater motion than just from the elbow joint. This is where the hump comes in (the raised vertebral spines). It does just that, raising the body high enough to permit a freer swing of the forelimbs. So a gallop of a large African antelope will not be the same as a thoroughbred horse's. During a gallop, an animal will lift its head up and down in a compensatory, weight-balancing action.

Figure | 9-5 |

One-suspension gallop—horse; two-suspension gallop—dog.

Animals obviously also move about in ways that are not always running. Walks are limited by the amount of arc that a leg can perform relative to its fixed joint position. Without an extra jolt or push, the walk can be only so fast and go only so far. The velocity of a walk or run is stride rate times stride length. If the stride can only go so far, the speed is clearly limited. A walk for a biped is gravity assisted and so is fairly energy efficient. For a quadruped, the walking gait is muscle-produced. For them, the gait is a four-beat symmetrical gait. The legs move in a repeated pattern in time and position.

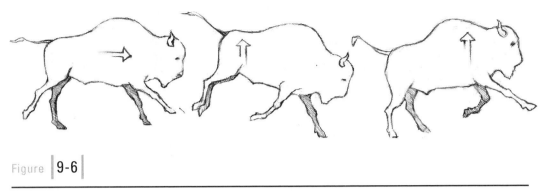

Figure | 9-6 |

Bison running: hump spines help front legs lift.

Figure | 9-7 |

Four-beat symmetrical gait; walk of horse.

At this point we need to point out another gait speed, that of the trot and pace (or rack). These involve suspension but are symmetrical in time for footfalls. They fall in between walks and gallops in velocity. Several variations of this speed are used by different animals. A trot involves a transverse gait and the pace or rack a rotary gait. The trot of a camel is a rotary pace. Although camels are capable of a transverse gallop, they seem to prefer the rack mode for running. This makes for a very uncomfortable ride!

We have more diagrams in Figure 9-8 to illustrate this important section on locomotion. What is doubly important here is that if you are an animator (or even illustrator) showing animals or humans in motion, you will need to understand at least in basic terms how each animal solves the problem of locomotion.

PLEASE TAKE NOTE!

Animals of differing sizes actually perform in similar ways mechanically. There is a mathematical formula that can be applied to locomotion. It is called the *Froude number*, and it is derived by using the following formula: u^2/gl, where in locomotion u equals forward velocity, l equals leg length, and g is the acceleration of gravity. Animals as small as mice and as large as donkeys use comparable gaits and have a ratio of leg length to stride length that is about the same. That is, a mouse will run rather like a horse and its stride length is related to its leg length in the same way a horse's is. Certain Froude numbers signify when an animal will change gait for efficiency reasons: if the Froude number is between 2 and 3, then a gait change will probably occur.

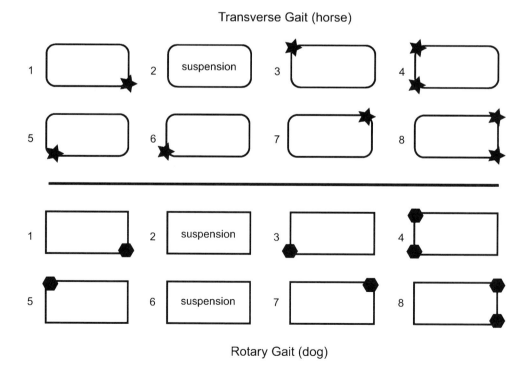

Transverse Gait (horse)

Rotary Gait (dog)

Figure 9-8

Transverse gait and rotary gait diagrams.

Bipedal Built for Two

Humans as bipeds have a walk cycle that is essentially an inverted pendulum. Pushing over a stiffened leg, the body launches forward, and would fall flat if it were not for the pulling up and planting of the opposite leg in front, allowing another pendulum swing of the body, repeated endlessly. The comical image of the forgotten step and face-plant or the banana peel slip gives slap-stick comedy much material. Unlike most other animals, humans walk and run *planti-grade*: flat-footed. This produces a somewhat different overall look and motion because the leg does not have the "double" bend of quadrupeds.

In animation, walk cycles can be created in a variety of steps, or in-betweens. As is the rule in animation, more in-betweens equals smoother action when filmed, but eventually, too many in-betweens causes a slow-motion effect. Our interest here, however, is in the basic mechanics of a walk. Humans walk in a variety of ways, depending upon height, leg length, speed, general build, and gender. Generally, the pelvis is required to move in a figure-eight (actually a dumb-bell shape) while the body is walking. This allows each succeeding leg to move into position under the body for planting the foot while the leg just used is raised and rotated back into planting position again.

The pelvis rocks left and right, up and down, and forward and backward in a smooth three-dimensional figure eight. Each leg bends just enough to allow the foot to clear the ground as it goes through its piston-like cycle to return to a planting position. The foot plants on the heel, followed by the side and front of the foot in an almost rocking motion. Because of the wider set of women's hips, the pelvic rotation and in-turning of the leg is exaggerated. Each leg is forced inward at the knee because of the wider displacement of the hip joint. Male walks tend to be stiffer, often accompanied by lax bending of the knee during strides. A sample walk cycle for each is demonstrated in Figure 9-10.

As the legs move, the torso adjusts to the forward and side motions of the pelvis and legs, sometimes with a gentle forward "bob" as each step commences. The head, too, can "give" a bit with each stride. It is the shoulders that move in a miniature imitation of the pelvic pattern. When

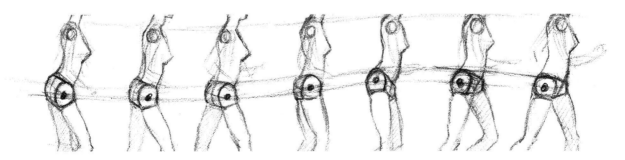

Figure **9-9**

Human walk cycle.

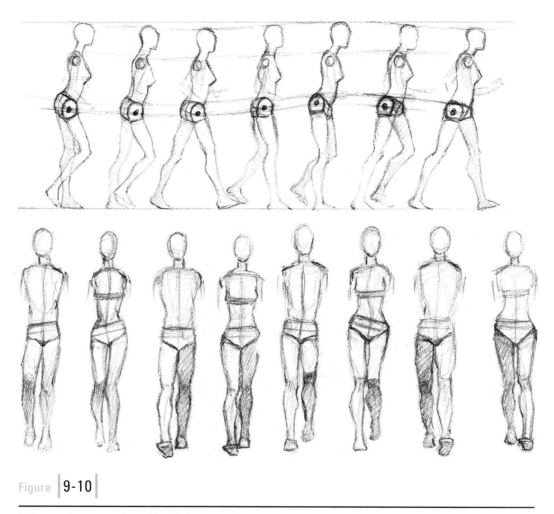

Figure 9-10

Difference between male and female human walks.

one iliac crest is at its most forward position for the pelvis, the opposite shoulder moves forward to compensate. Each arm swings forward in turn, matching the opposite leg, with the upper arm stopping motion just at the front of the torso and the lower arm continuing upward for a bit. This countermotion helps balance the weight distribution of each leg displacement.

Muscles involved in this motion are as follows: when a leg swings forward, the hamstrings in the back upper leg, gemelli, gluteus maximus (fanny), and quadriceps (upper leg front) contract; now the leg, lifting off the ground, uses the contraction of the quadriceps and rectus femoris in particular (upper-middle quad) to first pull the leg and hold it and then to extend the lower leg out (and thus forward). Now the leg is under the body again after planting, and lateral muscles of the hip and knee help keep the leg (and us) stable.

Running for humans involves a similar motion, but with the proviso that at some point both feet are off the ground, due to the larger push-off and exaggerated motions involved. The faster the run, the longer the stride, and the higher the lift on the legs.

Figure **9-11**

Run cycle for human.

Walking produces an up and down bobbing motion for bipeds, whereas running, because of its need for forward momentum efficiency, reduces this motion to some extent in humans, but not necessarily in quadrupeds.

Udder Land Critters

For limbed vertebrates like the salamanders, three legs are in contact with the ground, allowing the fourth to move forward. This is forced by the extremely wide stance of the legs outward from the torso. Changes in speed for these animals is, to a great extent, simply an acceleration of the rate of foot strike, rather than a change of gait.

Some animals, as we have noted, use an undulatory motion in their spine to aid in locomotion. There are two prime examples of this movement: one is legless, the other has limbs. Snakes move by crawling, which is really bending the body and by the contraction of sequences of muscles, producing a sine wave motion the travels along the body, propelling it forward. Snakes basically do not have a reverse gear. Some amphibians and lizards also undulate the spine/torso, but

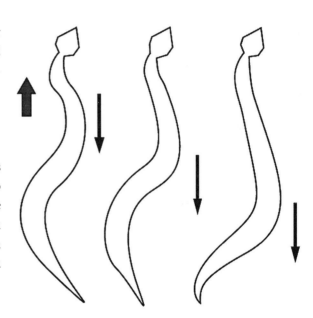

Traveling Wave

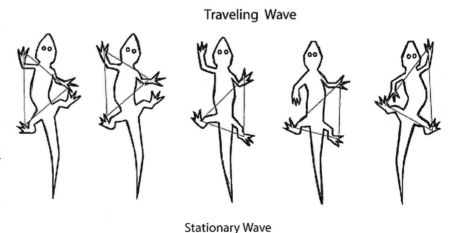

Stationary Wave

Figure **9-12**

Snake locomotion and lizard locomotion with traveling and stationary waves respectively.

Figure | 9-13 |

Kangaroo hop.

with a different mode. They are literally placing the opposite pairs of legs and feet in closed and open positions in order to advance forward. Snakes use a traveling wave along the body, whereas amphibians and lizards use a stationary wave. Figure 9-12 illustrates each of these modes.

Kangaroos, mice, humans, and many birds often or always use hopping as a locomotive mode. *Hopping* is the use of both hind legs simultaneously to push the body forward. It is, to some extent, a combination of running and walking. The same storage of kinetic energy in the Achilles tendon is responsible for the resultant thrust. Each landing stores anew the kinetic energy for the next push. Hopping (or *bounding* or *pronking* in quadrupeds) occurs when vertical position exceeds the body weight: the center of gravity, which was relatively constant when running, now elevates in a parabolic curve. Obviously, this gait has suspension. The animal is literally propelled into the air. Although the stride rate is reduced because of the vertical component, the length of the stride compensates for this by being extra long. By using both feet and legs, extra power is inserted into the push-off part of the gait. Landing and "flight" are stabilized by this two-foot mode as well.

Other terrestrial modes of locomotion include the "one-anchor" used by such creatures as the mussel (shelled creature like a clam), in which a "foot" is extended, the end spread out, and then contracted to pull the creature along the line of the foot. Clearly there is no sprinting here. Some caterpillars and worms use a "two-anchor" mode of locomotion, involving back and front ends of the creature. In this mode, the body is contracted upward with the front end anchored, allowing the back end to lift and move forward and anchor in turn. Then the front disengages, moves forward with the body descending flat, and the whole process starts over again.

Peristalsis is another means for moving small, soft-bodied animals to a destination. Muscles that circle the body contract and extend the anterior part of the animal (like an earthworm) while segments of the body contract in a wave in the opposite direction down the body, pushing the whole creature forward. These are specialized movements appropriate to the body types and have stood the test of time for millions of years.

Davy Jones' Locker

Moving through water presents a totally different set of problems for animals. The most well known denizen of the oceans, lakes, and rivers of earth is the fish. Fish present a basic body plan that has some variations from species to species, and in these variations we find responses to the needs of ecologic niches and the issue of locomotion, producing some wonderful and visually beautiful forms of fish. Because they are in water, fish (and all other sea and fresh water animals) must contend with a material approximately 800 times as dense as air. Because this is nearly the density of animals, the effects of gravity are nearly negated. The downside is that water presents a more difficult medium to travel through because of its density. Animals must be streamlined

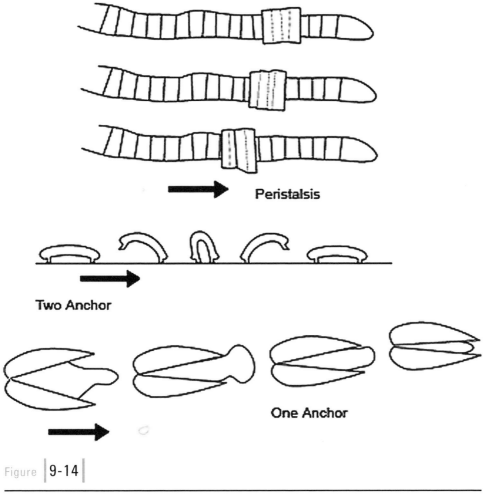

Figure **9-14**

One-anchor, two-anchor, and peristalsis locomotion modes.

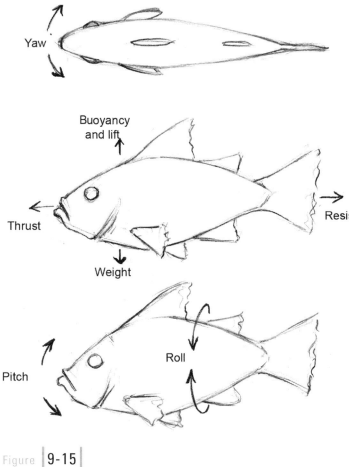

Figure 9-15

Fish diagram with yaw, pitch, roll, and other parameters of motion.

and have bodies and motility suited to movement easily through liquid. Some fish, of course, are dwellers of coral or the bottom, and may not move quickly relative to the fish we will describe in a moment. We leave these slower animals for the reader to investigate, because their locomotion is not nearly as dramatic or interesting.

Water-dwelling animals have three issues in moving through water. The skin of the animals has friction with the surrounding water, water is pushed aside by the shape of the animal (streamlining), and vortices are formed by larger fins that cause drag. These issues are overcome by acceleration reaction, lift, and drag forces. Besides having efficient shapes, fish create lift perpendicular to their flow direction with asymmetric movement of water past them (one side unequal to the other side, causing lift). Acceleration reaction, which is greatly influenced by the scale of the animal, has to do with inertial forces generated from either the animal or water being in acceleration relative to the other. The animal's buoyancy, weight, and hydrodynamic lift affect its vertical motion, while the horizontal motion is subject to thrust and resistance. And like aircraft, the fish is subject to yaw, pitch, and roll stresses.

Unless an artist is involved in a technical study, these factors can, to a great extent, be dealt with in a cursory manner. Fortunately for fish, these issues are handled instinctively through their anatomy and neural patterning. Otherwise, they would be so dumbfounded as to sit in a stunned stupor, never moving an inch, because the math and engineering are so daunting.

Below is a generic diagram of a fish. The terms used are cited in the section on locomotion coming up shortly.

Our concern here is with swimming locomotion, rather than with burrowing or gliding and the like. Fish, like other animals, have both sustained and non-steady locomotion. Watching a football halfback weaving his way through tacklers, one can see that there are bursts of forward

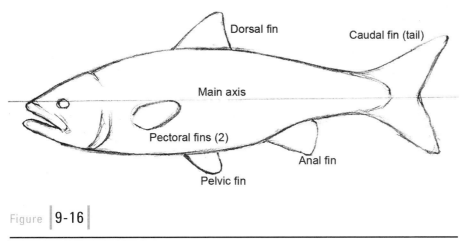

Dorsal fin

Caudal fin (tail)

Main axis

Pectoral fins (2)

Anal fin

Pelvic fin

Figure | 9-16 |

Fish diagram, generic.

sprinting, evasive maneuvers, and interrupted gaits. Fish, too, can exhibit this behavior, given the proper circumstance. So we can see that there are longer, repeated "gaits" in fish as well as shorter, nonrepeated locomotive techniques. For general purposes of this book, we will look only at generic motion types, and not deal with the technical issues connected with sustained and interrupted locomotion.

Fish can be divided into two main camps for locomotion: (1) body or caudal fin locomotion (BCF), and (2) median or paired fin (MPF) locomotion. Some fish use one mode for some activity and the other for other activities, while other fish may share features of both systems. In the first mode (BCF), fish bend their bodies, producing a wave that moves to the rear, culminating in *caudal* (tail) fin motion. Some only move the caudal fin, and others use their bodies only moderately in this action. In MPF locomotion, along with body motion, the paired fins providing most of the thrust are the pectorals. Cluttering this up further, *undulatory* and *oscillating* modes (a traveling wave and anchored swiveling propulsor) can be included here. Further muddying the water, fins can have undulatory waves for propulsion as well. The body wave described in BCF mode can take four major forms. These are *anguilliform, subcarangiform, carangiform*, and *thunniform* (with an additional oscillatory type we'll not cover called ostraciform). The ultimate mode for fish appears to be *thunniform*, used by many marine animals such as sharks, some sea mammals, and teleost fish such as tuna. In it, the main motion occurs in the caudal (tail) fin and the immediate preceding peduncle (slender body transition into the caudal fin). It allows great speed and endurance.

| NOTE |

Each of these locomotive types has a differing amount of involvement with the body; in order of oscillatory magnitude they are as follows:

1. Anguilliform: trunk undulated one wavelength or more

2. Subcarangiform: trunk undulated between one-half but less than one wavelength

3. Carangiform: caudal fin (tail) plus undulate body less than one-half wavelength; fin provides propulsive force

4. Thunniform: oscillate caudal fin (tail) with minimum of body undulation

The following illustrations show how these appear and function:

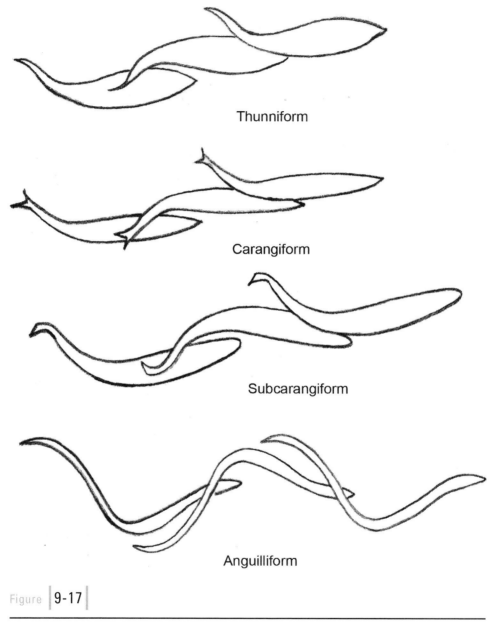

Thunniform

Carangiform

Subcarangiform

Anguilliform

Figure | 9-17 |

Fish locomotion modes.

Undulatory fin motions are: *balistiform* (anal and dorsal fins), *gymnotiform* (anal fin), *rajiform* and *diodontiform* (pectoral fin), and *amiiform* (dorsal fin; seahorses use this mode). *Labriform* uses the pectoral fins for propulsion by a rowing motion. Usually the fins used in these modes are elongated or enlarged in order to utilize their particular motion.

Sea mammals also use a vertical body wave stroke for propulsion, as opposed to the side to side motion found in most fish. Whales, manatees, and dolphins depend upon this vertical motion to push them forward in their liquid environment. Because of their varied mass, the motion can be fairly rapid, as in a dolphin, or rather lazy, as in a blue whale. The tail area is horizontally formed to accommodate this propulsive motion. Fur seals and sea lions use their flippers for the main propulsion, with the rear flipper acting more as a rudder. Phocids, or true seals, use their rear flippers and body in a side-to-side sculling motion, with the foreflippers either held against the body or used for guidance in turning and maneuvering.

Penguins literally "fly" through the water, with the main propulsion coming from their wings/flippers and some body undulation. From a clumsy surface animal, the penguin transforms into an amazing underwater acrobat. Sea turtles also use their flippers for the main propulsion, but because of their size and rigidity, the momentum is far less. There has been much speculation on how the prehistoric plesiosaurs moved through water. One school says that an alternating front and back flipper stroke was the main mode, while others maintain that the size and maneuverability of the hind flippers precluded anything much beyond a role as rudders.

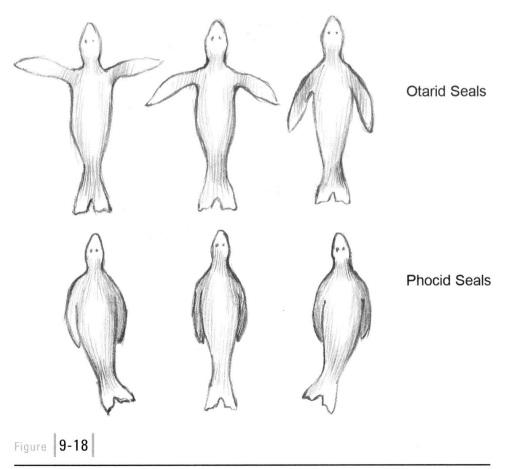

Otarid Seals

Phocid Seals

Figure |9-18|

Seal locomotion.

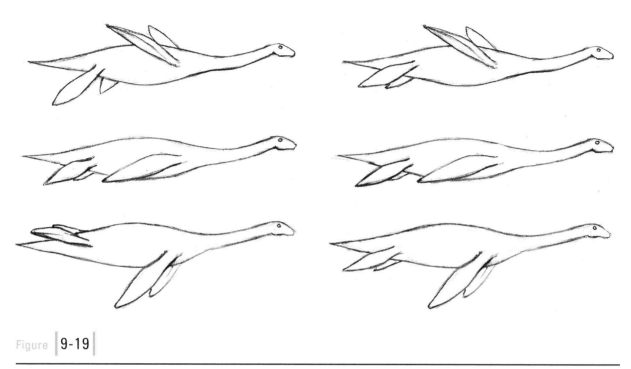

Figure **9-19**

Plesiosaur locomotion.

The truth probably lies somewhere in between, although we have noted that excluding behavior and locomotive modes is more likely to be in error, given the broad flexibility that most creatures exhibit in responding to their environment.

Flying Revisited

There are four basic types of flight in animals, both vertebrate (with backbones) and invertebrate (such as insects). They are listed below:

1. Active flight: In this mode, the animal actually beats or flaps its wings to produce thrust, lift, and flight. Animals that are capable of this include most birds, some insects, bats, and in ancient times, the pterosaurs.

2. Dead drop or parachuting: This is where an animal literally falls and uses its body surface as a wind brake. Any animal can do this, as long as the fall is more than 45 degrees relative to the horizontal axis.

3. Gliding: This is like using a parachute but with the animal able to generate lift with its body design, allowing a descent less than 45 degrees, and enabling it to travel over longer distances. Flying squirrels are an example of this mode of flight.

4. Soaring: Few animals do this type of flight, which uses a large surface area to allow the animal to lift vertically on thermals, the hot columns of air that rise and can actually bear an animal with the right combination of weight and surface area. Some birds (and extinct pterosaurs) use this type of flight, with minor active flight being needed for adjusting, takeoff, and landing.

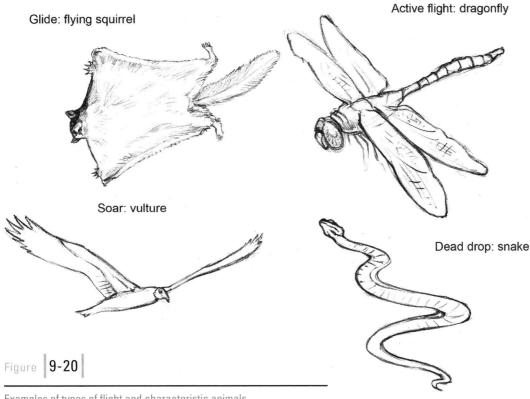

Glide: flying squirrel

Active flight: dragonfly

Soar: vulture

Dead drop: snake

Figure **9-20**

Examples of types of flight and characteristic animals.

Interestingly, each category still contains optional ways of achieving the flight mode. An eagle, a hummingbird, and a bat all fly actively, but they all have somewhat different techniques for achieving the same end. Part of the reason for this is their particular lifestyle and its demands, and the other is how they evolutionarily solved the problem of flight anatomically. For a character or creature designer, the anatomy is probably the foremost issue. We want to make something that will work (and function with our design) and we want something with visual appeal, frankly, really *sweet*.

In other sections of this book, we look at wings and character design where functionality (does it work?) doesn't much matter. This is a legitimate design mode, but has certain drawbacks in believability and appeal in the long run. Right now, we'd like to examine just how these animals are put together, and how that might be modified and applied to our characters and creatures. Once we've seen how they are built, we can look at some representative wing beat cycles that might apply to animated characters. We'll also take a brief look at powered assistance using technology.

Let's first take a look at the most familiar flying animals for most people: birds, bats, and the extinct flying reptiles. We have a diagram below that illustrates their basic design skeletally. Note in birds and pterodactyls, the enlarged sternum, or breastbone, where powerful flight muscles are attached and have become enlarged to accommodate this fact.

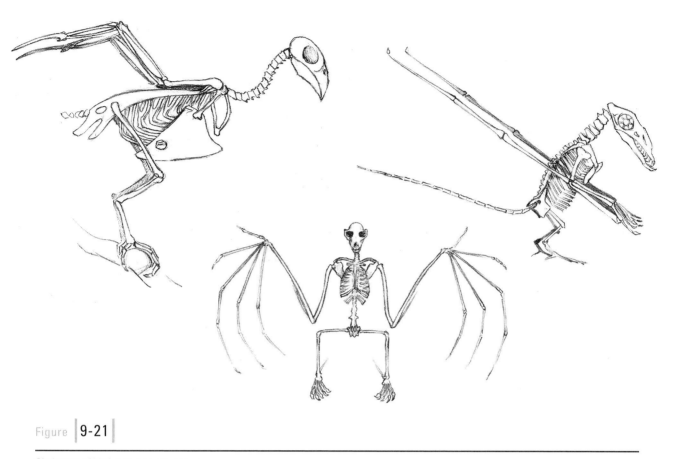

Figure **9-21**

Skeletons of bird, bat, and pterosaur.

So as not to make this a scientific monograph, but a useful tool for artists, let's just cover some basics here. It's clear that mammals, birds, and reptiles share certain features, but they also have some pretty significant differences. All three have a modified and/or enlarged sternum with a heavy keel to attach flight muscles. It's instructive to compare all three with a human arm.

Goin' Batty

Chiroptera, the scientific name for bats, means "hand-wing," which pretty much describes their mechanism for flight. The arms of the bat are an extremely elongated set of arm bones and fingers, allowing bats to form a functional wing when a membrane, the *patagium*, is attached, and it is where the fingers are that the thrust for flight happens. Two membranes are interconnected by tiny muscles and are filled as well with elastic blood vessels and elastic fibers. These muscles and fibers help keep the wing tight during flight. The patagium connects all the way from the third finger tip to the ankle of the hind leg. Between the hind leg and the tail is another small membrane, the *uropatagium*, probably used for stabilization. Part of the function of this membrane is to scoop prey as well during flight for transport to the mouth. This membrane, supported by special foot bones, resembles glider animal design. The sternum has a keel, albeit

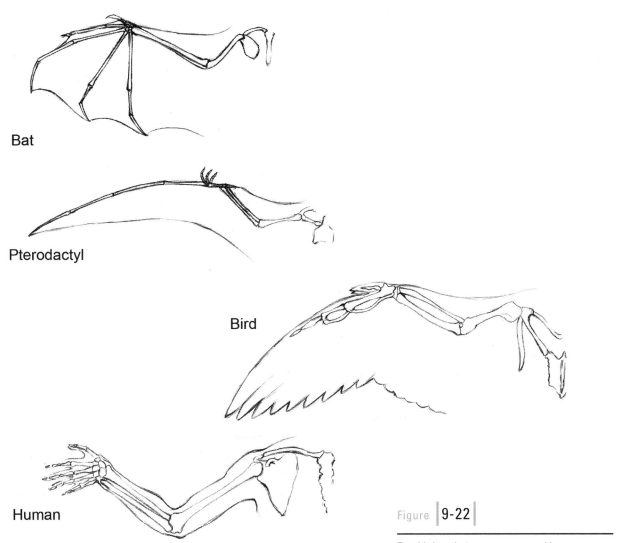

Bat

Pterodactyl

Bird

Human

Figure **9-22**

Bat, bird, and pterosaur arms and human arm.

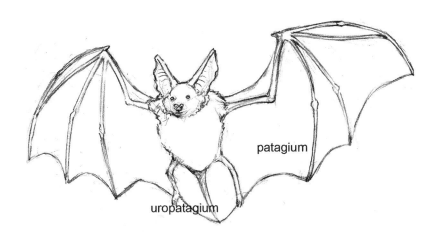

patagium

uropatagium

Figure **9-23**

Further look at bat wings and bodies in diagram.

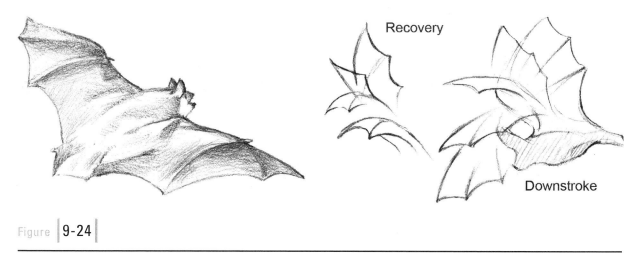

Recovery

Downstroke

Figure | **9-24**

Bat in flight.

much smaller than birds, for flight muscle attachment. The radius and ulna are tiny, very short, and thin. Their pelvic girdle is basically fused, giving a solid support to the base of the skeletal structure. Bat wings are relatively large outstretched in comparison to the body of the animal.

The motion of the bat wing corresponds pretty well to basic bird flight, except that the motion is more one of rowing because the lift generated by bat wings and bodies is not nearly as great as that of some birds. A normal bat wing is about as efficient as a pigeon's in its lift/drag ratio. They literally power themselves through the air. Flight muscles for the downstroke in flight are the pectoralis major, subscapularis, part of the deltoid, and part of the serratus anterior. For the upstroke, the rest of the deltoid, the trapezius, rhomboids, infraspinatus, and supraspinatus are used. The scapula in the back moves across the back in a mobile fashion during flight, and is important as an attachment point for many flight muscles. These muscles correspond to those in almost all mammals. It is interesting to see how they have been modified for use in flight.

Downstrokes in bats have fully extended wings that move down and forward. Once the nose is cleared by the wing tips, the upstroke takes over, with a partial folding of the wings and bending of the wrists and elbows. In the downstroke, the leading edge of the wing bends, or has *camber*, toward the tip. The downstroke is responsible for moving forward and lift.

For the Birds

Birds form the most familiar family of flying animals on earth. Classified as *Aves,* birds vary from large flying/gliding animals such as an eagle, to the tiny hummingbird. Their configuration of feathers allows a sophisticated means of modifying the flight surface of the wing for many types of aerial maneuvers. The wing of a bird differs substantially from that of a bat. Whereas the bat used its fingers to stretch a membrane for purposes of a wing, a bird has a much more arm-like affair, with the shortened humerus, and strong ulna and fibula, ending in a modified "hand." Flight muscles attach to the arm and hand, and some reach back to connect to a large sternum with a raised keel. Primary flight feathers, attached to the hand, are angled

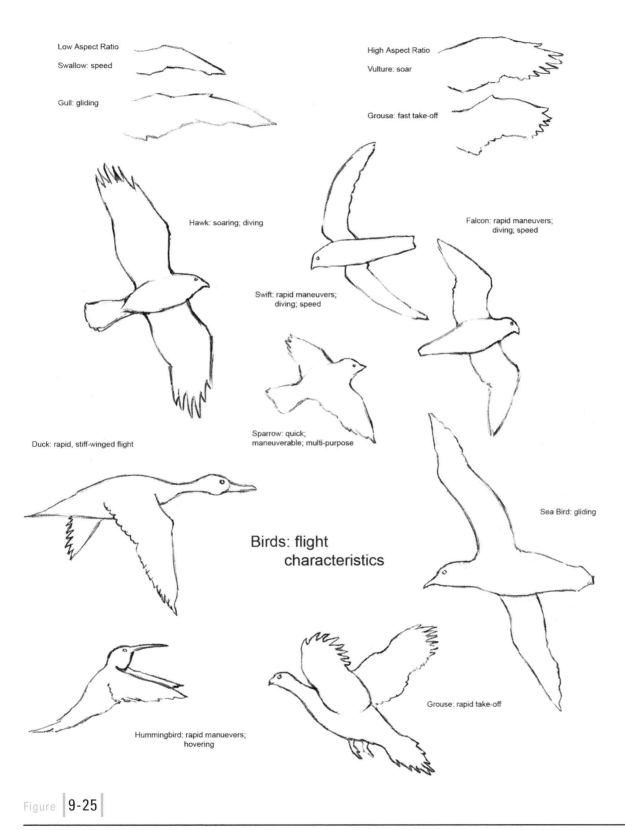

Low Aspect Ratio

Swallow: speed

Gull: gliding

High Aspect Ratio

Vulture: soar

Grouse: fast take-off

Hawk: soaring; diving

Falcon: rapid maneuvers;
diving; speed

Swift: rapid maneuvers;
diving; speed

Sparrow: quick;
maneuverable; multi-purpose

Duck: rapid, stiff-winged flight

Birds: flight
characteristics

Sea Bird: gliding

Hummingbird: rapid manuevers;
hovering

Grouse: rapid take-off

Figure **9-25**

Various birds showing differing flight types—gliding, hummingbirds, hawks, sparrows, and so on.

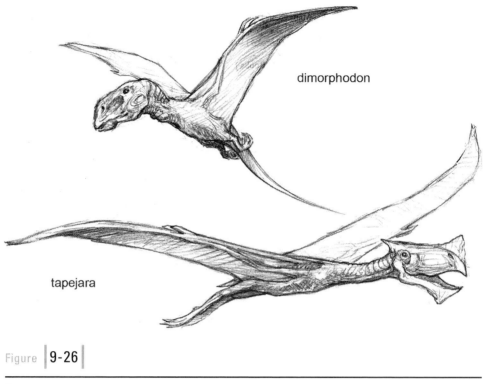

dimorphodon

tapejara

Figure | 9-26 |

Some pterosaurs.

to produce a low pressure zone in front of the bird when in a downstroke. This pulls the bird forward, while the upstroke, with partly bent wing, utilizes the secondary flight feathers for lift. These are attached to the arm. Hollow bones in birds allow a great reduction in weight, which is necessary to be able to produce enough lift to leave the ground and fly.

Birds come in a wild variety of sizes and wing shapes. Although they share certain basic loco-motive modes, it is clear that some birds are more suited to quick maneuvering (e.g., hummingbirds, swallows) and others for less spectacular flight (e.g., ducks, swans). Some are gliders and soarers (e.g., vultures, albatross) and some have various modes (e.g., eagles).

That pterosaurs flew it is certain. However, the exact nature of that flight is still speculative. Based upon the radically differing sizes of these creatures (from sparrow to small plane size), we can presume that the different spans of wings and body weights included everything from very active pursuit flight to simple soaring and gliding.

Arthropods I Have Known

Most of the animals on earth are insects. Their structural relatives, arachnids, make up another sizable bite of the animal pie. Insects move by two basic means on the ground. The first is called *metachronal wave gait*. In it, on alternating sides of the insect, the legs move in a wave from front to back, with one side ahead of the other, giving the forward propulsion necessary.

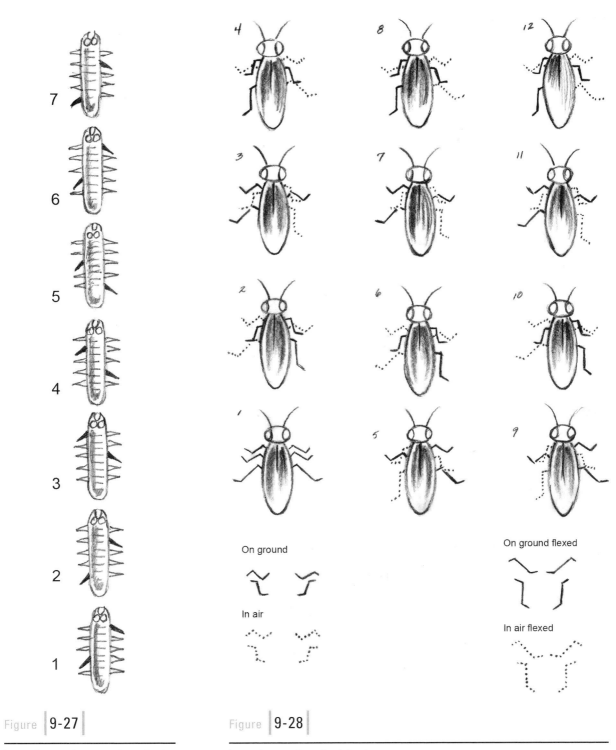

On ground

In air

On ground flexed

In air flexed

Figure | 9-27 |

Insect locomotion: metachronal gait.

Figure | 9-28 |

Insect locomotion: tripodal gait.

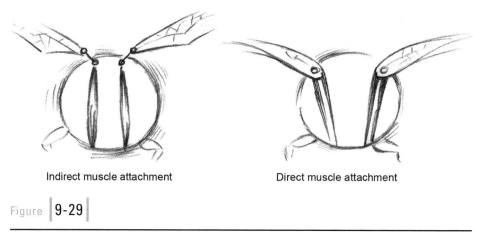

Indirect muscle attachment   Direct muscle attachment

Figure **9-29**

Direct and indirect insect wing attachment diagrams.

The other form of locomotion is a *tripod gait*. In it, alternating from one side to the other, a stable moving tripod of legs give the insect forward momentum.

Tripodal gaits are by far the fastest, and metachronal the slowest. Many insects move between the two gaits, depending upon the speed needed (and the number of legs they have). In the tripodal, there are always three legs on the ground, one on one side and two (split) on the other, giving the great stability of the triangle. The three legs that remain on the ground will move backward, and the three legs that are raised will move forward, then to descend and start the process over again. The basic rule here is the insect can't raise a leg unless the leg behind it can support the insect, and legs on opposite sides of the insect (i.e., the pairs) will be going different directions, one back and one up and forward. Soft-bodied insects like larval stage caterpillars must move via *peristaltic* action; the rear prolegs are pulled forward, tugging the surface and thence pulling the creature forward in a "wave" of these actions from back to front.

Swimming insects are of two types. One can retain air by use of gills or siphon tubes or a contained bubble. They move using oar strokes through the liquid environment. Surface walkers depend upon the surface tension and their relative light weight to, in a sense, skate over the surface, although they don't lift their legs as human skaters do.

Insect flyers are the first flying animals on earth. Some attained enormous size, such as the Meganeura dragonfly that had a wingspan of two feet! They worked out the first winged muscle attachments, which were of two kinds. One was direct and the other indirect. What this meant was the muscle on the first was internal, attached to the inner part of the exoskeleton and the wing (which was located at an opening on the exoskeleton). The other method involved a structure mediating between the wing and the muscle; this allowed a much higher wing beat frequency.

The actual motions of the wings are highly complicated, involving rotation, figure eight paths, and so on. A butterfly actually can use three or four different flight modes in a row while navigating about. Unless you are going to be working on military applications for miniature spy equipment, it is unlikely that you will need to study these modes too much in depth. Structurally, the wings are supported by "veins" that act as rigid radiating rods that keep the wing shape stable. Wings for insects can actually bend while moving, allowing complex patterns and the lift necessary for flight.

SUMMARY

In conclusion we can see that our dialogue about anatomy and locomotion barely touches the tip of an enormous iceberg of information on these subjects. What we present in this chapter gives the artist a basic working overview of the issues and fundamental modes that commonly occur in character and creature design.

Character and creature designers must take into account the anatomic and locomotive properties of their creations, at least to the extent that they wish believability and authenticity to register with the audience. The anatomy of the animal is linked both to its stationary appearance and its movement and locomotion. By understanding the one, an artist will have a good clue as to the aspect of the other. Some similarly constructed animals, however, move in surprising ways, and it is here that a more in-depth study is necessary. For great action poses and animation, a study of locomotion is a necessity; for the sense of validity in appearance, an understanding of some anatomy is required. To usefully pursue synthesis in designing these characters and animals, knowledge of the parts and their purpose gives a better understanding of how to recombine and modify existing anatomy. Ignorance of these subjects leads to dead, clichéd and amateuresque design.

exercises

1. Compare and contrast the gallop of dogs and horses. Draw a character in motion that uses one gait or the other.

2. Design a flying creature that uses the winged structure of a bat; take care to preserve a convincing wing/weight ratio.

3. Construct a character based upon a mix of the anatomy of two separate species; show how the locomotion of each is combined into a coherent whole.

4. Design an underwater creature that uses carangiform or thunniform locomotion and animate it in motion for a short sequence.

in review

1. What are the four basic modes of flight?

2. What is the fastest swimming mode called and name one example of an animal that uses it?

3. Name an animal whose walk is mechanically like an inverted pendulum.

4. An earthworm uses what mode for locomotion?

5. Digitigrade and plantigrade refer to what?

6. Tripodal gait is the fastest for what animal?

notes

_____
_____
_____
_____
_____
_____
_____
_____
_____
_____
_____
_____
_____
_____
_____
_____
_____
_____
_____
_____

objectives

Demonstrate how one type of research category can be used in depth.

Gain an understanding of the usefulness and variety of prehistoric resources for construction of fantasy characters and creatures.

Gain an introduction to several categories of possible sources of prehistoric imagery.

Gather ideas about the application of prehistoric resources into the visual design of characters and creatures.

Gain a visual overview of how visual resource elements relate to prehistoric creatures.

Introduction

When we use a research category for character or creature design, we often think of only the most obvious images or sources, those with which we are the most familiar. In fact, all of the category outlines in Chapter Two have enormous and varied types of information. An example of this is the subject of prehistoric animals as a source for character development imagery. By examining this source in more depth, we can show again, as we did with mythology, a better understanding of how categories can be used. In addition, this category is one of the better ones for creature design resource, and as such deserves a closer look for the artist and designer. It is also important to realize how the sciences of biology and paleontology affect the character design process as it applies to prehistoric creatures.

One of the underused and obvious sources for fantasy illustration in "monster" or creature design is the wealth of prehistoric animal resources available through various media. Probably the reason that this fund of knowledge is less used than it should be is the nature of the sources themselves. Museums often publish specialized monographs on extinct animals that are expensive or hard to come by. Popular books on the subject generally, although not always, concentrate on animals with which we are more familiar, such as the venerable Tyrannosaurus rex or stegosaurus.

Some animation/special effects studios keep on their staff designers or artists whose background provides experience in scientific illustration and animal physiology. Their expertise often includes some training in paleontology or anatomy studies. On such films as *Jurassic Park*, in which a high level of anatomic accuracy is necessary to bring believable dinosaurs to life, producers brought in real-life paleontologists to render aid via consultation to 3D modelers and animators.

Research is vital for transferring science fact into the stuff of animation, illustration, or visual effects. For instance, the stop-motion animation models of dinosaurs and other once-living creatures created for the landmark motion picture *King Kong* (by artist Marcel Delgado) were considered to be anatomically and scientifically accurate by the standards of prehistoric animal reconstruction circa 1933. The primeval animals featured in the film were largely based on the authentic dinosaur imagery of Charles R. Knight. Knight, one of the foremost natural history illustrators of the turn of the century (nineteenth and twentieth centuries, that is), created a plethora of paintings for the American Museum of Natural History in New York City. Although not regarded now as representing the cutting edge of current paleontologic knowledge, Knight's work is still considered to be amongst the finest of its kind. It is interesting to note that some incorrect dinosaur descriptions can also be of value as resource material.

With the advent of the internet, accessing some of this information is now not quite as difficult as it was in the past. Many educational institutions have web space devoted to prehistoric flora and fauna of the world including updated information on recent discoveries. In addition, libraries still have lending programs linked to other institutions that can lead to books and smaller publications not normally found on the shelves. Be on the lookout for skeletal reconstructions of ancient animals because these are most helpful in the visual restoration of such creatures and are the first choice as reference for recreating extinct animals.

Ultimately, all artists worth their salt stand on the collective shoulders of lots of people, including other artists and researchers. It's the same in music, literature, and all other creative endeavors; even science. Trying to go it alone isn't a very good strategy. As long as you give credit where it is due, an artist can "mine" this wealth of information. Previously created imagery of prehistoric fauna is a great reference for jump-starting the imagination. Be cautious, however, that you are using the most accurate reference available when reconstructing ancient critters. Don't multiply the mistakes of other artists by using preexisting imagery without comparing and contrasting these sources with related and available scientific resources.

In our appendix, we list several sources for information on prehistoric fauna, and recommend that the artist intent on pursuing this avenue of creativity look into these resources.

Why? Why Not!

Why use extinct animals for visual resources at all? Why not just make up everything? One good answer is that the past provides real surprises that we might never come up with ourselves. Waiting for inspirations can be a long and lonely enterprise.

Some animals from the past are so weird that it is difficult to imagine that they were denizens of this planet and not some fauna from another world.

Because they offer great sources for visual ideas, prehistoric creatures cannot only be used interestingly "as-is" (with addition of some distinct character qualities like unique coloring, a broken tusk, a scrawny body, or battle scars), but provide an exceptional source of strange anatomies that can be applied to new creature creations. The "how to use it" issues really are these: configuration (overall shape and pose probabilities), surfaces, smaller parts (like teeth, antennae, or horns), locomotion (getting from point A to point B) modes, size (think sauropods), tails or wings, or other uniquely ancient physical traits. These are categorical breakdowns of raw information derived from any animal group. Each can be applied individually or in combination with the other variables to produce design variations and solutions. By synthesizing some elements, these traits can be further extended. Poses invite the analysis of what the actual physical capabilities of the animal are, and that begs the question of anatomy.

Figure | **10-1** |

Waiting for inspiration.

Surfaces are the part that the audience sees in large part as the "whole" design and are thus extraordinarily important in the appeal factor. Texture mapping, texture in general, color, and pattern become vital to the success of the creature design. Smaller parts such as teeth can signal roles or emotional potential, or the difference between old and new, or friendly or dangerous, or attractive or repulsive. All other parts are equally able to transform the design in an endless series of permutations.

As we have said before, try one change at a time, because multiple changes exponentially modify (in quite unpredictable and uncontrol-

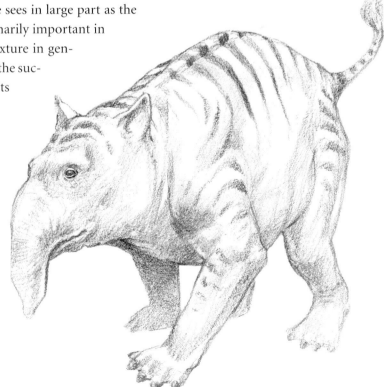

Figure | **10-2** |

Palorchestes azael: a marsupial tapir.

PHANERAZOIC PHUN OR NAME THAT EPOCH!

Before we continue through this chapter and start bandying about such 25-cent words as *Pennsylvanian*, *Cambrian*, and the ever popular *Triassic*, let us outline the basic geologic time scale. We hope that this will help you, gentle reader, to comprehend the relationship of the existence of a multitude of prehistoric fauna to the grand chronologic stretch of which they have been a part:

**Phanerozoic "Eon of Multicellular Life"
    (544 MYA to Present)**

**Precambrian "Age of Hidden Life"
    (4600 to 550 MYA)**

**Paleozoic "Age of Ancient Life"
    (550 to 248 MYA)**

Cambrian (550 to 505 MYA)

- Early
- Middle
- Late

Ordovician (505 to 438 MYA)

- Early
- Middle
- Late

Silurian (438 to 408 MYA)

- Early
- Middle
- Late

Devonian (408 to 360 MYA)

- Early
- Middle
- Late

Carboniferous (360 to 286 MYA)

Mississippian (360 to 320 MYA)

- Early
- Late

Pennsylvanian (320 to 286 MYA)

- Early
- Middle
- Late

Permian (286 to 248 MYA)

Mesozoic "Age of Dinosaurs" (248 to 65 MYA)

Triassic (248 to 208 MYA)

- Lower
- Middle
- Upper

Jurassic (208 to 144 MYA)

- Lower
- Middle
- Upper

Cretaceous (144 to 65 MYA)

- Lower
- Upper

Cenozoic "Age of Mammals" (65 MYA to Present)

Tertiary (65 to 2 MYA)

- Paleocene
- Eocene
- Oligocene
- Miocene
- Pliocene

Quaternary (2 MYA to Present)

- Pleistocene
- Holocene

By the way "MYA" refers to "millions of years ago."

Our research showed that there are many chronologic variations of this time scale, with ours being acceptably correct. What's a million years between friends, anyway?

lable ways) a design. Ultimately, the rationale behind using animals that no longer exist is precisely because of their appearances and substructures that are *different*. By following the path of technique as practiced and applied to many exercises and projects, the artist will find that this avenue of research can be of great value. It really *does* work to try research and synthesis, to use a sketchbook, to practice life drawing, and to attempt animal studies. By trial and error the artist will gain confidence and experience in what works and what does not work. Now we'll walk a bit further in the realm of prehistory by visiting how things are categorized.

Wild Kingdoms!

Let's step back for a moment and delve into the classification of living forms to give you some perspective on the breadth and relationships of our prehistoric resources. Animals in general can be divided into groups convenient for anatomists and biologists. A cat, for example, belongs to the largest group called a *kingdom*: Animalia (animals, not plants). Next, it is sorted into the *phylum*, for example Chordata (vertebrates, animals with backbones), then *class*, Mammalia (mammals, animals that give live birth) , then *order*: Carnivora (meat eaters), *family*: Felidae (cats), *genus*: Smilodon (extinct saber-toothed cat), and finally *species*: fatalis (such as the saber-toothed cats from the La Brea tar pits near Los Angeles). If you're really interested in classification of life forms, you can delve into such areas as suborders and even cladistics, but we don't have enough pages to do so here.

Although knowing all of this isn't always necessary from an artist's point of view, not knowing any of it can cause some problems when a script or other specialized application of the information calls for it. Take, for example, using animals from different periods in the same scene, as in *Jurassic Park*, or taking license with the shapes and sizes of tyrannosaurs or smaller theropods. These design decisions actually occurred, and must be justified, at least within the creative level they were aspiring to; poor movies suffer because they simply don't care, and put ludicrous designs and combinations in front of the audience. They "dumb down," so to speak.

Some animals have "equipment" or anatomic specializations that make distinct differences, morphologically speaking. (Morphology, or the study of form, comes from *morphe*, the Greek word for shape.) For instance, certain deer are distinguished partly from the differences in their horns. Other differences come from color, lengths of forms like legs or necks, part shapes such as noses or ears, and so on. Some examples follow.

mule deer - tines not off main beam...

white-tailed deer - tines off main beam...

Figure **10-3**

Comparative deer heads.

Figure | 10-4 |

Gigantopithecus blackii: the original King Kong.

Disney studios, when drawing Bambi, had to research particular deer types and decide on one configuration to follow. When using extinct animals or animals that may not have any living close relatives, some of these form distinctions become more difficult to figure out, even for anatomists. However, because many living animals share features with extinct ones, some good educated sleuthing can result in probable "looks" for the long-dead animal. The point here is not to become just a paleontologic detective who attempts to figure out how extinct animals looked, but rather to find others' work in this area that may be then applied to a design problem. A good artist can help in reconstruction of extinct animals. Sometimes the information gathered through the study of fossil evidence can be "underwhelming." Here's an example of such a "missing link" in scientific information. *Gigantopithecus blackii* was an extinct ape about the size of Mighty Joe Young (cousin of King Kong). This mighty anthropoid, all 10 feet of him, is certainly a marvelous creature and the visuals depicting *Gigantopithecus* are mostly imagined in reconstructions because the only skeletal remnants we have are jawbones and teeth. Lack of post-cranial anatomy (anything else) leaves some guesswork in deciding how this creature looked when alive.

Meanwhile, Back at the Cretaceous

As fantasy artists, we may be more interested in what is useful for our designs, not specific questions regarding species assignation or other related scientific requirements. Our goal in applying this reference to character design is two-fold: get visual information from a new source that extends the possibility of our designs or use that information in a modified form to develop extinct creatures as characters.

Figure **10-5**

Mosasaurs, icthyosaur, and plesiosaur.

Because a lot of what we do as artists involves synthesis (combining different things to make new things, as we talked about in Chapter Five), ancient animals provide parts or even whole pose configurations from which we can borrow bits and pieces to make something new. Animals come in groups, as we said, and scientists have categorized them in great detail. For artists, however, it is probably more useful to think in more general categories, like *dinosaur*, *prosimian*, or *flying reptile*.

Extinct animals still share many features with the living animals of today. So if we are looking for something in the reptile groups that might fit a character we are building, then it would be useful to check up on dinosaurs, of course, but maybe also sea reptiles like mosasaurs, icthyosaurs, and plesiosaurs.

The menacing "croc"-like phytosaurs are an excellent resource for creating the denizens of a menacing menagerie.

Beyond that, there are flying reptiles of all sizes and shapes: the pterosaurs (see figure 10-7). We discuss more on these creatures a bit later.

The strange predinosaur therapsids of the Permian period seemed to be as much mammal as they were reptile (see figure 10-8). Permian South Africa could produce the terrible *gorgonopsids*, ferocious, 10-foot long eating machines and great subjects for characterization.

Once we've determined what ancient beast we want to develop, we must then decide what elements of prehistoric animal anatomy we want to use in our creation of creatures. Tail, jowl, eyes, scales, or teeth? Or perhaps what we want is an odd, long, and toothy overall feel to the figure, as seen in the appearance of a nothosaur (Figure 10-9).

Figure 10-7

Weird pterosaur: Thalassodromeus.

Figure | 10-8 |

Inostrancevia alexandri: a mammal-like reptile.

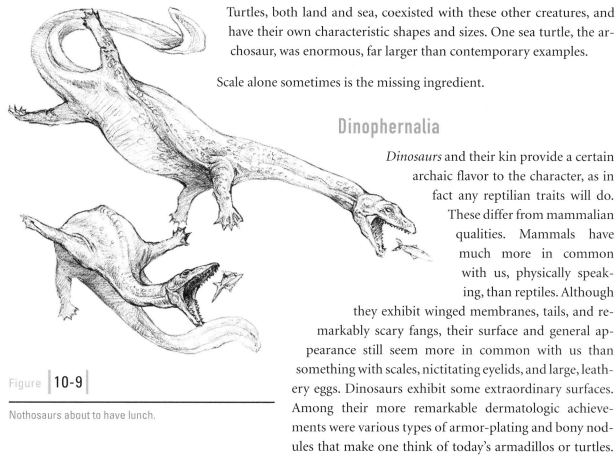

Figure | 10-9 |

Nothosaurs about to have lunch.

Turtles, both land and sea, coexisted with these other creatures, and have their own characteristic shapes and sizes. One sea turtle, the archosaur, was enormous, far larger than contemporary examples.

Scale alone sometimes is the missing ingredient.

Dinophernalia

Dinosaurs and their kin provide a certain archaic flavor to the character, as in fact any reptilian traits will do. These differ from mammalian qualities. Mammals have much more in common with us, physically speaking, than reptiles. Although they exhibit winged membranes, tails, and remarkably scary fangs, their surface and general appearance still seem more in common with us than something with scales, nictitating eyelids, and large, leathery eggs. Dinosaurs exhibit some extraordinary surfaces. Among their more remarkable dermatologic achievements were various types of armor-plating and bony nodules that make one think of today's armadillos or turtles. These skin surface variations make for inviting artistic mayhem when applied to a character that needs some kind of interesting outer covering. One might try a combination of large and small scale platelets, or even a pebble-like skin reminiscent of *Iguanodon*.

Other relatives of the *Iguanodon*, such as *Lambeosaurus*, *Corythosaurus*, and *Parasaurolophus*, had odd heads and crests probably used for mating and courtship display. Their bodies most likely were usually on all fours, but had the capability of being upright to feed. Others have been found with extensive nesting sites complete with eggs and newly hatched and unhatched young.

In addition to the aforementioned details, we may extrapolate that older reptiles had throaty sacs like frogs, spiny extrusions like iguanas, and coloration adapted to forest or open land, that is, camouflage. Savage claws on feet and paws can provide a character with an anatomic arsenal. Applying some of these more "dangerous" traits from a prehistoric predator like a *Deinonychus* could give a character some extra zing. Elements from a *Charcarodontosaurus* skull (say, the jaws with their terrifying teeth) could enhance an alien head, rendering it carnivorous, instead of just menacing. This is a newly discovered meat-eater from Africa the size of a Tyrannosaurus rex! Another enormous newly found theropod is the *Giganotosaurus* from Argentina. Other more gracile theropods such as *Afrovenator abakensis* and *Deltadromeus agilis* have been found, giving an eerie, almost greyhound feel to such dangerous animals.

The comparison of extant reptile traits with those of dinosaurs shows the visual advantage of utilizing the prehistoric animal's anatomy as character reference. The difference between a theropod skull and that of a contemporary alligator is both size and structure. The dinosaur, with its monstrous dentition (teeth) and gaping fenestrae (holes), has a look that is not as recognizable as the elements of the more familiar swamp-dwelling carnivore. All the other reptilian critters mentioned also have an eerie, somehow alien sense to their appearances that are no longer common in contemporary animals, such as inordinate scale, bony protuberances, and steak knives for teeth.

Crocodile-like reptiles from the dinosaur era, the *phytosaurs*, while similar in many ways to our contemporary swamp and river dwellers, add to the dangerous feel of our own crocs and 'gators with their size, robust snouts and teeth, and remarkable surfaces. Some of these fellows were 50 feet long. One croc relative recently found from the dinosaur era was the massive, 40-foot long *Sarchosuchus*, with a bulb on its snout and a size that would threaten *any* animal.

Figure **10-10**

Archelon.

Another way of using ancient reptiles (and any other extinct animal, for that matter) is to give the character we are designing a similar overall structure. For this we need at least a skeleton view or some valid reconstruction to look at. As we have already mentioned, some reptiles had strange or incredibly robust appearances that could enhance our character's appearance through configuration. A *Camarasaurus*, as well as other enormous plant-eating sauropods, had such chunky and massive bodies and legs that they would redefine a character or creature character completely if we applied the same length-to-diameter ratios to their limbs and bodies. In plain language, a really stocky leg combined with great length makes for a powerful impact. The feet and even extrapolated skin could be included as well. Other wild examples of these long-necked animals were *Brachiosaurus* and *Diplodocus*. Their bulk alone provides (and provided) artists with a wonderful scale exaggeration to work from.

Fins and sails have found their way onto many reptiles backs. Early in the reptile era, before the dinosaurs, *Dimetrodon* and *Edaphosaurus* had huge, apparently heat-regulating sails on their backs. Later carnivorous dinosaurs, such as the enormous *Tyrannosaurus rex*-sized *Spinosaurus* and *Acrocanthosaurus* had sails as well.

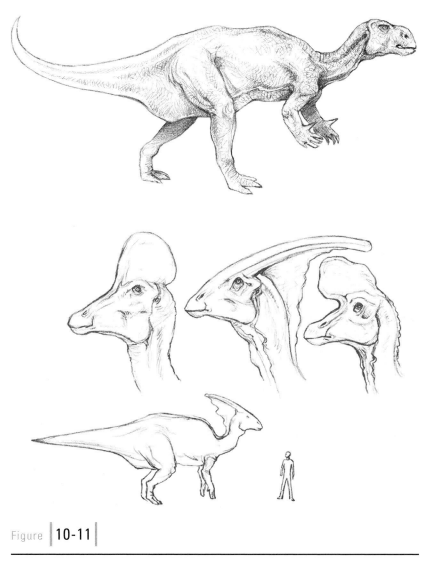

Figure | 10-11 |

Odd-crested and otherwise interesting dinosaurs.

Other representatives of this group include the *Ceratosaur*, with a horn on the nose, *Dilophosaurs*, with crests on their heads, and *Carnotaurs*, with oddly bull-like heads complete with horns! *Suchomimus*, found in Africa recently, sported a body like a theropod and almost crocodile-like head. The forward leaning postures now known to be correct for most theropods like *Tyrannosaurus rex* or *Allosaurus* could be combined with digitigrade (walking on their toes) legs/feet and employed on some creature, where a distinctly mobile look is needed. Poses possible with these body structures can also be effective design elements. In these cases, we are applying known anatomic elements to unknown creatures in order to create the idea that they are "biologically legitimate," that is, these imagined critters have anatomies that seem real to us because we have seen their like in extant living animals.

Figure 10-12

Menacing meat-eaters of the Mesozoic.

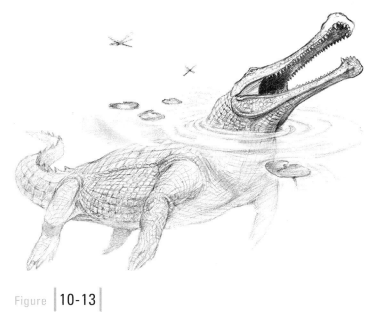

Figure | 10-13 |

Sarchosuchus.

Feathers and Color and Skin . . .oh my!

The physical appearance of vertebrates is necessarily caused by and is based on their skeletal and muscular systems. Inasmuch as anatomy is thus defined, it is possible to arrive at reasonably accurate reconstructions of prehistoric creatures based on comparative anatomy: not only observing the fossil remnants of ancient critters but also looking at the make-up of extant animals and applying their anatomic reference to their archaic relatives. For instance, large terrestrial mammals such as rhinos and elephants have folds of skin at limb joints that suggest flexibility. This premise could certainly be applied to ancient relatives of these beasties. Studying not only the anatomy but also the environment of animals relates to how they've adapted to exist successfully. These concepts can be applied to imaginary character and their habitats.

Surface structures and elements such as skin texture, coloration, and the possible existence of feathers (or feather-like structures) on extinct fauna is another whole "can of worms."

Fossil evidence of exterior anatomic features of prehistoric creatures, subject to the whimsy of the fossil record, ranges from significant to nonexistent. The availability of fossilized castings of skin, for instance, has given researchers a vital look at the outer surfaces of different types of prehistoric animals. The (mummified) remains of dinosaur skin have been found in fossil form for a number of species. Skin fossils from the gigantic sauropod Diplodocus sport a pattern of tiny bumps. There is fossil evidence that certain species of diplodocid and other sauropods had not only dermal spines but also bony scutes, which tend to put off the notion that these giant herbivorous animals were covered with gray, wrinkly elephant skin.

The dermal covering of the hadrosaur genus *Edmontosaurus* had a pebbled, leathery surface. Armored dinosaur species sported a menacing array of spikes, horns, and osteoderms that present exciting visual possibilities for character development. Various species of dinosaurs sported a variety of patterns for scales and tubercles: some small, as a general surface covering, and others larger, as grouped patches. Some experts speculate that scale patterns may have been enhanced for display (or even camouflage) by coloration.

The origin of epidermal skin scales in dinosaurs as a means of preventing desiccation in a terrestrial environment is a theory accepted by many paleontologists.

The direct relationship of dinosaurs, for instance, to birds and reptiles gives the character designer ideas for existing resources to observe while attempting to reconstruct the outer coverings of prehistoric beasties, or create skin for a new character based on this information. Looking at bird skin and feathers as a resource for decking out dinosaurs may not be as far off as you would imagine. Palaeontologic study over the past couple of decades has put forth the theory that dinosaurs are so closely related to birds that they should, in fact, be classified as avians.

The exposed derma of the ostrich, turkey, and cassowary are replete with interesting wrinkles, follicular bumps, and skin folds. The legs of birds, especially prominent in those of the large terrestrial variety, have protective "shin" and toe scales. Feathers are modified scales and fossil evidence preserving traces of fibrous, integumentary structures suggest that some dinosaurs may have been feathered or decked out with a "featheroid" covering.

Coloration and patterns for extinct animal skin (or fur) is a considerably more subjective issue. It is impossible to derive any direct evidence about the coloration of dinosaurs or other extinct fauna through the fossil record. We must therefore don our hound's-tooth deerstalker cap and search for clues in the form of circumstantial evidence and the comparative study of colors and patterns in extant critters.

There are two primary reasons for the development of patterns and coloration in animals and birds: camouflage and display. Predators need to hide their approach as they stalk their prey, while prey animals must be equipped to avoid becoming dinner (or brunch) for local carnivores. Animals also use color as a part of their repertoire for attracting mates. Both are key elements in species survival.

Now if animals (or their prey) can't see in color, that factor will certainly modify how color has been adapted into their camouflage/

Figure 10-14

Sauropods.

Figure | 10-15 |

Sailback beasties.

display systems. Some animal eyes are missing some or all of the cone cells that we humans use to perceive color. (Mind you, we are talking about the lens-and-retina vertebrate eye.) If the animal is brightly colored, then it is likely that that species sees in color. The exception would be nocturnal animals, which use rods (another kind of receptor cell in the eye) on the retina to distinguish colors. Most mammals see in color.

As color vision is known in modern birds, their relationship with dinosaurs, especially theropods and coelurosaurs, suggests that the latter critters may have been so equipped.

While most dinosaurs had eyes oriented on the sides of their heads, giving them a limited field of vision, certain carnivorous dinosaur genuses (like *Tyrannosaurus* and *Deinonychus*) had skulls with orbits suggesting their eyes had a forward-facing orientation that would give them stereoscopic vision. Such binocular vision is very useful for predators who gain an advantage through being able to perceive depth and distance with reasonable accuracy.

Recently, university researchers have inferred the DNA protein sequence for the vision pigment, rhodopsin, from dinosaur fossil information. This discovery suggests that archosaurs (dinosaur ancestors) may have had low-light vision.

Camouflage adaptations develop differently, depending on the animal's habitat, physiology, and behavior. What works for a tiger may not work for a toad. Certainly the simplest disguise technique for animals is to match the color (or value) of their background. Animals will not evolve camouflage modifications that do not assist their survival. In other words, a prey animal will not adopt "color-matching" camouflage if its natural enemy is colorblind.

It is interesting to note that very large, extant herbivores (rhinoceroses and elephants) tend to be dull in color with no skin patterns. Because big proboscideans and ungulates neither hunt nor have natural enemies as adults (due to their sheer size), they do not require the protection afforded by natural camouflage. Besides, it's difficult trying not to be seen when you're as big as the side of a barn!

In hairless critters, such as reptiles, fish, and amphibians, the coloration is affected by biochromes (microscopic natural pigments that alter coloration chemically) in living surface cells in the skin, or chromatophores, deeper-level pigment cells. With furry creatures, it's a different story. Because fur, like fingernails, is dead tissue, it has no living color-change cells. Animals like the arctic fox (brown fur in spring/summer and white in winter) must produce a whole new coat of fur thanks to chromatophores that affect fur color. These fur changes are hormonally stimulated by change in temperature or in the amount of daylight. This process also applies to some species of birds.

| NOTE |

Testing. . .1, 2, 3

How is the vision of modern animals tested? Behavioral tests are a common method developed to test the visual perception of animals. On a more anatomic level, researchers use an electroretinogram. An electroretinogram is a test that records the activity of cells in the eye in response to light flashes via a sensor attached to the cornea. With this test, researchers can tell if photoreceptors are responding to the light stimulus. This exam can be coupled with an electroencephalogram to determine whether the primary visual cortex of the brain is also responding to the visual information.

| NOTE |

Ring Around the Sclera!

Scleral ossicles, a ring of bony plates encircling the eye inside the sclera, are found amongst representatives from extant reptiles and birds, along with members of the Dinosauria. It has been hypothesized that the ossicles reinforce the "kink" where the cornea and sclera meet and retard damage that could be done by intraocular pressure.

Ossicles in birds, for example, allow the animal to adjust the shape of its cornea to alter the focusing power of the eye. Cool, huh?

| NOTE |

Ever notice that baby animals often have different coloration from their parents? They are usually more "camouflaged" than adults of their species. Why? Young animals have not yet fully developed the defense mechanisms of the grown-ups, like horns, antlers, and fleetness of foot, so they rely heavily on hiding.

The coloration changes as the animal grows and matures.

Some critters, like chameleons and cuttlefish, can actively restrict and expand their chromatophores via special muscles to provide a rather instantaneous color change. Certain invertebrates deposit pigment derived from their food sources directly into their skin so as to match the color of their supper, as it were.

Pattern variation in animal dermal/fur coverings is key element in the camouflage of herding animals. Zebras have "disruptive coloration": patches (in this case, stripes) of contrasting colors that break up the visual outline of the animal. This phenomenon is magnified by grouping the zebras, making it difficult for predators to figure out where one zebra ends and the next begins. Stripes and blotches also break up an animal's profile in environments like plains of tall grass or in a forest with dappled lighting. Additionally helpful for the zebra is the fact that lions are colorblind.

Following are some examples of extant animal patterns and how they might apply to extinct animals.

Mesozoic Mix-up?

The synthesis of elements for creating characters need not be limited to compositing organic entities. The overall configuration (that is, the overall look) of a prehistoric animal can be borrowed or "morphed" onto inanimate as well as living things. Imagine, if you will, a cyborg submarine that has *mosasaur* body parts grafted onto it! *Mosasaurs* such as *Tylosaurus* were marine reptiles that grew to 30 feet in length or more, terrifying the shallow inland oceans for millions of years. Along with the *mosasaurs*, the *plesiosaurs*, *pliosaurs* (short necked *plesiosaurs*), and *icthyosaurs* gorged themselves on fish (and each other) in a toothy competition in the seas. Some of these animals reached 50 feet in length, and some *plesiosaurs* (such as the *Elasmosaur*) had incredible, elongated necks attached to simpler, paddling body forms. *Liopleurodon*, a *pliosaur* and star of a recent animated documentary about prehistoric fauna from the United Kingdom, grew to enormous size, and had possibly the largest head ever for a carnivorous critter. One of the most fish-like dinosaurian relatives ever to roam the seas of the Mesozoic, the dolphin-like icthyosaurs, searched the oceans for prey. One variety, *Shonisaurus*, grew to 50 feet in length, an astonishing size for such an animal. Interestingly, the icthyosaurs gave birth live to their young (one skeleton was buried with the baby just emerging!).

Aircraft would have an extremely appealing and almost alive sense if they were "married" to *pterosaurs* in their appearance. This would be another example of a hybrid design possibility us-

Figure |10-16|

More menacing meat-eaters of the Mesozoic.

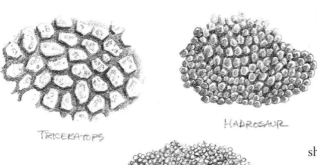

TRICERATOPS

HADROSAUR

DIPLODOCUS

Figure **10-17**

Dinosaur skin.

ing animate and inanimate sources. *Pterosaurs* were the first vertebrate animals to fly with any skill, and had many representatives, from the smaller, toothy *rhamphorhyncoids* to *Quetzalcoatlus* and *Pteranodon*, great soaring cousins of these smaller flyers. Pterosaurs had a wild variety of crests, beak, and head shapes, and tooth configurations. The different shapes coincided with their differing life-styles. Some were more land oriented. Others scooped fish from the oceans, much the same as some sea birds do today. Pterosaurs probably evolved from simpler gliding reptiles such as *Archaeopteryx*, which looks like a wild combination of lizard and bird rolled into one. Other possibly feathered early reptiles have been found recently in China. Flight for the *pterosaurs* was possible due to their extremely light bodies. An elongated finger from their "hands" allowed a membrane to be stretched from this outward point back to their hind legs (we think in most cases). This wing was their tool for flight.

The possibilities of adapting these anatomic shapes are limited only by source and imagination.

The Spider that Ate Hoboken

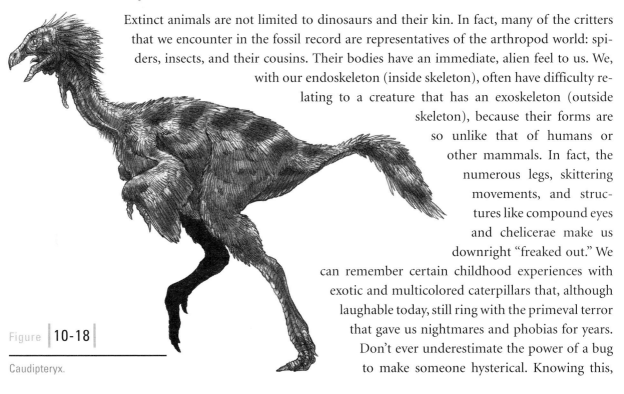

Extinct animals are not limited to dinosaurs and their kin. In fact, many of the critters that we encounter in the fossil record are representatives of the arthropod world: spiders, insects, and their cousins. Their bodies have an immediate, alien feel to us. We, with our endoskeleton (inside skeleton), often have difficulty relating to a creature that has an exoskeleton (outside skeleton), because their forms are so unlike that of humans or other mammals. In fact, the numerous legs, skittering movements, and structures like compound eyes and chelicerae make us downright "freaked out." We can remember certain childhood experiences with exotic and multicolored caterpillars that, although laughable today, still ring with the primeval terror that gave us nightmares and phobias for years. Don't ever underestimate the power of a bug to make someone hysterical. Knowing this,

Figure **10-18**

Caudipteryx.

Figure | 10-19 |

Figure | 10-19 |

Decorative.

our search back in time reveals insects and arachnids (those other leggy creatures like spiders, lobsters, and centipedes) of both scale and anatomic design every bit as frightening and fascinating as reptiles of the Mesozoic. The *Megarachne*, a spider-like eight-legger from the *Pennsylvania*n period forests millions of years ago, spanned 20 inches from leg tip to leg tip. It probably ate whatever it could get its, well, legs on. Some other arachnids reached several feet in length and looked quite hideous. There was an enormous giant millipede that reached 6 to 8 feet in length. Each of these gives multitudes of visual ingredients for character formation. Pterygotus, a 7½-foot long sort of scorpion-like animal, ruled the shallow seas.

Arthropod's segmentation, hard outer surface, and odd proportions can be used in characters or creatures needing an alien feel, or even a quasi-mechanical appearance. Part of what horrifies is, we think, this almost soulless, utterly inhuman look

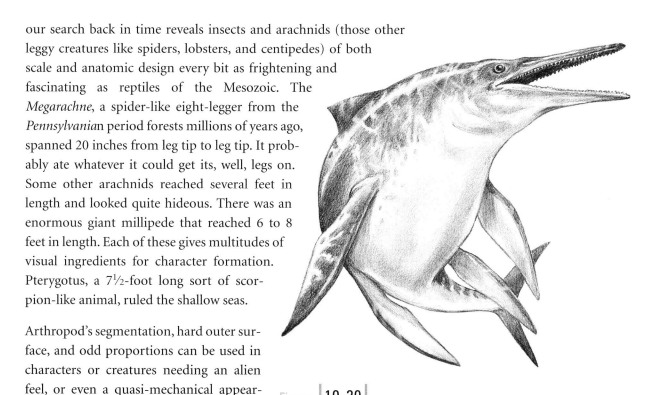

Figure | 10-20 |

Shonisaurus.

Figure **10-21**

Fantastic flying reptiles.

that insects have. They appear to be a kind of biomorphic machine, and a malevolent one at that. The dragonflies and mayflies that we see hovering in antic acrobatics over our swimming pools were preceded in history by enormous versions. One antediluvian gliding dragonfly (*Meganeura*) had a wingspan of 2 feet.

Scaling up, or humanizing, such a creature seems reminiscent of B-movie horror flicks from the 1950s about radiation-mutated insects.

The difference here is that the ancient "bugs" actually existed. This type of animal could be used whole, unaltered, for some designs. Its scale alone gives one the chills. Relating other normally scaled characters to such a monstrosity would give the scene being portrayed an ominously surreal aspect.

Warm and Fuzzy (or not)

Mammals are by no means useless for archaic resources. Many of the extinct mammals found in the fossil record seem, in their own way, as bizarre as the strange Permian reptiles or flying reptiles with huge head crests and outsized "wings." Among these are *saber-toothed cats*, *creodonts*, *mesonychids*, and early *proboscideans* (elephants).

All of these mammalian groups have representatives that could give a nice artistic touch to a character or creature design. The saber-toothed cats (called, improperly, tigers) like *Smilodon* or *Homotherium* had such outlandish canines that the teeth themselves become the subject, due to their relative hugeness in otherwise "'normal'" jaws. *Barbourofelis* and *Machairodon* are other, stunning examples of the saber-toothed cat type.

Mesonychids, a primitive mammal group, included the *Andrewsarchus*, which is known only from its skull—but what a skull! Fully 3 feet long, it is the largest mammalian carnivore skull ever found. This prompts us to think perhaps in terms of both the shape of the skull and its proportional relation to the rest of the body to define a very menacing aspect to one of the largest terrestrial predators in the fossil record. Another monstrous omnivore is *Megistotherium*, with a skull as large as the *Andrewsarchus*.

In character design, proportion is just as important as the individual elements themselves. By giving the viewer an outlandish skull or head (such as an *Andrewsarchus*-like one) atop a more mundane sized body, the artist has introduced a sense of deliberate imbalance and emphasis upon the function of the head as opposed to the rest of the character/creature.

Figure **10-22**

Megarachne and Pterygotus.

Figure **10-23**

Meganeura.

Some early transitional sea mammals had bodies and heads that only a committee could dream up. They could provide unique ideas for futuristic or alien mammal-like creatures.

The largest land mammal of all time, the *Indricotherium*, was a type of hornless rhino creature that stood 18 feet at the *shoulder*. *Arsinoitherium*, a huge double-horned rhino-like animal provides another outsized source for images. Various early primitive elephants had shovel tusks and other odd configurations that seem almost impossible to imagine as having possibly existed.

Once again, the sheer scale of a creature design could be borrowed in the context of an already known entity. Massive, elephantine legs would be quite something on a pig or bovine critter. Its front shoulder area, if borrowed from the *Indricotherium* and so being higher than the rear pelvic zone, could also become the model for similar, weighty creatures.

Marsupials, mammals that give birth to tiny, barely recognizable infants that live in the females' pouches for some time until they have matured, have come into the spotlight lately, as Australia has given us some remarkable new fossils of extinct, large, marsupial lion-like animals (*Thylacoleo*) and 9-foot tall flat-faced kangaroos (*Procoptodon goliah*). Some kangaroos were carnivorous, and there was even a marsupial saber-toothed "tiger," the *Thylacosmilus*.

Amphibious Assault or Warts and All

If your taste runs to slimy and grotesque, then ancient amphibians are your cup of tea. *Eryops*, *Seymouria*, *Icthyostega*, or *Diplocaulus* (not to be confused with the similarly spelled dinosaur, *Diplodocus*) provide almost unreal visions of squat water- and land-dwelling animals.

Besides often being carnivores (and effective ones at that, for the time), these beings exhibited such features as enormous,

Figure | 10-24 |

Bug-eyed monster: human & dragonfly

Figure | 10-25 |

Saber-toothed cats.

flattened heads, or legs articulating sideways from the body, plus flattened or squat body types just begging to be part of some water world creature invention.

In their case, the locomotion itself suggests many possible adaptations to a creature design. The primitive, out-jutting legs, moving with deliberate pace, would give a kind of ponderous, menacing drama to an animal. In the water, their ability to swim more swiftly would invert this into a potentially fast, lethal animal. Modern amphibians have glistening, patterned skin, and this could be extrapolated into these extinct forms safely.

Wonderful Water Weirdness

Other possible sources for image ideas include prehistoric fish, squid, ammonites, nautiloids, trilobites, and other sea dwellers. Because of their evolution in water, these animals have quite different body designs from terrestrial animals. Some are almost entirely water, like jellyfish. These are nearly transparent, sometimes deadly colonies of cells that have an unearthly beauty to them.

Figure | 10-26 |

Andrewsarchus (top right and bottom) and megistotherium (top left).

Some ancient fish, like *Dunkleosteus*, had enormous heads and bodies, plated with armor, and possessing jaws that were themselves sharpened and jagged instead of containing conventional teeth.

Other armored fish include *Hemicyclaspis* and *Bothryolepis*; the names alone warrant a look. Besides being among the more terrifying animals to grace this earth, the sheer novelty of their appearance alone would lend itself to creature design.

Some prehistoric sea dwelling creatures have already found their way into some major studio designs and animated motion pictures. The animated Disney film *Fantasia* is one example that shows various early fish, trilobites and other prehistoric sea creatures. *Trilobites*, relatively familiar to fossil lovers and laymen alike, give an unusual, three-part division of the body lengthwise, as opposed to the insect, which is in three parts head to abdomen.

Figure | 10-27 |

Therocephalus
imaginarius.

Sea-floor dwellers for millions of years, the trilobites came in various sizes, from fingernail size to a yard long. Their unusual organization gives rise to design ideas unlike contemporary animals. Some of the tentacled creatures had shells that curled into enormous, several-foot diameter spiral discs, or 10-foot long pointed tubes (*nautiloids*). These cephalopods (literally "head/foot") evolved into an astonishing variety of shelled (and unshelled), tentacled monstrosities.

One shark apparently had a curled, jaw-like apparatus with saw teeth. Another, *Orthacanthus*, an extinct fresh water shark, had a spike jutting out of the back of its skull. The ancient shark *Carcharodon megalodon* probably was 50 feet long, and had a mouth several feet in diameter when open.

A good rule of thumb to use when choosing prehistoric creatures to develop in visual imagery would be to pick the weirdest and least used or seen. The overall expanse of natural oddness in the fossil record far outweighs the number of prehistoric beasts known to the general populace. Virtually everyone knows what a *Triceratops* looks like. Few folks are likely familiar with *Placerias gigas*, the lumbering, tusked dicynodont: a veritable "bovine" of the *Triassic* period.

Figure | 10-28 |

Strange proto-whale
beast: Ambulocetus.

Figure | **10-29** |

Arsinoitherium and Indricotherium.

Birds of a Feather

Prehistoric birds supply another arena of visual source material. Flightless birds such as the carnivorous ostrich-sized *Diatryma* and *Phororhacos* terrorized ancient plains.

While some of these flightless birds were not carnivorous, they reached gigantic sizes, as with the New Zealand *Moa*, which reached upwards of 12 feet in height at its greatest. Similarly, the Australian *Dromonrnis stirtoni*, weighed an unbelievable 1100 pounds. *Teratornis*, an extinct soaring bird, may have had a wingspan of 25 feet. This archaic relative of the vulture is a frequent fossil find in California's ancient tar pits, giving us some clues to its predatory or carrion-eating habits. A wonderfully animated gigantic version of *Teratornis* (or its ilk) can be seen converted into the guise of a stop-motion creature by Ray Harryhausen in the film "Clash of the Titans."

The Story of Og

People are not exempt from prehistory. Fossil evidence is abundant of a myriad of fascinating "semihumans" and distant relations. Whatever your take on the theological/metaphysical implications of these "creatures," their fossils and reconstructions provide another resource path for the creative artist. Primitive humans and humanoids are found in relative abundance. One of the chief figures in this collection is the *Neanderthal*, an apparently separate species of hominoid, but a very close cousin to us "modern humans," also known as *Homo sapiens*. Other names that might be recognizable to the casual investigator of man's prehistory are *Australop-*

Figure | **10-30**

Procoptodon goliah and Thylacosmilus.

ithecines, more ape-like relatives whose existence dates from millions of years ago, and *Pithecanthropus*, the "Java Man," an antediluvian character that caught the public eye in the early part of the twentieth century. Among the more remarkable fossils that are found amongst the extinct members of the primate families are *Gigantopithecus blackii*, which we have previously discussed, and *Theropithecus oswaldi*, a marvelous gorilla-sized baboon.

Neanderthals have been well reconstructed, showing a distinct series of anatomic traits: large brain case, large nose, long-headed/short-chinned humanoid skull, and very stout limbs. Their brain case, interestingly enough, was slightly larger than our own. *Cro-Magnon* man of 50,000 to 100,000 years ago was essentially identical in form to modern man, but some early hominids and relatives had flatter heads, large protruding eyebrow ridges (as did Neanderthal), and smaller brains. Their overall look, while human-like, was defined by heavy and more primitive facial features.

Figure | 10-31 |

Eryops, Seymouria, Icthyostega, and Diplocaulus.

Early reconstructions of Neanderthals in both popular culture and the scientific community have often resulted in a brutally apish humanoid; a veritable simian in rudimentary skin garments. Whereas a living Neanderthal (dressed in modern-day garb) may be able to blend in with a bustling crowd of New Yorkers, the archetype "caveman" is often more suitable to characterization because of the exaggerated features. Even so, we must always observe the anatomy and current scientific reconstruction of fossil beings before modifying their appearance. A basis in reality always serves as the best foundation for character creation.

There has been an explosion of hominid finds in East Africa in the past few years, and re-dated fossil finds in Indonesian Java are now estimated at a remarkable 500,000 to 1,000,000 years old! In venerable Georgia (formerly of the U.S.S.R., not U.S.A.), finds have been found of *Homo erectus* that are a half million years old. All of these exhibit the beetling brow, smaller brain case, and (when actually found) generally smaller bodies, although one remarkable skeleton in Africa has a "primitive" hominid head on a modern human sized body! Truth is stranger than fiction, as the saying goes.

Figure | **10-32** |

Dunkleosteus: armored and dangerous.

The obvious relationship of their more primitive features and possible character design is clear: "Savagery" or human variation present available elements that stem from our own fossil record.

Postosuchus from Teeth to Tuchus

Characterization is a key part of fantasy design work as it applies to creatures, and is an oft forgotten piece in the development of prehistoric fauna as characters. These animals, as part of the imagery that is relating a story to the viewer, must be visually enticing. In our experience, the artistic question in this scenario has two distinct elements: Do you develop a prehistoric beast solely based upon the very latest scientific data (yes, if you're creating a reconstruction for scientific literature or display or for science animation and illustration) or do you create a "symbolic" form of the animal based on our general idea about the appearance of the creature? The answer is neither.

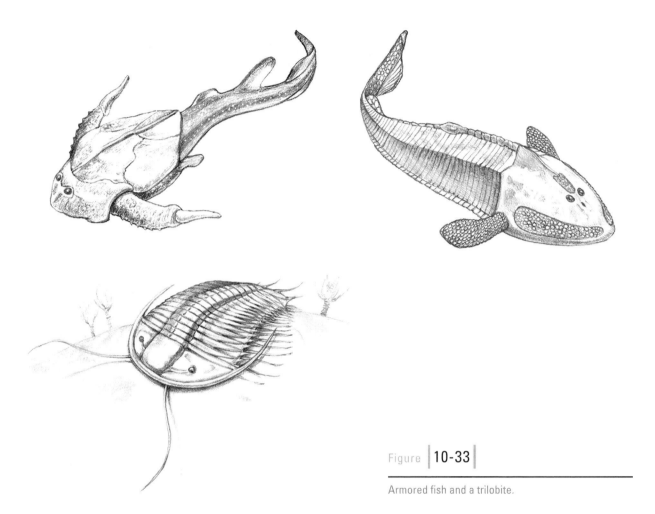

Figure **10-33**

Armored fish and a trilobite.

The first step is to gather available research and reference materials on the particular animal. The next step is to address the problem of character design and how it applies to this creature. "Characterization" means defining and designing a creature that is different, unique, and appropriate in the visual media for which it is being produced. For instance, let's imagine that an artist is designing prehistoric characters for an animated film that takes place in the late *Triassic* of Arizona. What type of creature would make an appropriate villain? Well, the top terrestrial predator of the time, *Postosuchus*, a predominantly quadrupedal archosaur with a mouthful of nasty teeth, might be a likely candidate.

Figure **10-34**

Nautiloid.

Once we've rendered a basic drawing of a *Postosuchus*, if that's what we chose, we can modify it to suit our character-driven needs. Scowling brow ridges and larger teeth can make him look meaner. Perhaps this *Postosuchus* has been in a fight with a predatory competitor and is missing an eye or the end of his tail.

By taking our own reasonable license with some anatomic details, we can retain the biological integrity of our prehistoric carnivore, while adding elements that make him an individual. These are "character traits": physiologic (and often psychological) qualities that give a person or creature a distinct persona. Our *Postosuchus* is now recognizable and different from others of his kind.

When animation artists work on a film such as Disney's "Dinosaur," they are responsible not only for creating dinosaurs and extinct animals that are physically acceptable representatives of the genuses or species, but also for creating good characters that have audience appeal and can tell a story. Hyper-realistic dinosaurs would have been ineffective as "actors" in such a film. In the case of "Dinosaur," the characters had to be able to deliver dialogue, which is another whole can of worms to open. Remember: Characters drive the story.

Now, we'll contradict ourselves by mentioning that the animated dinosaurs from the "Jurassic Park" films would have been ineffectual if characterized in a similar manner. These beasts were essentially forces of nature in creature form, acting as the antagonists (usually) in each film—an important story role, no doubt, but not "acted out" in the same fashion as the animated antics of the aforementioned Disney flick. The animated "Jurassic Park" dinosaurs acted as we imagine their extinct counterparts would have in similarly proscribed scenarios.

Figure | **10-35**

Before Jaws: Orthacanthus and Carcharodon megalodon.

"What Now?" Revisited

To reiterate, for using all of this enormous, varied visual information, we recommend first getting good images of these creatures, and then, in sketchbooks, trying to combine differing elements from one creature to another. This synthesis of looks, as we have spoken of before, is something like the "meat and potatoes" of fantasy design. By combining unexpected parts of differing species (especially extinct ones) as we have indicated, a totally new and fascinating being evolves. Selecting various elements from prehistoric beasts and applying them to "generic" figures, or substituting them for already existing parts of a design follow our synthesis plan that we outlined in Chapter Five. Exterior anatomic elements, such as surfaces and textures, in general follow this same methodology. The ability to successfully make

Figure | **10-36** |

Triceratops and Placerias gigas.

Figure | **10-37** |

Terror birds!

Figure | 10-38 |

More ancient avians.

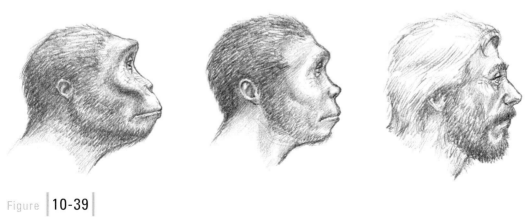

Figure | 10-39 |

Hominid heads.

Figure | **10-40** |

Neanderthal woman.

Figure |10-41|

Postosuchus

something really new is exciting, and quite frankly, a bit ego-inflating for artists. This method of using prehistoric resources is one way to accomplish that aim.

Ready, Set. . .Draw!

Obviously, the culmination of all this research into prehistoric monstrosities must be the development of some visual design. Following, we will show the application process of prehistoric imagery to a character design drawing.

This is our procedure:

1. We first create a series of rough "thumbnail" sketches to begin developing a visual idea for our character. A synthesis of the anatomies of a variety of prehistoric critters provides the basis for our ideas. Variations in scale and configuration are keys to preliminary design process.

2. Based on a chosen "thumbnail," we create a concept drawing to enlarge and refine our sketchy and cursory original drawing. Try enlarging your thumbnails on a photocopier and tracing them as a basis for starting concept studies.

Figure **10-42**

Postosuchus revisited.

At this point, we want to address key character design elements that we can modify and enhance, such as physical scale, texture, anatomy, and props. Our character here is sort of a pseudo-dinosaurian centaur. We can change the size of relative parts (upper torso, head, lower body/limbs), modify his or her weaponry, add or subtract horns, scales, and teeth, and define anatomic details as they apply to this conglomerate critter. In this case, we've grabbed constituent parts from a variety of prehistoric sources: "humanized" head/upper torso from a theropod mixed with a *Dimetrodon* undercarriage, and a few tail spikes from a *stegosaur*.

3. At this point, we've refined our character concept sketch into a fully developed black-and-white illustration. As you may recall from our earlier discussion, refining the character drawing means cleaning up unnecessary line work, smudges, or scribbles, defining necessary line work, and making final drawing changes. The last step is to render the image in its final form: in this case a clean pencil drawing. Voila!

Lastly, if we take one of our previous critters, *Dimetrodon*, and "monsterize" it (by changing the scale of various body parts, giving it an upright stance and a smidgeon of artistic license), we have a beast capable of trashing Tokyo with the best of 'em.

"DIMETROTAUR" THUMBNAILS

Figure | 10-43 |

"Thumbnail" character sketches.

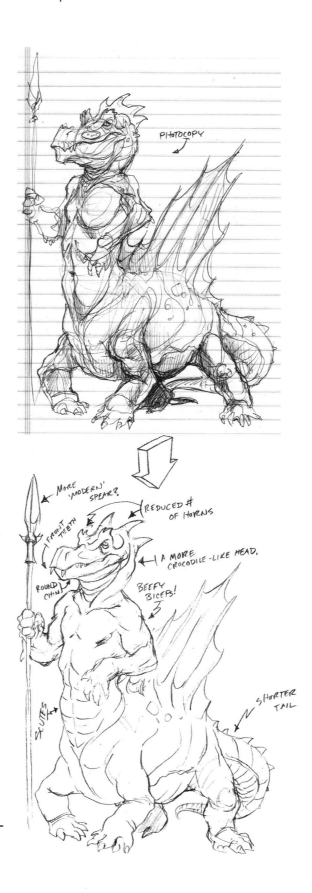

Figure | 10-44 |

Rough character sketches refined.

Figure | 10-45 |

Dimetrotaur.

Figure | 10-46 |

Run away! It's Dimetrozilla!

SUMMARY

In Chapter Ten, we discussed the use of prehistoric fauna as an example of one type of category research and application. It is, in itself, a wonderful visual springboard for creating unique character and creature designs. Epitomizing the phrase "Truth is stranger than fiction," ancient animals often offer a weird variety of anatomic structure that provide interesting visual material in this designing process. The size, ferocity, and "alien" aspects of many prehistoric creatures make them prime monstrous character or creature candidates with some minor modifications. Additional modifications can further "characterize" such creatures. The concept of mixing, matching, and synthesizing physical elements of ancient animals can be an important and powerful tool in character and creature design.

exercises

1. Visit a museum collection that displays mounted fossil animals and do a variety of sketches of the skeletons from different vantage points. You might even include some museum visitors in the sketch to show relative scale!

2. Research an extinct reptile, insect, amphibian arachnid, mammal, or other animal, finding good visuals from book and internet sources. Analyze the general anatomy, structure, and surface detail and then draw a detailed restoration of the creature based on the gathered information.

3. Draw a series of character thumbnail sketches of the animal chosen in exercise 2. Make modifications to the creature's structure to develop it as a character while maintaining its basic anatomy.

4. Using the sketches from the extinct animal done in exercise 1, apply to and refine the drawing into a final design for the character. Create a "turn-around" model sheet of the final character design depicting four different views of the creature.

5. Try making hybrid variations on extinct animals in thumbnail sketch form: change, add, mix, or edit out parts of each animal. Don't be too conservative; the more ideas tried the better. Try changing one variable (head, legs, coloration, etc.) at a time, seeing how it affects your own character or creature.

6. Build your own character design-related vocabulary by consulting a dictionary or encyclopedia to look up any unfamiliar words regarding prehistoric creatures that you've run across in Chapter Ten.

in review

1. How do we define characterization as it relates to creature design?

2. Why would extinct (or prehistoric) species give an artist unique visual resources?

3. How does synthesis work in respect to the use of prehistoric animals as visual resources?

4. Name some of the possible kinds of prehistoric animal groups that could be used for character design.

5. How were reptiles, mammals, and birds different from insects, jellyfish, and squids in terms of design for characters?

6. By what two methods can an artist translate prehistoric animal resources into character designs?

research not of this earth: alien design

objectives

Learn about potential alien design types.

Understand how alien designs might vary from standard character design.

Explore the relationship between alien world environments and alien design.

Examine stereotyping in alien design.

Gain an introduction to developmental traits applicable to alien entity design.

Explore alien design project demonstrations.

Learn how comparative anatomy applies to alien character design.

introduction

One of the major arenas of character and creature design is the world of alien creations. By this we mean any character or creature that does not originate from Earth. This obviously covers a lot of territory with numerous possibilities. This chapter gives certain examples and shows how story needs, creative anatomy, and alien environments come together to produce a design product. Designs for alien typologies are driven by the particular needs of a story, script, or scenario. Such designs are constrained by the environment of that alien's origin and its anatomic considerations. A host of other details (intelligence, motive, technology or lack of technology, history) flesh out the particular character or creature. What mainly differentiates an alien character or creature from other creations is its visual (and perhaps functional) uniqueness, that is, how it is different from earthly beings. This chapter explores some of the ways this information can be analyzed and put to use in a character design context.

The concept of "alien" or "extraterrestrial," that is, the way we perceive and visualize the idea, has been pounded into the collective conscious of earth's populace by the massive onslaught of the science-fiction film, TV shows, comic books, and so on. Over the last hundred years, the movie industry and multitudinous reputed UFO and alien sightings have developed pre-existing notions for us as to the appearance of these creatures. This massive backlog of imagery has greatly increased the number of design "rip-offs" and bad stereotypes in the area of alien design.

Xenomorphus Repetitus or Cliché What?

We should probably start by looking at some stereotypical alien design solutions, because this is what most readers are familiar with and use as a starting point for reference. The most well known is probably the so-called grey, a variant of the little green men in flying saucers. A grey is a sentient biped, with a large head, extremely large eyes, small or nonexistent nose, mouth and ears, no hair, thin limbs, and long , slender hands. This being is highly intelligent, flies elaborate spaceships, and is from another planet. As seen on numerous television programs and various films, this character is a derivative of both anecdotal tales of "visitations" and art directors' projections of human form onto an alien personage. This is where we begin our understanding. This character shares most, if not all, of our common human features and anatomy, albeit in somewhat modified form. People transfer human traits to creatures and aliens, both behaviorally and physically. This is called *anthropomorphism*. Much of character design involves this mechanism. In it we attribute qualities that are human based to characters and creatures that are clearly not human. A good example of this would be the animal characters in Disney films who exhibit intelligence, emotional states, and even some physical traits that are derived from human beings.

As a device to create characters, anthropomorphism is a useful one, but it has its drawbacks as well. One advantage is that the audience can identify motives and emotions with which they are familiar, and thus become involved in a story line that otherwise might seem abstract or difficult to understand. The disadvantage is that these characters or creatures can be *too* familiar. Perhaps we really don't want always to hand the audience everything on a platter. Maybe we really need something clearly so un-human in its actions and motives that it presents the element of mystery and anxiety that would make our film/game/television show/illustration more menacing. And this is where the artist, director, and art director need, within the bounds of a script or idea, to come up with a viable solution.

This subject of cliché or stereotypical images is perhaps one of the core ones any artist encounters. How do we, as artists, both create an individually distinct image yet meet the general expectations of a, perhaps, less than sophisticated audience? To this end our entire book is dedicated.

The process of creating designs for alien characters is especially problematic for releasing a host of "imitation demons" to pester and browbeat the character designer. We often fall prey to the tendency to try to create something "cool" or interesting that is derivative of extraterrestrial critters we've seen on TV or in a comic book.

The reality of the situation is that we (as artists) are living in a world of influences. You will experience "design crossover" even unintentionally. Let's say you come up with a reptilian humanoid creature armed with a repertoire of martial arts weapons and suddenly someone draws the conclusion that you're trying to reinvent one of the Teenage Mutant Ninja Turtles! While these things happen, we can offset the probability of being derivative by setting up a procedure for planning the attributes of your alien.

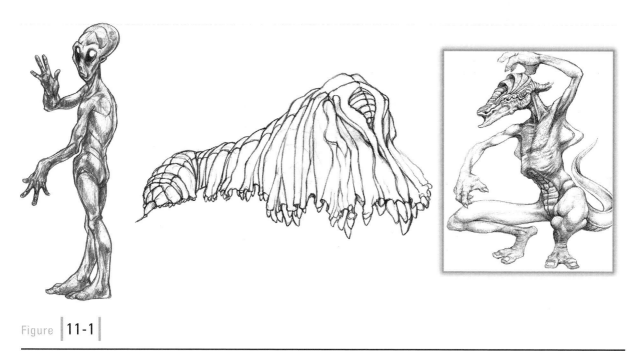

Figure | 11-1 |

Grey alien with non-anthropomorphic/anthropomorphic pals.

Beyond our tendency to rely on specific character solutions, there is an overwhelming tendency to create critters that are carnivorous killing machines, bristling with weapons, claws, fangs, and other dangerous paraphernalia. This concept is overused and represents only a fraction of the possibilities within the realm of alien life forms. Pacifist herbivores come to mind as an alternative.

The groundwork for generating alien creatures is laid by asking a series of questions that define the "natural history" of the character in question. Living organisms do not develop productive forms erroneously or by happenstance. Our assertion for these alien creations is that they have followed a natural selection process (a lá Charles Darwin) or perhaps have been genetically engineered from some other form. You may come up with other ideas for how your creation came into being, but the process of using developmental characteristics always applies.

When, as designers, we begin to address inquiries into the character's habitat and activities, then the creatures begin to design themselves. We'll discuss both potential environmental influences and possible alien designs, taking into account such things as locomotion, habitat, body type, and related issues. The following sections of this chapter are informational categories that the character designer should be aware of when designing aliens.

The Measure of an Inhuman

Alien genres of design are both broader and more ambiguous than earth-bound counterparts. They may be presented as a special case of hybrids or synthetic designs, because much of what we conjecture about them involves creatures we are familiar with here on earth and how they interact with their environment. On the other hand, because of how much we *don't* know about what is possible for life in various off-earth contexts, there is a lot of "wiggle room" for design. The assumption that all life is carbon-based may prove erroneous, and silicon-based creatures have been proposed by scientists based upon what that material is capable of doing. Nevertheless, shapes are what they are, and the designer still can only play with elements that humans can perceive and understand.

We can understand alien types in a couple of different ways. In one, we consider the images that have already been evolved by cover artists, movie studios, and effects studios like those run by visual effects master Stan Winston or movie make-up guru Rick Baker. These are well-known creature designers with successful track records in the entertainment industry. The second major group of aliens would be represented by unpublished or non-mainstream imagery. Really, what we are saying here is images already conceived (and thus in the public awareness, often becoming stock types of designs) and images that are fairly new and original.

Figure **11-2**

Weird, yet imaginative extraterrestrials.

Other means of constructing alien types (which is discussed forthwith) are to involve the elements we have talked about before, namely, sentience, environment, and ecologic role and evolutionary status. Thus, brains or self-awareness and reasoning power, the type of environment (e.g., a methane atmosphere or frequent sulfur lava eruptions), the way the character or creature interacts with and fits into the environmental ecology, and where the same critter stands in its own planet's life evolutionary chain, all affect the nature of the design.

Extraterrestrial Developmental Characteristics and Other 25-Cent Words

In order to simplify the creation of alien characters and creatures, the authors have developed a listing of eight basic traits found in living entities that can be applied to alien life-form design. By answering questions related to these characteristics, a basic framework for creature design emerges and allows us to develop our character on a foundation more solid than pure guesswork. The traits are as follows and are discussed in further detail as this chapter progresses:

1. Core structure: organic/inorganic
2. Locomotion
3. Habitat
4. Food
5. Attack/defense modes
6. Sentience
7. Reproduction
8. Culture

Animal, Vegetable, or Mineral?

The first and most basic choice that we can make regarding the core structure of our alien characters is whether it is organic or inorganic.

If a character is organic, we must ask further questions such as "Is it multicellular or like a giant amoeba?" "Is it humanoid?" "Is it insect-like?" The list of questions can go on and on.

We are used to thinking about living beings as having an organic base, being made up of flesh, blood, muscle, and bone. Thinking "animocentrically" is understandable because we humans are such life forms. However, the possibilities of creatures existing in our universe or in our imaginations (that have developed an existence thoroughly foreign to our origins) are quite likely.

An inorganic life form might take the form of some crystalline matrix that exhibits behavior patterns or reactions to its environment, such as fluorescence as a result of some external stimulus.

Figure |11-3|

Inorganic "thingies."

Perhaps a creature may be some sort of noncorporeal energy presence, like the "will-o-the-wisp." A super-intelligent energy being may choose to use telekinetic powers to build a "body" out of rocks or other inanimate flotsam. Why? That's for you the designer to decide!

By the way, robotic or other artificially created organisms would qualify as inorganic entities.

What's My Anatomy?

The anatomic development of an alien character is predicated on environmental origin, physical nature, and survival requirements. Creatures don't just develop in such a manner so as to "look cool," but evolve in response to particular needs. A primary requirement for the continued existence of most entities is the ability to move around their respective environments, so they can engage in such activities as hunting, mating, and avoiding predators. That being said, some creatures may have a symbiotic relationship with their environment that has allowed them to stay put, like plants rooted in the soil.

One notion for developing alien fauna (or flora) is to use the "What If?" method as it applies to comparative life-form development on Earth. This conceptualization technique occurs when the character designer asks what would happen if a particular animal developed under such-and-such a series of circumstances. What kind of critter would be the end result? Here's an example of this kind of character conceptualization: What if a group of simians on another earth-like planet had to adapt to survive in an environment where much of their habitat is comprised of great savannas and populated by herds of herbivorous beasts? What if these simians took on the ecologic niche of "alpha predator" within the said environment, and, if so, how would this have modified the development of their physical characteristics?

Figure **11-4**

Mad, man-eatin' monkey: a "what if" scenario.

Now let's try to answer the question by comparing our imaginary simians to known primates from our world.

Earth primates are omnivorous. Capuchin monkeys will kill and eat small animals and birds if they can catch them. Chimpanzees will devour everything from insects to small primates, in addition to the vegetable matter portion of their diet. It does not require a great leap of imagination to dream up a wholly carnivorous "primatoid."

The monkeys and apes that we know and love engage in existences both arboreal (live in the trees) and terrestrial (live on the ground). If our imaginary ape critters came from arboreal stock and now had to chase and kill herd animals, their anatomy would reflect such modifications. Limbs might become stronger and heavier, somewhat less flexible, and more adapted to running (heavy foot pads), like those of a big hunting cat. Instead of a prehensile tail, our ape creature's posterior appendage may now be stiffened and thicker, acting as a counterbalance to support swift ground movement, quick turns, and leaping. Perhaps this critter's canine teeth would become elongated to provide a powerful killing bite, such as those delivered by our prehistory's "saber-toothed" felids. Once again, we are drawing upon "real-world" research and observation of animal anatomy and behavior to create the conceptual framework for an alien critter creation.

Habitat for Inhumanity

Environment is undoubtedly the greatest contributing factor to the survival and development of the living organism. Creatures develop anatomic responses and changes over a long period of time as a reaction to outside influences. For instance, a desert-dwelling character may benefit from some moisture/food source storage area, like a camel's hump. This character's progenitors may have had some centralized area of body fat that had greater capacity than those accumulations in competitors within their own species. Other specializations would be helpful for denizens of warm to hot climates, especially if one is endothermic. For example, the sail-back synapsids of earth's Permian period, such as Dimetrodon, developed skin-covered, elongated neural spines that are believed to have acted as heat-exchangers. By giving their sails full sun, these creatures could effectively warm their "cold" blood.

What types of environments are available from which to develop our alien critters? To be honest, a lot of this is conjectural or educated guesses, but we can outline some possible worlds that could harbor life. The variables are numerous, but would include most of the following:

1. Type of sun the world revolves around (if there is indeed a sun for the home)

2. Number of suns the world has and their types

3. Size of planet

4. Existence or nonexistence of solid surface

5. Crust (earth component) and its composition and quantity and stability

6. Moons, rings, and other planetary accouterments

7. Atmosphere (or lack of) and type of gases available

8. Liquid components of environment (lakes, oceans, rivers) and what the liquid consists of

9. Temperature range (surface, atmosphere, night/day)

10. Volcanism

11. Weather

12. Seasons

13. Orbital period and eccentricities in same

14. Plate tectonics

15. Atmospheric winds and their frequency, velocity, and so on.

16. Age of the world and its status within a solar system

17. Rogue worlds that have no attached sun or other physical "systems"

18. Distance from center of galaxy, or position with star clusters or other types of multistar systems, or completely separate from any star systems

19. Stellar neighborhood issues (gas or dust clouds, comets, asteroids/meteors, radiation, gamma ray bursts)

20. Gravitational field (pull) of the planet

21. Atmospheric density

22. Rotational period of planet

All of these factors (and more) would be involved in setting the parameters for any alien design. Obviously, we don't have to consider all of them for much fantasy or science-fiction work, but for authenticity and sheer ability to increase the image options, these environmental variables would weigh heavily.

Once these issues have been examined, we can look at what types of local environments exist, and what life/ecological systems have evolved to acclimate to them. Our normal categories of plant, animal, bacterial, viral, and other types of living things we are familiar with might not apply as well in an alien environment. They might have attributes that look plant-like in some respects and animal-like in others, or they might have characteristics that don't resemble either closely because of the particular needs of their environment. Mutually interactive colonies of sentient clouds of protein-like motes could exist, floating in liquid or gaseous environments, using chemical or electromagnetic communication. Just this example gives the reader a glimpse of how far-ranging the options are. Apart from the physical aspects, we can imagine (or can't) how different their behavior, motives, and emotions (if they have any) could be.

Figure | 11-5 |

Alien critters from strange environments.

Chow Time!

Animal and plant life-forms require some type of sustenance in order to survive. The methodology by which this process is implemented follows some basic guidelines (along with your imagination), which can certainly be applied to alien character designs.

Plants (as we earthlings know them) usually derive nutrients via sunlight from the photo-chemical process of photosynthesis. The physical result of this vegetable development is the evolution of leaves, carrying the apparatus for converting light into energy. Other plant forms are carnivorous, preying on insects and small animals. The infamous Venus flytrap has spe-cialized folding leaves that secrete a sticky substance and have sensitive "hairs" that signal the arrival of some hapless and unsuspecting insect, then. . .snap! The leaves close on the prey and it is dissolved by digestive juices. A "man-eating" alien plant might exhibit a similar method of food procurement. More on deadly plants a little later, though.

Animals (as we know them) are herbivores (plant eaters), carnivores (meat eaters), or omni-vores ("variety" eaters). Herbivores eat plant material and derive energy and nutrients from the internal processing of the said substance. Carnivores eat and process other creatures (meat) for the same purpose. Omnivores do likewise with both plant and animal materials (e.g., bears).

Because plant material "cellulose" is a less efficient, harder to process energy source, herbivores (like gorillas) forage all the time for food. Meat eaters (like the lion) get more "bang for the buck" food-wise from the odd gazelle or slow-footed wildebeest.

Related to food consumption and processing is a creature's metabolism: endothermic (warm blooded) or ectothermic (cold blooded). Warm-blooded critters have a metabolism that allows them to keep a constant body temperature in relation to their environment. The trade-off: More body heat and activity equals the need for more food consumption. Cold-blooded crit-ters (lizards, for instance) need to eat less but rely on old Sol to warm up their core tempera-ture so that activity is possible.

Alien eating habits and metabolism affect their anatomic structure and relationship to their re-spective environments. Herbivores might have flat teeth and heavy jaws for grinding up woody branches to a pulp. Cold-blooded creatures may be reptilian and slow-moving. Omnivorous creatures might have tusks for digging "insectoids" from the mud, along with sharp claws and equally sharp carnassials for ripping and gnawing meat from rotting carcasses. While we don't eat carrion, human mastication equipment is designed for processing a variety of foods. Hu-manoid aliens might have similar "eating anatomy."

The following illustrations suggest solutions to alien creature designs capable of acquiring and processing a variety of forms of sustenance and functioning as ectotherms/endotherms.

Hit and Miss or Duck and Cover

Most creatures have, by virtue of natural selection, developed some method for protecting themselves from being killed or eaten by each other or other critters. These protective solutions are also typically related to environmental factors in their development. For instance, camou-flage as a defense mode is related to a creature's surroundings, in that it may have developed a texture or color to help it blend into its natural surroundings. Intelligent, technically advanced alien species may have developed some sort of invisibility device to afford them the protection of not being seen.

Figure | 11-6 |

Alien endotherms, ectotherms, and eating apparatuses.

Figure | 11-6 |

Continued from page 316.

Figure | 11-7 |

Attack of the Bladder Plant!

A creature might develop some variety of natural armor to act as protection from predators, like our Cretaceous ankylosaurs or modern armadillos. Intelligent aliens may create artificial suits of armor as a protective covering. Meanwhile, here are some other thoughts on how alien creatures might defend themselves:

- Out-running, out-swimming, out-flying, or otherwise out-pacing predators through sheer speed of locomotion, coupled with maneuverability.

- Emitting a defensive liquid spray, projectile, or odor, such as used by the bombardier beetle, porcupine, and skunk, respectively.

Figure | 11-8 |

Aliens: Big claws, sticky tongues, fleet feet, and heavy armor.

- Giving off a poisonous secretion that renders them "unappetizing." The South American poison arrow frogs have bright coloration that signals their poisonous nature to other animals.

- Burrowing. 'Nuff said on that one. . .

- Making itself look bigger, meaner, or just plain hard to swallow. The critter might have an expanding head frill or may blow itself up like the puffer fish and even wedge its body tightly in a stony crevice like the chuckwalla.

Figure | 11-8 |

Continued from page 319.

- Defensive posturing and sound emanation (like a hiss or rattle).
- Being immense. This trait is likely to fend off even the most stalwart bearers of ill will.

Creatures, alien or not, also have tools (teeth, claws, sticky webs, and so on) that allow them to effectively hunt (assuming that they are carnivores); these provide a valuable asset when in conflict with other critters. Both alien flora and fauna could exhibit a variety of strange and not-so-strange prey-acquisition attributes. For instance, imagine this alien plant hunting method: the aforementioned plant has developed a series of membranous gas bags (or blad-

Figure |11-8|

Continued from page 319.

ders) and tendrils that radiate from a central stalk lying on the ground surface. A weird flower pod tops the central stalk. The plant's "head" is filled with poisonous dart-like spores and is connected to each bladder with a thin, sinewy vine-like strand. An animal steps on the bladder, which simultaneously tugs the sinewy strand and "aims" the "head" at the critter, while sending a burst of compressed gas through the hollow stalk, firing the poison spore-darts into the hapless animal. The body of the animal acts as "fertilizer" for the new plants that grow from the spores, and juices from the decomposing carcass are absorbed as nutrients through the

Figure | 11-8 |

Continued from page 319.

root-like tendrils of the parent plant. Perhaps absorbed decaying animal matter created gases that could reinflate the bladders; or maybe it's a "one-shot" plant. These are the concerns and conundrums faced by the character designer!

Moving on to fauna, we can use comparative anatomy to look at attack/killing modes of earth predators. Most terrestrial predators rely on a healthy set of fangs and claws to catch and slay prey, and to defend themselves from attack. The teeth of big cats are designed to stab into soft throats while canids have teeth to rip at soft underbellies and crush bone—allowing the latter to be more effective scavengers (e.g., the hyena). The predator's "design" must fit its hunting and eating methods and anatomy.

A variety of other "attack" modes exist in our animal world:

- Poison: Scorpions and spiders sting prey and respond thusly in defense.

Figure | **11-8** |

Continued from page 319.

- Constriction: Pythons crush the life out of their prey before swallowing the hapless victim whole!

- Pecking: Birds peck, stab, and tear with their hard, sharp beaks.

- Projectiles: The shooting tongue of the chameleon nabs insects, while spat water globs do the same for the archer fish.

- Weapons: Intelligent life forms could create artificial killing tools from sharpened sticks to energy weapons.

Figure | 11-9 |

Aliens exhibiting a range of mental acuity.

Design your own alien feeding frenzy solutions by researching creatures from our own planet. Ask questions! How would a blood-sucking alien critter attack its prey? Would it use a sharp proboscis like a mosquito or would it alight on the back of a larger creature where it could cling, biting through hide and licking up gore (or ichor) from the host like a vampire bat?

The following illustrations give us glimpses of the possibilities of alien attack and defense possibilities.

Thoughts or Not

Animal forms, as we know them, respond to their environment and situations therein based on their relative intelligence, instincts, or direct sensory input from their immediate surroundings. The lower the intellect of the critter, the more likely it is to act as a result of direct physical stimuli. All lesser animals (below human intellect) function on instinct: the "fight or flight" response.

Tool use (also related to cultural development) is a key factor that usually signifies a major leap in the cognitive processes of a species. Along with this, the ability to reason and to think of and understand abstract concepts (not to mention the opposable thumb) separates human beings from the rest of the bestiary. Also, intelligent critters tend to have bigger and more complex brains.

Figure | 11-10 |

Advanced cartography and herding in extraterrestrials.

Figure **11-11**

Beware of cleverly disguised alien invaders!

The level of sentience of a character defines how it can and will react to a given stimulus situation, alien or not.

Almost Everything You Wanted to Know about Alien Sex, but Were Afraid to Ask

Propagation, like gathering nutrients or breathing, is a key component to the survival of a species. Nature has come up with a variety of unique methods by which living organisms can replicate themselves on our planet (assuming our general readership also resides hereabouts); once again we shall use comparative anatomy to conceptualize how alien species make babies. The romantic or ritual aspects of mating would be related to cultural behavior; we confine ourselves at this point to looking at known biological reproductive methods.

First, we can separate these baby producing methods as sexual and asexual. Sexual reproduction requires male and female partners (or at least their respective anatomies), one being an egg carrier and the other being the "fertilizer" (not to be confused with manure of the same moniker). Through the process of copulation or other physical interaction, the eggs become fertilized and spawning follows. People and animals mate in this form without great "thematic" variations. As mentioned, the process of sexual reproduction ends up with an egg being fertilized and the biology of the critter in question dictates how the eggs will develop into a birthed offspring. The following list describes major known egg-processing methods, as applicable to animals:

- **Oviparous:** Birthing offspring via eggs that hatch after being laid by the parent animal (e.g., birds)
- **Ovoviviparous:** Birthing offspring via eggs that are hatched inside the body of the parent animal (e.g., some snakes)
- **Viviparous:** Birthing live offspring that have developed inside the body of the parent animal

Asexual reproduction refers to a biological system wherein a creature singly carries both sperm and eggs for self propagation or is otherwise able to spin off its genetic material in the form of offspring. Following are a series of asexual reproductive methods that can be used as referential possibilities for alien creature birthing. We focus on these particular forms because of their odd variations as applicable to interesting creature reproduction and may relate to plants and even unicellular organisms:

- **Apogamy:** Growth of an embryo without fertilization.
- **Parthenogenesis:** Development of an unfertilized egg into a new individual (e.g., many insects along with some additional arthropods)
- **Fission:** Reproduction exclusive of the fusion of sperm and ovum
- **Schizogony:** Reproduction by manifold fission (e.g., minute, unicellular-type critters)
- **Blastogenesis:** Reproduction by budding
- **Sporulation:** Reproduction by the creation and discharge of spores

Research on reproductive methods for flora and fauna will reveal interesting possibilities about how your character design can and must evolve.

Getting Cultured

How does a species develop the concept and application of culture? A primary component in the process of reaching such societal development is the factor of intelligence. In order to develop an advanced society, living entities have to have an intellect capable of comprehending abstract ideas like teamwork, religion, politics, and sophisticated tool use. This determination is necessary when planning a character design, because aspects of culture affect everything from clothing style (or lack thereof), to motivation, belief systems, and even food preference. The rudiments of culture come from a series of basic behaviors displayed by "lesser" types of creatures. Insects, like bees, work together for the good of the hive while serving a central authority: the queen, who exerts matriarchal control.

Herding, seen (for instance) in the behavior of many ruminant animals is a pattern of action in which individual animals move and live in groups that provide them protection in numbers, especially for the good of younger animals. Herds can set up defensive perimeters, sound alarms, and bring "alpha"/"bull" beasts to bear on roving predators. Herds may also share in the care of infant animals, or nesting areas.

Pack behavior similar to herding gathers animals not only in a familial group but also as a hunting group.

Groups of creatures that are capable of exhibiting sophisticated collective behavior patterns (like primates) typically create ever more complex hierarchies and "rules." If intellect progresses through evolution, we see tribal activity—where the collective shares responsibilities that support the entire group, like hunting/gathering. The greater the intellectual capacity of the creatures, the greater the capability of developing advanced cultural systems through the comprehension and development of abstract ideas like politics, religion, social mores, and such.

Alien cultural preoccupation can vary as much as the cultures themselves. Some advanced alien beings may be interested in collecting maps and charting their known world, whereas others may wish to develop the means for galactic conquest.

Sci-Fi: Why?

What's the definition of *science fiction* as a genre and how is it related to alien character design? Science fiction stories typically take place in an environment where the evolution of scientific thought has progressed beyond the realm of contemporary human culture, whether it is related to the culture in the story or that of the world around us. Scientific advancement impacts a couple of key cultural areas: general knowledge and technology. It's a symbiotic relationship between the two. For instance, we have developed space vehicles capable of deploying an advanced telescope into earth's orbit, and by using that "eye-in-the-sky," we are able to gain further knowledge about the heavens through more effective exploration.

Our association of advanced technology with alien species as a creative concept is derived from the idea that explorers from a far-off planet would require some fantastic means of interstellar travel (a flying saucer, perhaps?) in order to visit and/or terrorize our unsuspecting world. Space invaders in popular culture often exhibit superior weaponry along with virtually impregnable defenses. Like living mummies and most vampires, star-spawned creatures tend to be impervious to small arms fire, but may at anytime succumb to the common cold. Which reminds us to remind you, gentle reader, that suitable heroes and villains (alien or not) must have reasonable (and hopefully interesting) strengths and weaknesses: it's just a part of good storytelling!

Earth folks are always on the lookout for technology that will enable them to make themselves richer, stronger, and healthier. Stories about earthling and alien dealings may also be fueled by the hope of sharing such knowledge. An alien culture may be able to provide significant information on scientific advancements that would solve earth's energy or medical problems. This is a situation in which extraterrestrials represent a positive influence on mankind. Just watch out for any hidden alien agendas or evil reptilian humanoids cleverly disguised in rubber "people" masks.

STUDENT SHOWCASE

Ramon Hippolito

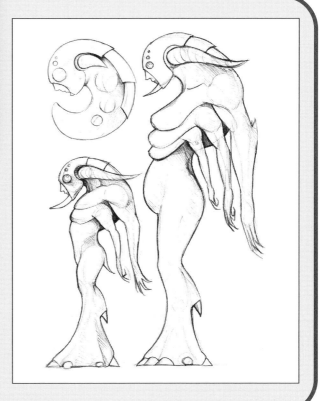

Student artwork by Ramon Hippolito: Male and female versions of an alien. As an example of a possible alien design, Hippolito uses synthesis and repetition to create two believable but disturbing aliens, one of each gender, and what appears to be their offspring.

SUMMARY

Creating alien character designs is a great challenge for artists due to the pitfalls of stereotyping fueled by decades of previously generated extraterrestrials in the annals of popular culture. A key factor for artists to understand in the process of inventing alien characters is how to use developmental characteristics to generate life-form parameters. These design boundaries include the following: organic/inorganic structure: locomotion, habitat, food, attack/defense modes, sentience, reproduction, and culture. It is important that alien characters be designed based on the research of comparative anatomy and behavior of existing living entities to help ensure their overall plausibility.

exercises

1. Construct an alien using a terrestrial model (creature or creatures). Apply synthesis rules from Chapter Five and the developmental characteristics from this chapter.

2. Develop an alien world with its own weather and rules. Devise some derivative aliens that would inhabit this world using the developmental characteristics from this chapter.

3. Create an alien that could not live on Earth using the developmental characteristics from this chapter.

4. Create an alien that is technologically advanced but thoroughly nonhuman, using the developmental characteristics from this chapter.

5. Assuming that an alternate Earth exists where similar animals evolved differently, create an alien animal using the "What If" method and the developmental characteristics from this chapter (e.g., an aquatic lion, a terrestrial bat, a flying primate, and so on).

6. Set up an alien world as in number 2. What happens to your inhabitants when the world is changed by natural disaster? How do they adapt?

in review

1. What are the eight alien developmental characteristics named in this chapter?

2. What would be an example of a stereotypical alien being as defined by modern culture?

3. How does comparative anatomy relate to alien creature creation?

4. How does the genre of science fiction (e.g., films, writing) relate to alien character design?

5. What is meant by the "What If" method as used in character design?

PROFILE

David Dawson

"I received my BA in December of 1992 from Baylor University in Visual Arts. After my BA I went back to school to pursue an Associates Degree of Applied Arts in Computer Animation at the Art Institute of Dallas, from which I graduated in December of 1996. Shortly after graduation I began my involvement in teaching. In December, 2004, I earned my MFA in Computer Arts from Florida Atlantic University.

"For the past five years I have been working as a full-time instructor. I began my academic career at the Art Institute of Dallas, teaching in the Computer Animation Program. From Dallas I moved to Los Angeles and began teaching in the Animation program at Mount San Antonio Community college. I finally landed in Phoenix where I am currently teaching in the Game Art and Design program at the Art Institute of Phoenix.

"I strive to stay in touch with the industry by doing freelance work whenever possible. My first job in the Video Game industry was as a Concept Artist for Mesa Logic, a third-party development company for Atari, developing arcade games. The year following this I was offered a position in a company called Liquid Pictures. I did a great deal of retouching, comp work and 3D illustration for print, most of which was for the Frito Lay Company. The year following this I was offered a position as a Senior Animator at Paradigm Entertainment developing games for the Nintendo platform. Recently I did some character work for Farsight studios, a game developer in Big Bear, California. Teaching has turned out to be my true calling in life, but I am first and foremost an artist. I learned what I know about character design from other artists I have met, colleagues I have worked with, and teachers I have taken classes with over the years. I truly enjoyed my time in the game art industry and it is my experiences there that helped define me as an instructor.

"The following process is what I use when I am designing a character that starts at the 2D level and then is translated into a 3D design:

Make sure that your design looks good from every possible angle. For example, some 2D design elements such as Bart Simpson's hair don't translate well into 3D.

Start with your character's basic shape; have this shape convey the character's personality.

A character is an icon, or symbol for something (Charles Zembillas told me this and it was like a light going on in my head).

Be very deliberate with your designs. Try to create an engaging character that has a clear cut motivation or role to play out (Villain, Hero).

When drawing your designs, utilize squares, spheres, triangles and other geometric shapes. This drawing process is used so that your designs can easily be broken down into simple shapes.

I can't remember who said this or where I heard it but I think its dead on: Characters that have been filtered down to their essence read better on the monitor.

Spheres tend to denote soft, delicate characters. Squares tend to denote strength and dependability. Triangles are aggressive.

Use scale to create interest and variety in proportion. Do this by creating a dominant mass or feature such as the torso or head. Break down the various elements that make up your character such as the arms, hands, feet and the like in the same way. For example, is the eyeline high or low on the head?

Try and say as much as possible with as little possible. I strive to not burden the design with unnecessary details.

Avoid letting the limitations of the software define your designs.

The 3D design process is very much like creating a 2D character without the concerns of such things as straight and curved lines, as well as other 2D elements that don't easily translate to 3D."

Tips for students entering this field:

If you are a student wanting to get into character design, my advice is to DRAW all the time (8–10 hours a week of figure drawing class). Know your anatomy!

Keep a sketchbook with you; draw from life constantly. Drawing is a language, and when you draw from life you constantly learn a new visual vocabulary. There can be no growth visually if you draw only familiar things.

Don't settle for your first design, but thumbnail, thumbnail, thumbnail, thumbnail. Try changing such things as the dominant mass, the scale of the features in relationship to each other, the character's age, weight or other essential elements that make up the character's look."

12

in conclusion: the power of design and final thoughts with
demonstrations and illustrations

Discover how the various design themes presented in this book work together as a means for visually developing characters and creatures.

Learn about general concepts regarding inanimate and animal character design.

Explore examples of step-by-step construction of various characters and creatures.

Examine a gallery of sample character designs.

introduction

As the reader has discovered, character (and creature) design is far from a simple matter. Although it is entirely possible to be a successful artist without knowing much in the way of theory, sooner or later such artists will find themselves in a dead-end stylistically or creatively, and unable to claw their way out to a new solution. Many of our students have complained that they "just want to draw" and the rest of the information hurts their heads. Unfortunately, their success or lack of it (and limitations) are all too predictable. Frankly, they just don't know enough. Many historically famous designers had good practical grounding even if their education wasn't academically formal. This training got them through many a tough spot, and it will do the same for any aspiring artist as well, whether in college, secondary school, or out working.

Knots to You or Tying It All Together

We'd like to discuss how all of the issues covered in this book relate to one another and are directed toward design success. To sum up what we have talked about in this text, the following topics were covered in detail: concept development; research methodology and related arenas; construction techniques; types of characters; style issues; synthesis and creativity; expression; anatomy and locomotion; alien design issues; and prehistoric resources. It seems logical to begin by reiterating what a character is (and what "character creatures" therefore are): A character is an individual entity, man, woman, beast, alien, or the like that can be derived from the story, but sometimes stands alone from an overall story line, and is usually the central focus of story development. Characters are what the audience follows in an emotional way: loving them, hating them, or just being fascinated by them, and in any case, identifying with them (see Chapter One). To create a character or creature design requires, for lifelong professional competence, a working knowledge of how design techniques dovetail with broader knowledge bases. Let's look at how we arrived at a basic set of techniques for accomplishing this. How do all our varied topics fit together to fulfill this creative quest?

- Before anything else is possible, you have to have an idea (concept) that contains the root of character development, such as a story or ad campaign. The idea is developed to show possible visual solutions that help tell the story. Among these solutions are the characters, backgrounds, and effects that give language literal meaning for the eye. We have dealt with the character (and related creature) designs in this book.

- After the idea or concept is resolved to the satisfaction of author, script writer, director, artist, and any other production personnel, it becomes immediately obvious that a lot of research will have to go into producing a visual product. Many things may have to be considered. Historical accuracy, anatomic problems (like making a dragon fly), costume choices, and relationship to environment are but a few possible problems that could be encountered. Verbal and pictorial resources need to be digested, and examples for the artist to work from should be available. Research is critical in making a valid and believable design solution, and often helps avoid clichés, copyright issues, and logical integration with the story.

- Now types of characters and style considerations come into play. What or who will fill the roles needed for characters and creatures in the story or visual context? Hero, villain, geek, fool, babe, monster, old codger? And when this is determined, what style will the production insist upon? For the whole project to be successful, a consistent and appealing style must be decided upon and used throughout the designs. The characters involved in the story now must be clothed in a visual style that will appeal to the chosen audience and must in themselves complete the story and be innately interesting.

- Construction techniques and synthesis are tools by which character (and creature) choices can be made and original approaches instituted for a particular project. How you construct your art is directly related to the style chosen, and synthesis is the ultimate tool for leapfrogging over stale, old ideas. Combining new and unexpected visuals into an original design solution can take even a completely familiar story and make it fresh again. Modular, cartoon methods will produce results far different from more linear, realistic approaches, and each must be considered in how it would solve the project's needs.

- Understanding expression and how it applies to characters is vital to making them grab the attention of the audience. Without convincing emotional visuals, characters remain cardboard cutouts that quickly bore the viewer. Particular audiences may need special types of signals, for example, working out designs for young children rather than for more mature audiences. Cultural expectations must also be considered if the project is intended for a more narrow viewing niche.

- If animation is core to the project, or if the character or creature is to be taken as authentic in stand-alone images, then knowledge of anatomy and locomotion become essential. Poor analysis of a walk can doom a character's appeal because of its affect upon a visual sequence, and faulty anatomy can make a character or creature laughable rather than heroic or sinister. Each plays its part in producing convincing and interesting characters, and cannot be ignored for expediency.

- Contemporary artists are commonly called upon to invent alien characters and creatures; they will produce better and more interesting results if they understand just what alien qualities are and what type of environment ties to a particular alien. The relationship of environment to look and function gives the artist the ways and means to concoct valid alien designs.

- Prehistoric creatures are another popular realm for deriving creature design, and by a simple survey of what is available, an artist can exponentially increase their available visual resources.

We have also addressed human psychology, archetypes, and universal themes and how they show up in many seemingly varied story lines. The nature of the story and how it defines and shapes a character can be itself defined by its underlying psychological or archetypal structure. The three-act play structure commonly in use today also can contain the types of characters chosen. These and related structural parameters give energy to various ways of designing characters and creatures for public consumption.

Practical tips from various working artists have been introduced as well, and should be read carefully and related to the material covered in this text.

All these techniques and conceptual tools, when used together, can push the artist over design barriers and provide new and fascinating possibilities for visual solutions in many varied markets.

Thinking Final Thoughts

In our book, *Exploring Character Design*, we have tried to cover a broad range of topics relating to the creation of characters and creatures. These have included a very wide variety of subjects, from anatomy to style considerations. All this and more makes for a fairly comprehensive book, and it is easy to leave some arenas less fleshed out. Our emphasis on a good theoretical and practical foundation made this less an "eye-candy" text than a practical one. One area that we wanted to say a bit more about is the use of inanimate objects and animals as sources for character and creature design. Although they follow all the same rules of creations that we have already outlined in detail, their common usage begs a bit more attention in a section of their own. In addition, we wanted to give a few more demonstrations and finished examples of character and creature designs for the student to look at and use as a resource.

Inanimate Resources

Although the method for using inanimate objects as a source for character and creature design is basically the same as using any other source material, it is worth looking briefly into as a special niche source in and of itself. Inanimate sources include natural and man-made objects. In fact, the category is so broad that it would be impossible to do more than just indicate a number of subcategories and show a couple of demonstrations using inanimate objects as sources.

Because inanimate sources are, by definition, inorganic and nonsentient, we have to remember to use them for one of two purposes. One is to borrow their form and function as an addition to or foundation for a character or creature design. This means that we might use their shape and substance (and possibly how they work) to produce a character design. This produces results like the numerous children's book characters and animated film characters that are, in essence, live, sentient, and often human-like: teapots, trains, toy boats, even car engines, and shoes. The other means is to use them piece-meal; their form, or surface, or even molecular make-up are borrowed and merged with other elements to produce a character. This includes everything from robots and androids to any synthetic character or creature that uses some element that is inorganic.

To summarize: You can "bring to life" any inanimate object. Man-made ones are the easiest because their form is often more definite and design oriented than natural objects. Alternatively, you can use parts of objects, both natural and man-made, as part of the make-up of a character or creature design.

Below are examples of each of these methods:

Note that each depends upon the innate "look" of the inanimate source to enhance the design. Without the unique visual properties of the choice, there would be no reason to use any particular inanimate thing to produce character designs.

Critters as Visual Resources

As with inanimate resources, the possible number of sources among living things for character and creature design is staggering in number. We have already alluded to many of them in previous chapters, especially the chapter on prehistoric creature resources (Chapter Ten).

(1)

(2)

(3)

(4)

Figure |12-1|

A simple wine glass is slightly modified in shape, with stylized additions of flowery hair, olive eyes, and lemon-slice mouth. Add a couple of arms and hands, and voilá, a bar-babe. Inanimate source with a twist.

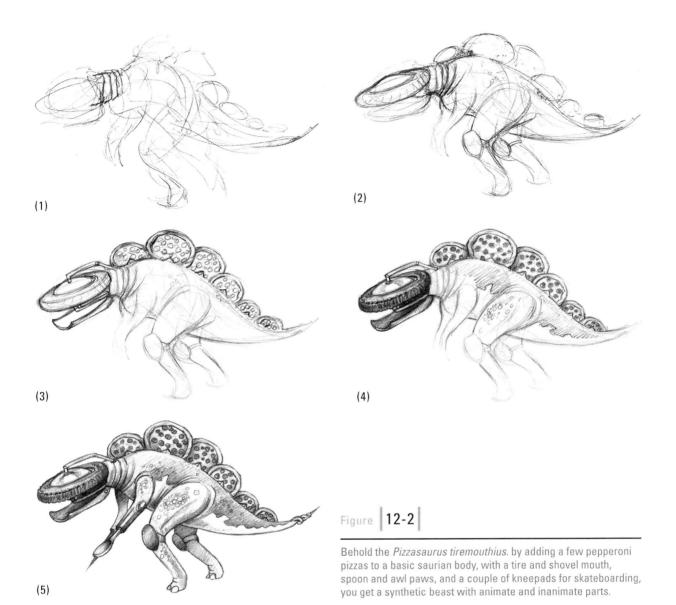

(1)

(2)

(3)

(4)

(5)

Figure | 12-2 |

Behold the *Pizzasaurus tiremouthius*. by adding a few pepperoni pizzas to a basic saurian body, with a tire and shovel mouth, spoon and awl paws, and a couple of kneepads for skateboarding, you get a synthetic beast with animate and inanimate parts.

Living things, especially animals, constitute a category of their own as visual resources. As with inanimate sources, they can be used or manipulated in many ways. In our chapter on synthesis (Chapter Five), we outlined some very specific means by which elements from living things can be used and blended with other sources to produce character and creature designs. Many creature designs are, to be quite honest, simply modifications of existing animals. This gives us a basic way to understand how to use such visuals: Use parts for synthesis or simply modify the whole creature. An example of each is included in the following illustrations.

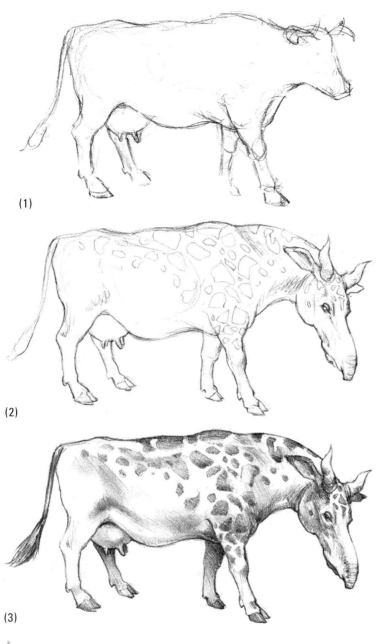

(1)

(2)

(3)

Figure |12-3|

What happens when cows stay out late and have too many drinks? Snoutitis. Changing the basic cow with a bit of nose magic and a few spots.

(1)

(2)

Figure | 12-4 |

More synthesis nightmares: Monkeys and hawks
get too friendly and produce hawnkeys.

(3)

Demonstrations and Illustrations

To conclude the chapter (and the book), we want to show some samples of the actual process of building a character or creature design, plus a small sampling of some finished designs that cover a wide variety of looks. Each of these is intended as only an example of one way to develop a design. There are as many viable ways as there are artists. We have found that the methods you will see below (and others that are sprinkled throughout the book) give a basic, practical roadmap to development. Look at them, copy them, disassemble them, and find a method that suits your talents and goals.

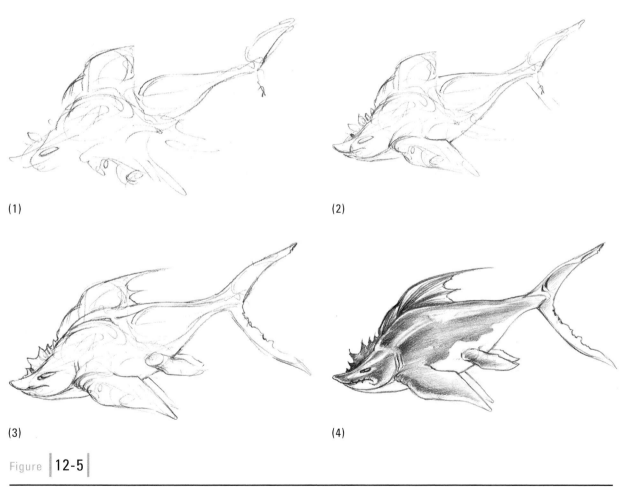

(1)

(2)

(3)

(4)

Figure | **12-5** |

Development of a sea creature roughly based on a shark in step-by-step construction.

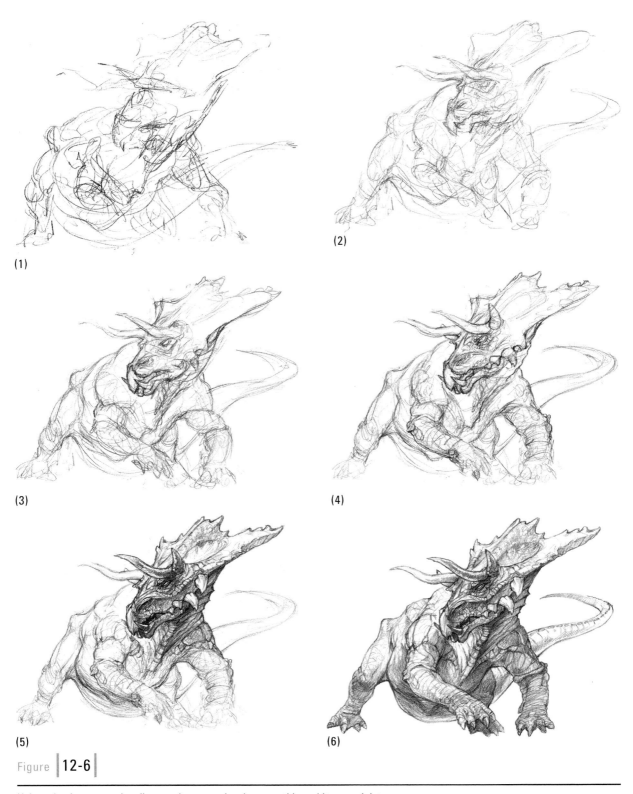

(1)

(2)

(3)

(4)

(5)

(6)

Figure | 12-6 |

Using a basic ceratopsian dinosaur base, we develop something a bit more sinister.

(1)

(2)

(3)

Figure | **12-7** |

Modular construction in three steps to produce a superhero.

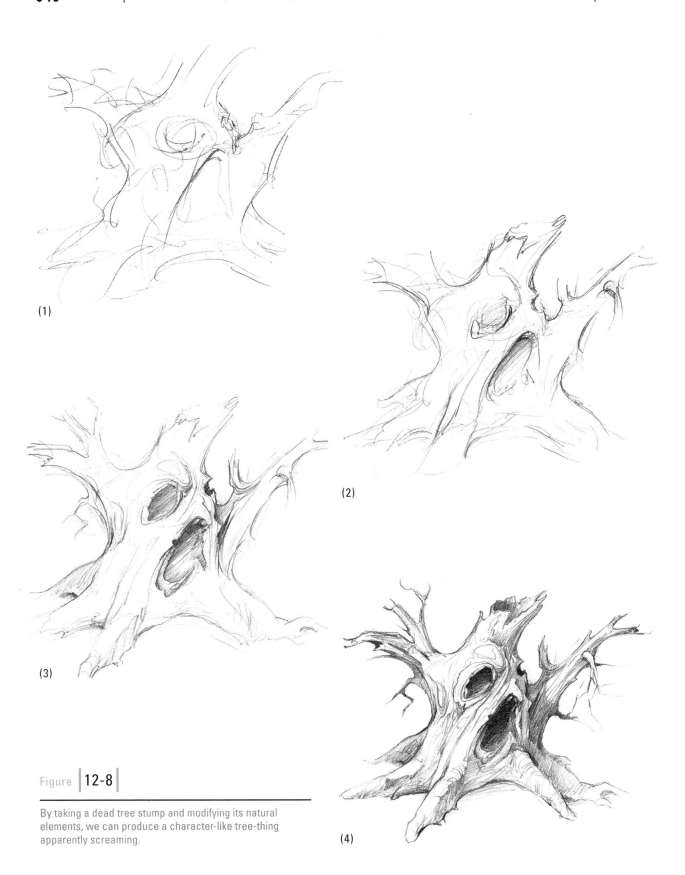

(1)

(2)

(3)

Figure | 12-8 |

By taking a dead tree stump and modifying its natural
elements, we can produce a character-like tree-thing
apparently screaming.

(4)

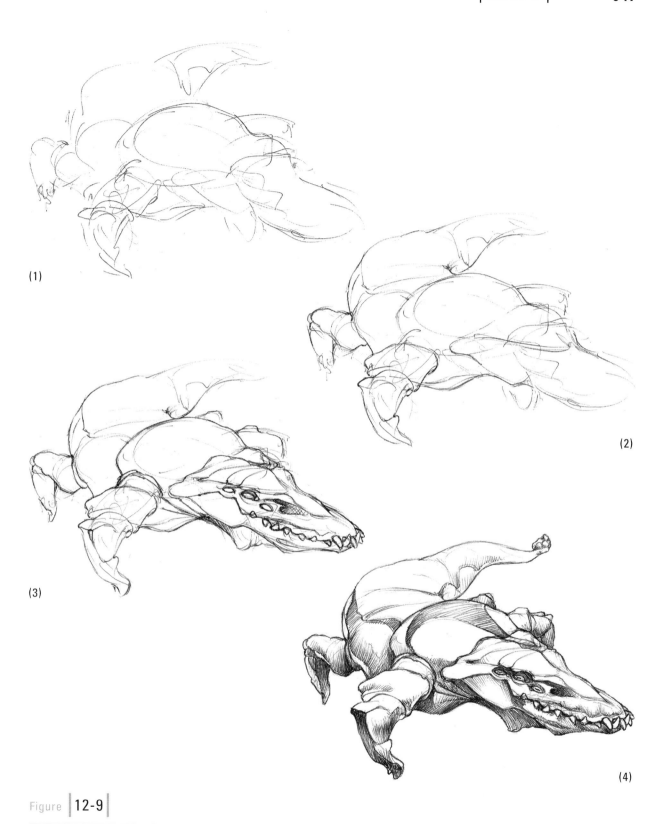

(1)

(2)

(3)

(4)

Figure | 12-9 |

A pen-and-ink demonstration: Using a gestural beginning, we concoct an insect-like crocodilian nightmare.

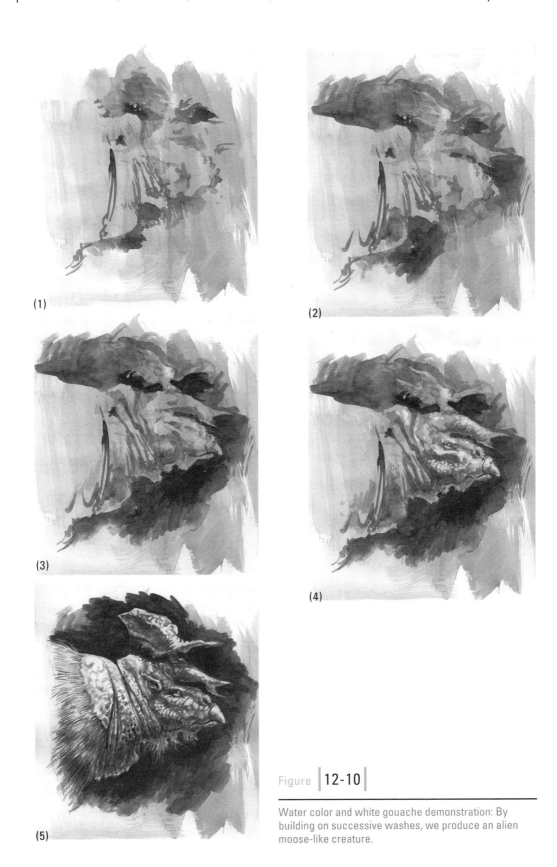

(1)

(2)

(3)

(4)

(5)

Figure | 12-10 |

Water color and white gouache demonstration: By building on successive washes, we produce an alien moose-like creature.

(1)

(2)

(3)

(4)

Figure | 12-11 |

A stylized hooded figure constructed from a gestural beginning, relying on experience in figure drawing for its validity visually.

Figure | 12-12 |

Alien fish design. It swims, but it won't win any beauty contests.

Figure | 12-13 |

Tonal pencil study for color post-apocalyptic figure.

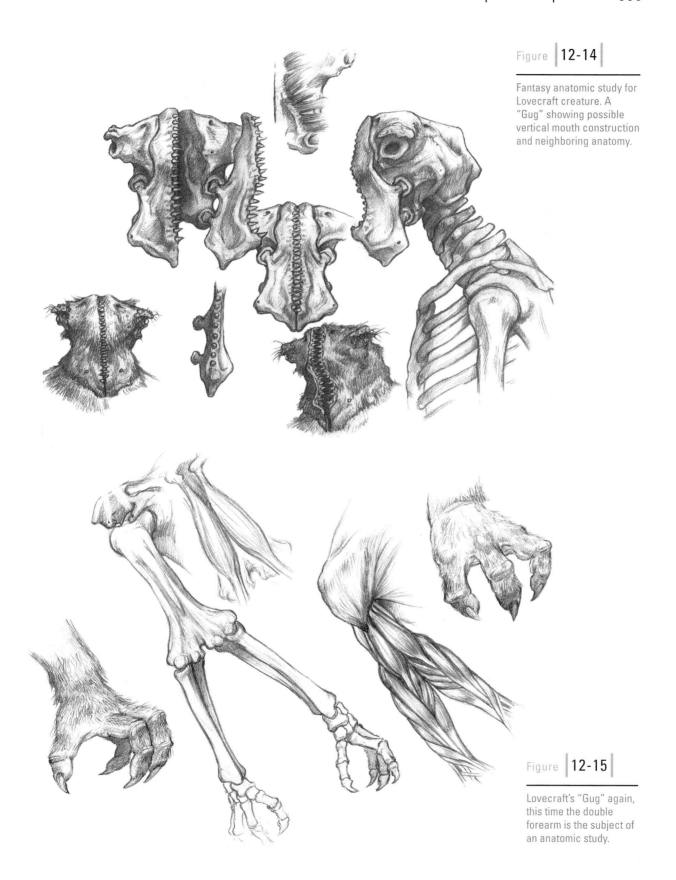

Figure |12-14|

Fantasy anatomic study for Lovecraft creature. A "Gug" showing possible vertical mouth construction and neighboring anatomy.

Figure |12-15|

Lovecraft's "Gug" again, this time the double forearm is the subject of an anatomic study.

Figure 12-16

Babes and dragons: one take on this timeless genre.

Figure 12-17

Alien or fantasy creature design. Surface articulation becomes an important part of the design solution.

Figure | 12-18 |

She's every alien's dream girl.

Figure | 12-19 |

Even fantasy characters get bored:
expression as a part of character design.

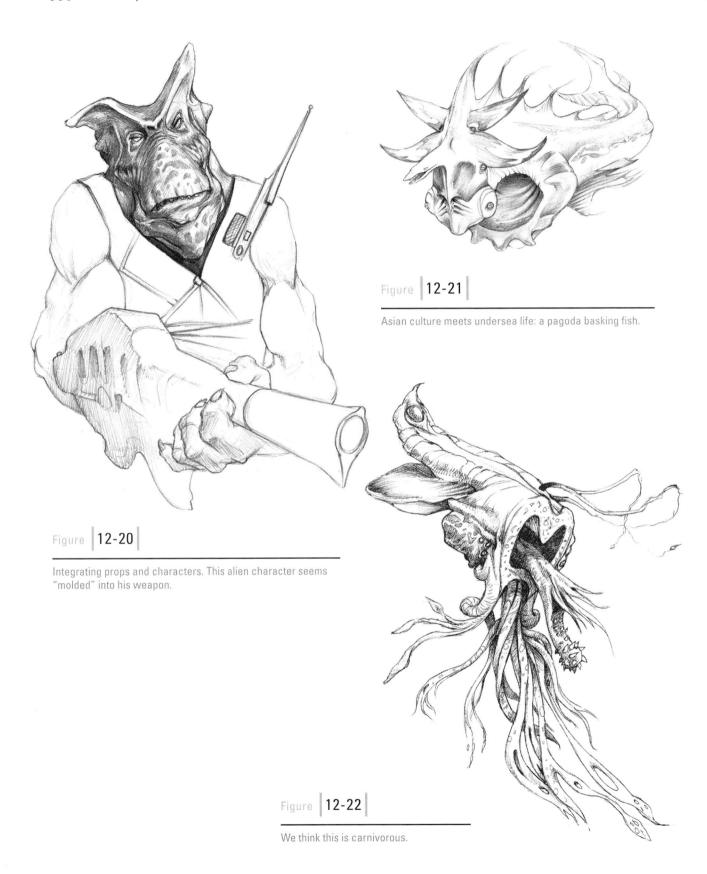

Figure | 12-20 |

Integrating props and characters. This alien character seems "molded" into his weapon.

Figure | 12-21 |

Asian culture meets undersea life: a pagoda basking fish.

Figure | 12-22 |

We think this is carnivorous.

STUDENT SHOWCASE

Yee, Thayn, Garza, Barker, Armstrong, and Campa

Yee, Thayn, Garza, Barker, Armstrong, and Daniel Campa show us various character and creature designs. In Yee's work, a cultural influence is subtly used to enhance each charac-ter's appearance. Thayn ventures into robotics with his bold style. Garza adds to his sea adventure series with young Cap'n Pete. Barker introduces an eerie were-wolfish thing and what appears to be perhaps a post-apocalyptic survivor; in his second effort we see two terrifying vampirish images. Armstrong weaves surface texture, costume, and props into an imposing warrior. In Campa's clown, the familiar jovial circus performer takes on less friendly overtones.

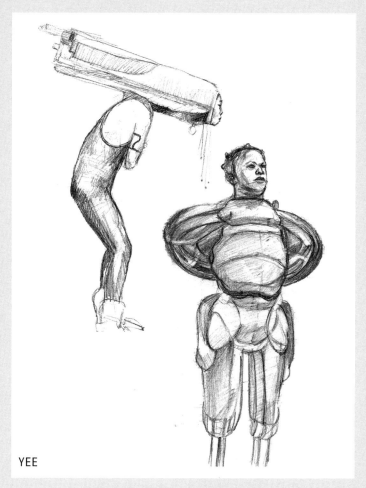

YEE

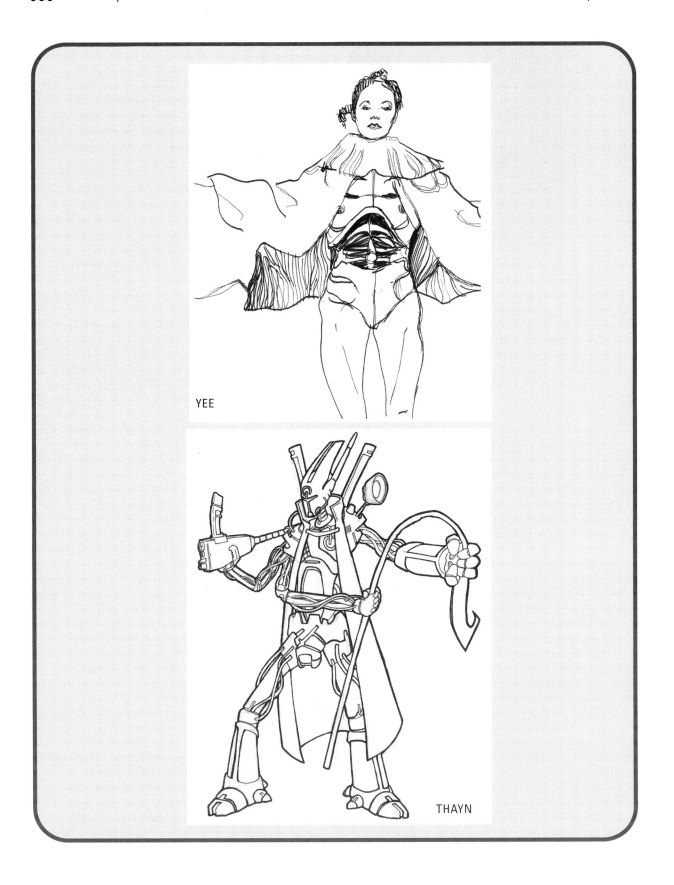

YEE

THAYN

GARZA

BARKER

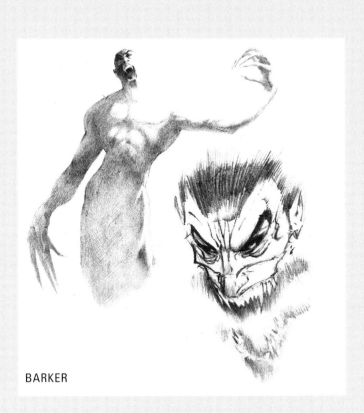

BARKER

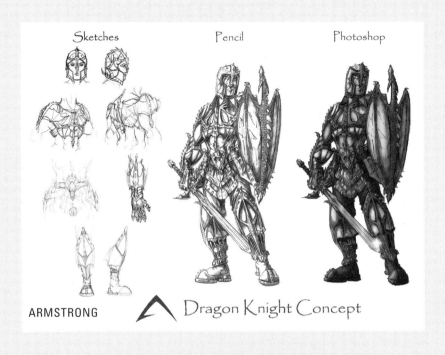

Sketches   Pencil   Photoshop

ARMSTRONG   Dragon Knight Concept

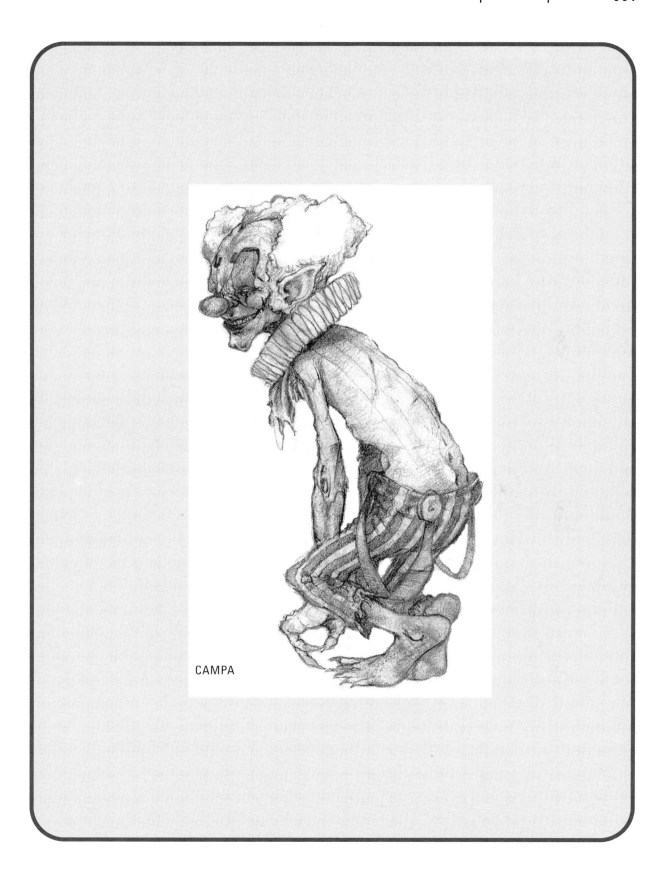

CAMPA

SUMMARY

Our book has given you a thorough map to follow for the creation of character and creature design. From conceptualization, research, and construction methods to an examination of the theory of synthesis, style usage, and character types, from expression, prehistory and alien sources, to anatomy and locomotion, we have traveled through the basics of creating a character or creature. Our intention was not to simply cover the pages with entertaining and exotic designs, but rather to give you the means by which to successfully make your own designs. This last chapter reviews a couple of categories that, by sheer volume of information covered in the book, we could only touch on during previous chapters. In addition, we wanted to conclude with some practical demonstrations and images that give, in a direct visual way, some hints to solving the design process and possible outcomes. We sincerely feel that we have put together the first true "how-to" text on designing characters and creatures, both in theory and practical, fundamental techniques. We hope it gives you the edge you need to become a successful artist in the field.

exercises

1. Construct a character design derived from a man-made object.

2. Design a creature based upon an existing earthly animal.

3. Imitating the methods and means of one of the demonstrations, draw and record, step by step, a character or creature design. Note how you arrived at each successive step. Are you shortchanging any of your design technique? Do you use thumbnails, gestures, or other preliminary means for designing?

in review

1. What are the two major methods of using inanimate objects for character or creature design?

2. What are two major means of using animals as visual resources for character or creature design?

index

index

Page numbers followed by *f* indicate figures; page numbers followed by *t* indicate tables; page numbers followed by *b* indicate boxes; page numbers followed by *n* indicate footnotes.

A

Acrocanthosaurus, 273
Acrylics, 117
Action pose sheet, 165f, 167
Adaptation, 78, 79
Adventure, 42b
Affinity, style with, 149, 168
Airbrush, 117
Alien design, 307–332, 339
    anatomy in, 312–314
    anthropomorphism in, 308–309, 309f
    attack/defense modes with, 317–327,
     320f–325f
    core structure in, 311–312, 312f
    culture with, 329–330
    environment for, 314–316, 316f
    fish, 352f
    food/sustenance with, 316–317, 318f, 319f
    habitat in, 314–316, 316f
    props in, 356f
    reproduction/propagation with, 328–329
    science fiction with, 330–331
    sentience with, 326f, 327–328, 328f
    stereotyping with, 308, 332
    surface articulation in, 354f
    tool use with, 327–328, 328f
    weapon in, 356f
    "What If?" method for, 313, 313f
Allosaurus, 274
American Museum of Natural History, 264
Amphibians
    gait of, 210–211, 211f
    prehistoric, 286–287, 292f
Analogous design, 21, 22
Anatomy, 92, 203–229
    addition/deletions to, 123–124
    alien, 312–314
    arachnid, 218

bat, 214, 215f
bird, 213–214, 214f, 215f
bone structure in, 205–213, 205f, 207f
changing ratio with, 124–125
dolphin, 216, 218f
fish, 215–218, 216f–218f
functional/dysfunctional, 123, 127f
general, 204
gesture drawing of, 97–98, 98f, 108
head, 223–229, 223f–229f
importance to design of, 203
insect, 218, 220f
jellyfish, 218, 220f
kangaroo, 217, 219f
modifying body parts with, 123–124
modular drawing with, 102–105, 105f
musculature in, 219–223, 221f, 222f
proportions in, 99b, 100f
sea animals, 215–218, 216f–218f, 220f
seal, 216
skeleton in, 98, 98f, 100f
snake, 217, 219f
spider, 218
spinal, 205–213, 205f, 207f
squid/octopi, 216, 217f
substitutions with, 123, 124f, 126f–129f
synthesis with, 122–126, 124f–127f
wallaby, 217
walrus, 216
whale, 216, 218f
woman/man in, 99b
Andrewsarchus, 285, 288f
Androids, 71, 73f
   synthesis with, 126–128
Anger, 183
Anguilliform, 247, 247n, 248f
Anima/Animus, 33b
Animals
   character, 67, 69f
   classification of, 267
   genetic material of, 79
   hybrid characters as, 73f, 74–75
   modification of, 79
   organ systems of, 79
Animation, 61, 131, 339
   concept art for, 150, 152
   drawing skill for, 154b
   line in, 144–145
   silhouettes in, 187, 191f
   translating from 2D design for, 334
   twelve principles of, 156
Animism, 5
Anthropomorphism, 308–309, 309f
Anubis, 37, 39f
Apathy, 183

Apes, 211f, 212f, 213, 213f, 214f
Apotheosis, 43b
Appeal
   defined, 155
   style with, 155–157, 155f
Arachnid, 218
   prehistoric, 282–285, 285f
Archetypes
   character development with, 58
   child, 33b
   defined, 58
   Egyptian/Mayan, 8
   Jung on, 32b–33b
   mental images as, 92
   Mr. Punch as, 8, 58
   origin of, 5, 8
Arms, 212f, 213, 213f
Armstrong, Landon, 118b, 169b, 169f, 357, 360f
Arness, James, 131
Art, prehistoric, 5–8
Arthropod. *See* Insect
Artist
   development of, 22–24
   humility of, 24
Artist's block, 92
Assignment, 94
Association game, 93
Attack modes, alien design, 317–327, 320f–325f
Audience, 193
Avalos, Cesar, 88b–89b

B
Baba Yaga, 47f, 48
Baby Huey, 22
Bacteria, 75
Baker, Rick, 310
Balder, 37
Bambi, 268
Barker, Joshua, 23b, 357, 359f, 360f
Bat
   anatomy, 214, 215f
   locomotion, 252–254, 252f–254f
   skeletal structure, 215f
Beer-bellied character, 105, 106f
Bill Plympton, 19
Biped
   anatomy, 205–206, 208–209, 209f, 211–212
   human resemblance of, 211
   limbs of, 208–209, 209f
   locomotion, 241–243, 241f–243f
   pelvises of, 205–206, 241, 241f
   spinal columns of, 212

Bird
    anatomy, 213–215, 214f, 215f
    leg, 214, 215f
    locomotion, 251f, 253f, 254–256, 255f,
        256f
    prehistoric, 290, 296f, 297f
    scleral ossicles with, 280n
Biv, Roy G., 154
Blackwood, Algernon, 29
Block, Bruce, 149
Body expression, 185–187, 186f, 187f, 188f,
    189f. *See also* Poses
Bone structure
    anatomy of, 205–213, 205f, 207f
    arms with, 212f, 213, 213f
    biped, 205–206, 208–209, 209f, 211–212
    breastbone with, 206, 206f
    coccyx of, 205
    feet with, 212–213, 212f
    head with, 209–210
    legs with, 210–212, 211f, 212f
    limbs with, 208–209, 208f, 209f
    pelvis of, 205–206
    quadruped, 205–206, 205f, 208–209,
        208f, 209f
    rib cage with, 206–207, 207f, 212
    scapulae with, 206
    shoulder girdle with, 206, 206f
    spinal column with, 212
    tails with, 210, 210f
    thorax of, 207
Bosch, Hieronymous, 46
Brachiosaurus, 273
Brahma, 38
Breastbone, 206, 206f
Breughel, Pieter, 46

C
Camarasaurus, 273
Cambrian age, 266
Camel, locomotion of, 236
Campa, Daniel, 357, 361f
Campbell, Joseph, 42b–43b
Carangiform, 247, 247n, 248f
Carboniferous age, 266
Cartoon design, 19
    line in, 145, 145f
    style, 157
Cartooning
    modular drawing as, 100, 101–102,
        102f
    realism v., 107–108, 109f, 111f
    stylization v., 101–102
Casein, 116
Cave paintings, 5, 6, 6f, 7, 7f

Cenozoic age, 266
Ceratosaur, 274
Changing ratio, 124–125
Character
    concept/construction of, 91–118
    defined, 3–4
    description, 80
    genre influencing, 13
    individual as, 11
    ingredients, 60–61
    look of, 12–13
    name of, 11
    qualities, 14, 14b
    real life, 45–46, 45f
    sketch pad derived, 11–12
    storyline for, 10–16, 61–62, 63
Characterization, prehistoric resources in,
    293–295, 299f, 300f
Charcarodontosaurus, 272
Charcoal, 116
Child archetype, 33b
Choosing process, 59–60
Chuck Amuck (Jones), 4
Circle, hero defined by, 142
Clavicle, 99b
Clichéd imagery, originality v., 20–22, 58,
    308, 332
Coccyx, 205
Color
    baby animals, 280n
    fish, 277
    repetition with, 149
    reptiles, 277
    style with, 149, 154
    surfaces with, 146
    synthesis with, 122, 125, 129f, 129n,
        131–132
Comic books, 51, 155
    aliens in, 308
    concept art for, 150
    line in, 145
    Mocarski, 174
Comic relief, 67
Compatibility, 78, 79f
Conan: The Barbarian, 88
Conceit, 183
Concept art, 150–154, 168
Conceptualization, 91–95, 117
    artist's block overcome with, 92
    association for, 93
    defined, 91
    gesture drawing for, 95
    ideation through, 91–95
    play-act stories for, 93
    problem solving with, 93–95

style with, 150–153, 153f
word play for, 93
Construction, 95–118
    gesture drawing for, 95–99, 96f–98f, 100f
    materials for, 115–118
    model sheet, 167–168, 167f
    modular drawing for, 99–113, 101f–112f
    sketchbook for, 113–115, 115f
Continuity, 78
Contrast, style with, 149–150, 149f, 150f,
    151f, 168
Cooper, Gary, 63
Copyrights, 22, 46
Corythosaurus, 272
Costumes, 14b, 23b, 61, 81–83, 82f, 83f, 84f,
    85f
    history of, 42
    seductive overtones of, 83
    synthesis with, 122, 132–133, 134f, 135f
    uniforms as, 82f, 83, 84f, 85f
Courage, 184
Cows, 343f
Crayons, 116
Crocodile, 349f
Crosshatching, 146
Culture
    alien, 329–330
    character influence of, 80–81
    character research with, 42–49, 50–52
    character's look influenced by, 13
    different expression with, 179–180, 179f
    emotion influenced by, 193, 199, 200
    sports, 52
    style creep from, 51
Cyclops, 35, 36f
Cynicism, 183

D
D'Arc, Rob, 147
Darwin, Charles, 180, 182, 309
D'Aulnoy, Marie-Catherine, 49
Dawson, David, 334–335
Deer head, 267, 267f
Defense modes, alien design, 317–327,
    320f–325f
Deinonychus, 272
Design, 17–19
    abstract elements in, 17
    analogous, 21, 22
    appropriate style for, 17
    cartoon, 19
    graphic novel, 19
    personal taste governing, 19
    real world images in, 17
    story-telling mode with, 17

stylistic modes within, 17–19
    surprise in, 21
    team approach to, 19
    theory, 122–123
    visual arts, 17
Desire, 183
Devonian age, 266
Digitigrade locomotion, 235
Dilophosaurs, 274
Dimetrodon, 273, 299–303, 301f–303f
Dimorphodon, 256f
Dinosaurs, 270, 272–283, 274f, 275f
    Acrocanthosaurus, 273
    Allosaurus, 274
    Brachiosaurus, 273
    Camarasaurus, 273
    ceratopsian, 346f
    Ceratosaur, 274
    character synthesis with, 280–282, 281f
    Charcarodontosaurus, 272
    Corythosaurus, 272
    Deinonychus, 272
    Dilophosaurs, 274
    Dimetrodon, 273
    Diplodocus, 273
    Disney film, 295
    Edaphosaurus, 273
    Edmontosaurus, 276
    feathers/color/skin of, 276–280, 277f,
      278f, 279n
    Giganotosaurus, 272
    Iguanodon, 272
    Jurassic Park, 295
    Lambeosaurus, 272
    Parasaurolophus, 272
    Phytosaurs, 273
    sailback, 278f
    Sarchosuchus, 276f
    Sauropods, 273
    Spinosaurus, 273
    Suchomimus, 274
    surface of, 272, 276–280, 277f, 278f,
      279n
    Tyrannosaurus rex, 273, 274
Diplodocus, 273
    locomotion, 234, 235f
Disgust, 184
Disney Studios, 33, 131, 156, 157, 268, 288,
    295, 308
Disney, Walt, 156
Distortion, 148, 148f
Dog, locomotion, 234, 235f, 237f, 238f
Dolphin, 216, 218f
    anatomy, 216, 218f
    locomotion, 249

Doré, Gustave, 28
Dracula, 29, 30b, 71
Drawing
    gesture, 95–99, 96f–98f, 100f
    modular, 99–113, 101f–112f
    prehistoric resources in, 299–303,
        301f–303f
    sketchbook for, 113–115, 115f
    style with, 154b
Dreams, 32b
    image conceptualization in, 92, 93
Durga, 38

E
Ecology, 76
Edaphosaurus, 273
Edda, 36
Education
    artist development from, 24
Emotion, 14b, 60, 61, 62–64, 177–200, 339
    anger, 183
    apathy, 183
    conceit, 183
    courage, 184
    cultural influence on, 193, 199, 200
    cynicism, 183
    desire, 183
    disgust, 184
    envy, 183
    facial expressions showing, 179–183,
        180f–182f, 184f, 185, 185f
    fear, 183, 187
    hands showing, 179f, 187, 191–192, 192f
    happiness, 183
    head/face showing, 178f, 179–183,
        180f–182f
    lighting influence with, 195, 196f–198f
    lust, 183
    poses showing, 185–187, 186f, 187f, 188f,
        189f
    power of, 178–179
    readability of, 192–194, 193f, 194f
    sadness, 183
    silhouettes in, 187, 191f
    sly, 184
    states of, 183–185, 184f, 185f
    surprise, 184
Environment, 78
    alien, 314–316, 316f
    character's look influenced by, 13
Envy, 183
Epic story, 29, 38, 47–48, 51. *See also*
  Mythology
Epoch, 266
Eros, 35

Exploring Drawing for Animation, 95, 185,
    219, 221
Expression, 177–200
    audience for, 193
    cultural differences with, 179, 179f
    defined, 177
    emotional states with, 183–185, 184f,
        185f
    fantasy character, 355f
    hand gestures showing, 179, 179f, 187,
        191–192, 192f
    head/face showing, 178f, 179–183,
        180f–182f
    hero/villain, 178f
    lighting influence with, 195, 196f–198f
    poses showing, 185–187, 186f, 187f
    readability of, 192–194, 193f, 194f
Expression sheet, 166f, 167
Extraterrestrial. *See* Alien design

F
Face, 9, 10f
    emotional states with, 183–185, 184f,
        185f
    expression with, 178f, 179–183,
        180f–182f, 184f, 185f
Fagin the thief, 29
Fairy tales, 47–48
    animals in, 67
Fangs, 270, 272
Fantasia, 33, 288
Fashion, style v., 142
Fear, 183, 187
Feet, 212–213, 212f
Fertility, 7
Film, 51
Fish
    alien, 352f
    anatomy, 215–216, 216f–218f
    anguilliform locomotion in, 247, 247n,
        248f
    body or caudal fin locomotion in, 247,
        248f
    carangiform locomotion in, 247, 247n,
        248f
    coloration of, 277
    locomotion, 245–248, 246f–250f, 247n
    median or paired fin locomotion in, 247
    pitch/yaw/roll of, 246, 246f
    prehistoric, 287–289, 293f, 294f, 295f
    subcarangiform locomotion in, 247,
        247n, 248f
    synthesis with, 356f
    thunniform locomotion in, 247, 247n,
        248f

undulatory fin motions of, 248

Flying, 250–259, 251f–258f
  active, 250, 251f
  bats, 252–254, 252f–254f
  bird, 251f, 253f, 254–256, 255f, 256f
  dead drop, 250, 251f
  four kinds of, 250, 251f
  gliding, 250, 251f
  insect, 251f, 256–259, 257f, 258f
  pterodactyl, 251, 253f
  pterosaur, 252f, 253f, 256, 256f
  reptile, 270, 270f, 284f
  soaring, 250, 251f

Food
  alien design with, 316–317, 318f, 319f
  chain, 77

Frankenstein, 71
Franklin, Ben, 45, 45f
Frazer, Sir James George, 33
Froude number, 240b
Frowning, 180, 180f, 181f

G

Gaia, 35, 37
Gait, 234–239, 237f–240f
  asymmetrical, 236–237
  defined, 234
  Froude number with, 240b
  metachronal wave, 256, 257f
  pace, 239
  rotary, 236, 239, 240f
  suspension, 237, 238f
  symmetrical, 238, 239f
  transverse, 236, 239
  tripodal, 257f, 258
  walking, 238, 239f

Gallop, 236–237, 238f
  four phases of, 236
  one-suspension, 237, 238f

Ganesha, 26f, 40f
Gardner, John, 62
Garza, Dan, 86b, 169b, 170f, 357, 359f
Gender, synthesis with, 122, 132, 135f
Generic figure, modular drawing of, 105, 105f, 106f
Genre, 155
Gesta Romanorum, 49
Gesture drawing, 95–99, 96f–98f, 100f, 157
  advantages of, 112–113
  anatomy in, 97–98, 98f, 108
  conceptualization through, 95
  defined, 95
  modular drawing combined with, 108–113, 114f

modular drawing developing out of, 102, 104f
  motion in, 98

Giganotosaurus, 272
Gigantopithecus blackii, 268, 268f, 269
Giraffes locomotion, 236
Gliding, 214
The Golden Bough, A Study in Magic and Religion (Frazer), 33
Golem, 41, 71
Gouache, 116, 157, 350f
Graphic novels, 19
Graphite, 116
Grendel (Gardner), 62
Grimace, 180f, 182
Grimm Brothers, 49

H

Habitat, 77
  alien design, 314–316, 316f
Hand gestures, 179, 179f, 187, 191–192, 192f
Happiness, 183
Harryhausen, Ray, 290
Harvey Comics, 22
Hatching, 146
Hathor, 37
The Haywain (Bosch), 46
Head, 209–210
  anatomy, 223–229, 223f–229f
  deer, 267, 267f
  expression with, 178f, 179–183, 180f–182f
  personality displayed in, 223
  scale with, 167f, 168

Heimdall, 37
Heracles, 35
Heroes, 63, 63f, 142, 347f
  expression of, 178f
  journey of, 42b–43b
  modular drawing of, 105, 106f

High Noon, 63
Hippolito, Ramon, 137, 169b, 171f, 331b
History
  archetype in, 58
  character, 61
  character influence of, 80
  character's look influenced by, 13
  costumes/weaponry in, 42
  prehistoric art, 5–8
  research into, 42–49

Horror, 155
Horse locomotion, 234, 236f–239f, 237
Horus, 37, 39f
Human
  prehistoric, 290–293, 297f, 298
  walk, 241–243, 241f–243f

Humility, artist, 24
Hwommy Klachnurt's Markers for the Right Brain, 115
Hybrid characters, 70–71, 70f, 71f, 72, 72f
 inanimate material with, 131–132, 133f
 plant/animal, 73f–76f, 74–80, 130–131, 131f, 132f
 robot/android, 72, 72f, 126–128, 130f
 spectators' expectations with, 129n
 synthesis with, 126–132, 131f, 132f, 133f
Hyenas locomotion, 236

I

Ice Age, 45, 46f
Iconography, 9
Icthyosaur, 269f
Idea urge, 94
Idealization, 58
Iguanodon, 272
Iliad (Homer), 35
Inanimate material, synthesis with, 131–132, 133f
Inanimate objects, 338, 339f
Indricotherium, 286, 290f
Ink, 116
Inostrancevia alexandri, 271f
Insect, 218, 220f
 flying, 258–259
 locomotion, 251f, 256–259, 257f, 258f
 prehistoric, 282–285, 285f
 swimming, 258
Internet research, 264
Isolation, 79, 81

J

Jellyfish, 218, 220f
Jones, Chuck, 4
Journals, character research with, 50
Jung, Carl, 32b–33b
Jurassic Park, 264, 267, 295

K

Kali, 38
Kangaroo, 217, 219f, 286
 anatomy, 217, 219f
 locomotion, 244, 244f
King Kong, 264, 268f, 269
Kingdom, 267
Knight, Charles R., 264
Kojiki, 39
Kokopelli, 40, 41f
Krishna, 38

L

Lambeosaurus, 272
Lascaux, caves of, 5, 7, 7f

Laughing, 180–181, 181f, 183
Leaves of Grass (Whitman), 29
Legs, 99b, 210–212, 211f, 212f
 locomotion with, 234–239, 235f–239f
Ligaments, 221
Lighting, 195, 196f–198f
 contrast, 195
 diffuse, 195
 types of, 195
Limbs, 97, 98, 208–209, 208f, 209f
Line, 144–145, 144f, 145f, 168
 of action, 98
 animation with, 144–145
 cartoon design with, 145, 145f
 comic books with, 145
Literature
 fairy tales as, 47–48
 reading list of, 30b
 scientific, 49–50
 world, 28–31
Living systems, 76–80
 continuity/compatibility of, 78
 ecology of, 76
 environment of, 78
 food chain of, 77
 habitat of, 77
 survival of, 79
Locomotion, 233–259
 anguilliform, 247, 247n, 248f
 backbone with, 234
 bat, 252–254, 252f–254f
 bipedal, 241–243, 241f–243f
 bird, 251f, 253f, 254–256, 255f, 256f
 body or caudal fin, 247, 248f
 camel, 236
 carangiform, 247, 247n, 248f
 caterpillar, 244
 defined, 234
 digitigrade, 235
 diplodocus, 234, 235f
 dog, 234, 235f, 237f, 238f
 dolphin, 249
 fish, 215–216, 245–248, 246f–250f, 247n
 flying, 250–259, 251f–258f
 Froude number with, 240b
 gait, 234–239, 237f–240f
 gallop, 236–237, 238f
 giraffes, 236
 hopping, 244, 244f
 horse, 234, 236f–239f, 237
 human, 241–243, 241f–243f, 244
 hyenas, 236
 insect, 251f, 256–259, 257f, 258f
 kangaroo, 244, 244f

legs in, 234–239, 235f–239f
median or paired fin, 247
metachronal wave gait, 256, 257f
muscles for, 219, 242
mussel, 244
one-anchor, 244, 245f
pelvis rocking with, 241, 241f, 242f
penguin, 249
peristalsis, 245, 245f
plantigrade, 241
plesiosaur, 249, 250f
pterodactyl, 251, 253f
pterosaur, 252f, 253f, 256, 256f
salamander, 243, 243f
sea animal, 245–250, 246f–250f, 247n
seal, 249, 249f
snake, 243–244, 243f
sprint, 236–237, 238f
stride, 234
subcarangiform, 247, 247n, 248f
thunniform, 247, 247n, 248f
tripodal gait, 257f, 258
two-anchor, 244, 245f
walk, 234, 238, 239f
whale, 249
worm, 244
Long John Silver, 28
The Lord of the Rings (Tolkien), 37, 42b
Lovecraft, H. P., 29, 30b, 80
Lust, 183

M
Magazines, character research with, 49
Mammoth, 6, 7f
Manga, 51
Markers, 116
Masks, 8–9
Materials, 115–118
    acrylics as, 117
    airbrush as, 117
    casein as, 116
    charcoal as, 116
    crayons as, 116
    gouache as, 116
    graphite as, 116
    ink as, 116
    markers as, 116
    pencil as, 115–116
    water colors as, 116
McQuarrie, Ralph, 152
Medusa, 41
Megistotherium, 285, 288f
Memories, 92
Mentoring, artist development from, 24
Mesonychids, 285

Mesozoic age, 266
Metachronal wave gait, 256, 257f
Metamorphosis, 35
Method, modular drawing, 106, 108
Migration, 79, 81
Mocarski, Matthew, 174–175
Model sheet, 160, 164–168, 164f–167f, 168
    action pose, 165f, 167
    Armstrong using, 169b, 169f
    construction, 167–168, 167f
    continuity tool of, 164
    drawing skill needed for, 164
    expression, 166f, 167
    Garza using, 169b, 170f
    Hippolito using, 169b, 171f
    styles of, 164–168, 164f–167f
    Thayn using, 169b, 171f
    turn-around, 164, 164f, 167
Modification
    changing ratio with, 124–125
    color, 122, 125, 129f, 129n, 131–132
    design synthesis with, 123–125
    spectators' expectations with, 129n
    substitution v., 125
    texture, 125, 129n, 131–132
Modular drawing, 99–113, 101f–112f
    advantages of, 109–112
    beer-bellied character in, 105, 106f
    body parts in, 102–105, 105f, 108
    cartooning as, 100, 101–102, 102f
    defined, 100
    emotion from, 105, 108f
    generic figure from, 105, 105f, 106f
    gesture drawing combined with, 102,
        104f, 108–113, 114f
    heroic character in, 105, 106f
    method for, 106, 108
    NBA character in, 105, 106f
    realistic v. stylized characters in, 106–107
    stylization as, 100–101
Monty Python and the Search for the Holy
    Grail, 42b
Morphology, 267
Mosasaurs, 269f
    character synthesis with, 280–282, 281f
Motion studies, gesture drawing of, 98
Motivations, 59
Mozart, Wolfgang Amadeus, 21
Muscles, 219–223, 221f, 222f
    abductor, 221
    adductor, 221
    depressor, 221
    erector, 221
    extensor, 221
    fixation, 222

flexor, 221, 222, 222f
levator, 221
locomotion from, 219, 242
prime mover, 222
pronator, 221
rotator, 221
supinator, 221
synergist, 222
tensor, 221
tone, 222
walking, 242
Mutation, 79, 79f
design synthesis with, 123, 124f,
126f–129f
Mythology, 5, 6, 53
Aztec, 40
Campbell on, 42b–43b
Chinese, 39–40
defined, 29, 32
Egyptian, 34, 37–38
Greek, 33–34, 34–36, 35f, 36f
Hindu, 38–39
Japanese, 39–40
Jung and, 32b–33b
Latin American, 40–41
Mayan, 40–41, 41f
Native American, 32, 34, 48
Norse, 5, 34, 36–37, 53
research using, 29–42
Roman, 33, 35–36
Zuni, 40

N

Name
character, 11, 60
National Geographic Magazine, 52
Natty Bumpo, 29
Natural systems, 76–80
NBA character, modular drawing of, 105,
106f
Neanderthal, 290–292, 298
The New Yorker, 157, 158
Njord, 37
Non-human/human-like characters, 70–71
Norse mythology, 5, 34, 36–37, 53
Nothosaur, 272f

O

Octopi, 216, 217f
Odin, 35
Odyssey (Homer), 35
Ordovician age, 266
Originality, cliché v., 20–22, 58, 308, 332
Osiris, 37
Osmosis Jones, 60

P

Paleozoic age, 266
Palorchestes azeal, 265f
Pan Gu, 39
Paradise Lost (Milton), 29
Parasaurolophus, 272
Pelvis, 205–206
biped, 205–206, 241, 241f
bone structure of, 205–206
locomotion with, 241, 241f, 242f
quadruped, 205–206, 205f
Pen-and-ink, 157
Pencil, 115–116
Penguin, locomotion, 249
Pennsylvanian age, 266
Peristalsis, 245, 245f
Permian age, 266
Perrault, Charles, 49
Personality, head showing, 223
Personification, 5–6
Phanerozoic age, 266
Photo-manipulation, 159
Phylum, 267
Phytosaurs, 273
Pixar studio, 158
Plague, 45, 46f
Plants
genetic material of, 79
hybrid characters, 75–80, 75f, 76f, 77f
modification of, 79
synthesis with, 130–131, 131f, 132f
Playboy, 157
The Pleasant Nights (Straparola), 49
Plesiosaur, 269f, 280
character synthesis with, 280–282, 281f
locomotion, 249, 250f
Plot, 80
Poetic Edda, 36
Popeye, 106
Popol Vuh, 40
Poses
closed, 186, 186f, 187f
expression in, 185–187, 186f, 187f, 188f,
189f
open, 186, 186f
static, 186–187, 189f
Postosuchus, 293–295, 299f, 300f
Practice, artist development from, 24
Precambrian age, 266
Predator, 63
Prehistoric art, 5–8
Prehistoric man, 6
Prehistoric resources, 263–304, 339. *See
also* Dinosaurs
amphibians as, 286–287, 292f

birds as, 290, 296f, 297f
character synthesis with, 280–282, 281f
characterization using, 293–295, 299f, 300f
Dimetrodon as, 299–303, 301f–303f
drawing from, 299–303, 301f–303f
fish as, 287–289, 293f, 294f, 295f
insects as, 282–285, 285f
man as, 290–293, 297f, 298
Postosuchus, 293–295, 299f, 300f
research using, 263–264
saber-toothed cat as, 285, 286, 287f, 291f
sea animals as, 287–289, 293f, 294f, 295f
spiders as, 282–285, 285f
surface of, 272, 276–280, 277f, 278f, 279n
surfaces with, 265
synthesizing with, 265, 270
Problem solving, 93–95
Project-driven creation, 59–60
Proportions, anatomic, 99b, 100f
Props, 14b, 23b, 81–83, 81f, 85f
alien design with, 356f
history of, 42
synthesis with, 122
Prosimian, 270
Protagonist, 142
Pterodactyl locomotion, 251, 253f
Pterosaur, 270, 270f
locomotion, 252f, 253f, 256, 256f
Punch, Mr., 8–9, 58
The Puppetry Journal, 147
Puppets, 147
Mr. Punch as, 8–9
origin of, 8–9
Puranas, 38
Pyle, Howard, 28

Q

Quadruped
anatomy of, 205–206, 205f, 208–209, 208f, 209f
limbs of, 208–209, 208f, 209f
pelvises of, 205–206, 205f

R

Ra, 37
Ralph Mayer's Handbook for the Artist, 115
Ratio
synthesis with, 122, 132, 134f
Refinement, 94
Religion, 5, 6, 8, 49
Rendering
prehistoric resources in, 299–303, 301f–303f
style, 157–159

Repetition
color with, 149
style with, 148–149, 168
Reptiles, 273
coloration of, 277
flying, 284f
gait of, 210–211, 211f
scleral ossicles with, 280n
Research, 28–52
culture, 42–49, 50–52
encyclopedias for, 42
history, 42–49
internet for, 264
mythology, 29–42
popular culture, 50–52
prehistoric resources for, 263–264
scientific literature, 49–50
sources for, 28
style out of, 159
world literature, 28–31
Rib cage, 97, 98, 103, 206–207, 207f, 212
Right-brain activity, 92
Robots, 71–73, 72f, 73f
origin of term, 72n
synthesis with, 126–128, 130f
Role-playing game, 62
Rumpelstiltskin, 48
Russian folklore, 48

S

Saber-toothed cat, 267, 285, 286, 287f, 291f
Sadness, 183
Saga of Volsungs, 36
Salamander locomotion, 243, 243f
Sauropods, 273, 277f
Scale, 335
head in, 167f, 168
repetition with, 149
synthesis with, 122, 132
Scapula, 99b, 206
Schwarzenegger, Arnold, 63, 72
Science fiction, 75
alien design with, 330–331
Scientific literature
magazines/journals/books as, 49–50
research through, 49–50
Scleral ossicles, 280n
Screaming, 180–182, 183
Scribbling, 146, 157
Sea animals, 345f
anatomy, 215–218, 216f–218f, 220f
anatomy of, 215–218, 216f–218f, 220f
locomotion, 245–250, 246f–250f, 247n
prehistoric, 287–289, 293f, 294f, 295f
undulatory fin motions of, 248

Seal, 216
    anatomy, 216
    locomotion, 249, 249f
Self, 33b
Self-interest-driven creation, 59
Shadow, 33b
Shamanism, 5
Shape, 142–144, 143f, 168
    hero defined by, 142
Sherlock Holmes, 28
Shiva, 38
Shoulder girdle, 206, 206f
Sidekick, 67
Silhouettes, 187, 191f
    readability of, 192
Silurian age, 266
Skeletal structure
    anatomy of, 205–213, 205f, 207f
    arms in, 212f, 213, 213f
    axial and appendicular, 98, 98f, 99, 100f
    biped, 205–206, 208–209, 209f, 211–212
    breastbone in, 206, 206f
    coccyx of, 205
    feet in, 212–213, 212f
    head in, 209–210
    legs in, 210–212, 211f, 212f
    limbs in, 208–209, 208f, 209f
    pelvis in, 205–206
    quadruped, 205–206, 205f, 208–209, 208f, 209f
    rib cage in, 206–207, 207f, 212
    scapulae in, 206
    shoulder girdle in, 206, 206f
    spinal column in, 212
    tails in, 210, 210f
    thorax in, 207
    woman/man measurements of, 99b
Sketch
    refined, 300, 302f
    thumbnail, 299, 301f
Sketchbooks, 113–115, 115f
    Dawson recommendation of, 335
    idea generation with, 113
    importance of, 113–115
    students' dread of, 113
    style out of, 159
Skin texture, dinosaurs, 276–280, 277f, 278f, 279n
Skull
    anatomy, 223f–228f, 225–228
    dog, 226f, 227, 228
    face bones of, 228
    frontal bone of, 228
    herbivore, 225, 225f
    human, 226f, 227, 227f

    lion, 226f, 227
    mandibula of, 227f, 228
    maxillae of, 227f, 228
    occipital, 227
    parietals, 227
    sphenoid bone of, 228
    superciliary crests of, 228
    temporals, 228
    zygomatics of, 228
Sleeping Beauty, 48
Sly expression, 184
Smiling, 180f, 181
Snake, 217, 219f
    locomotion, 243–244, 243f
Snarling, 180, 180f, 182
Snow White, 47
Soul Reaver, 174
Spider, 218
    prehistoric, 282–285, 285f
Spine, 97, 98
    column, 212
Spinosaurus, 273
Sporting News, 52
Sports, 52
Sports Illustrated, 52
Sprint, 236–237, 238f
Squid, 216, 217f
Squinting, 180–182, 181f, 182f
Squirrel, flying, 214, 215f
Star Wars, 42b, 152
Stegosaurus, 263
Stereotyping, 58
    alien design, 308, 332
The *Story of Civilization* (Durant), 42
Storyline
    character with, 10–16, 61–62, 63
    design relating to, 17
    plot in, 80
    synthesis and, 122
    theme with, 80
Straparola, Giovan Francesco, 49
Stride, 234
Style, 141–175
    affinity in, 149, 168
    appeal in, 155–157, 155f
    color for, 149, 154
    conceptualization for, 150–153, 153f, 168
    contrast in, 149–150, 149f, 150f, 151f, 168
    drawing skill for, 154b
    fashion v., 142
    genre with, 155
    line in, 144–145, 144f, 145f, 168
    model sheet used for, 160, 164–168, 164f–166f, 168
    rendering, 157–159

repetition in, 148–149, 168
shape in, 142–144, 143f, 168
sketchbook for, 159
steps creating character with, 159–160,
  161f–163f
surface in, 145–146, 168
symmetry in, 146–148, 147f, 148f, 168
synthesis with, 122, 132–137, 135f–136f
visual design in, 142
Style creep, 51
Stylization
cartooning v., 101–102
modular drawing as, 100–101
realism v., 106–107, 110f
Subcarangiform, 247, 247n, 248f
Substitution
anatomic, 123, 124f, 126f–129f
modification v., 125
Suchomimus, 274
Surfaces
color with, 146
dinosaurs skin, 276–280, 277f, 278f,
  279n
prehistoric resources with, 265
style with, 145–146, 168
texture, 146
Surprise, 184
Survival, 79
Symbolism, defined, 9
Symmetry
defined, 146
style with, 146–148, 147f, 148f, 168
Synthesis, 121–138, 338
anatomy with, 122–126, 124f–127f
color in, 122, 125, 129f, 129n, 131–132
costumes in, 122, 132–133, 134f, 135f
defined, 122
design theory with, 122–123
elements of, 122
fish/pagoda, 356f
gender in, 122, 132, 135f
inanimate material with, 131–132, 133f
modification in, 123–125
monkey/hawk, 344f
plants in, 130–131, 131f, 132f
prehistoric resources in, 265, 270,
  280–282, 281f
props in, 122
ratio in, 122, 132, 134f
robotic elements with, 126–128, 130f
scale in, 122, 132
spectators' expectations with, 129n
storyline and, 122
style in, 122, 133–137, 135f–136f

substitution in, 123, 124f, 126f–129f
texture in, 122, 125, 129n, 131–132
Syzygy, 33b

T
Tafoya, Cesar, 199b
Tails, 210, 210f, 270, 272
Tartarus, 35
Team approach, design with, 19
Tears, 180–181
Teenage Mutant Ninja Turtles, 22, 308
Teeth, 180f, 181
Tendons, 221
Terminator, 72
Texture, 122, 125, 129n, 131–132
mapping, 265
style with, 146
Thayn, Jamus, 53, 169b, 171f, 357, 358f
Theme, 81
The Thing, 75
The Thing from Outer Space, 131
Thor, 37, 53
Thorax, 207
Thoth, 37, 39f
Thunniform, 247, 247n, 248f
Thylacosmilus. See Saber-toothed cat
Tolkien, J. R. R., 37
Tom Thumb, 48
Tonal values, 146
Totemic figures, 8
Tree stump, 348f
Tripodal gait, 257f, 258
Turn-around model sheet, 164, 164f, 167
Turtles, 272
Twain, Mark, 22, 28
Tylosaurus, character synthesis with,
  280–282, 281f
Tyrannosaurus rex, 263, 267, 273, 274

U
UFO. *See* Alien design
Uniforms, 82f, 83, 84f, 85f

V
Value rendering methods, 146
Vampires, 71
Venus of Willendorf, 5, 6, 8f, 58
Video games, 174
Villains, 64–67, 64f
expression of, 178f
Viruses, 75
Vishnu, 38
Visual design, 142
Visual representation

character, 11–13
culture influencing, 13
design in, 17
environment influencing, 13
genre influencing, 13
history influencing, 13
time frame influencing, 13
The Visual Story, 149

W

Wagner, Richard, 22
Walk, 234, 238, 239f
Human, 241–243, 241f–243f
Wallaby, 217
Walrus, 216
War and Peace (Tolstoy), 28
Warner Brothers, 60
Water colors, 116, 157, 350f
Watership Down, 67
Weaponry, history of, 42

Whale, 216, 218f
anatomy, 216, 218f
locomotion, 249
"What If?" method, 313, 313f
Whitman, Walt, 29
The Willows (Blackwood), 29
Winnie the Pooh, 67
Winston, Stan, 310
Woman, 7
Wonder tales, 47–48
Word play, 93
World of Warcraft, 174
Wyeth, N. C., 28

Y

Yee, 357, 357f, 358f

Z

Zeus, 33, 35, 35f
Zuni, 40